My Kid is Back explains how family-based treatment can greatly reduce the severity of anorexia nervosa in children and adolescents, allowing the sufferer to return to normal eating patterns, and their families to return to normal family life.

In this book ten families share their experiences of living with anorexia. Parents describe their frustrations in seeking help for their child and dealing with their behaviour and sufferers discuss how the illness gets into their mind and takes over their personality.

By focusing on the Maudsley family approach and expert advice from Professor Daniel Le Grange, and including clear lists of illness symptoms, strategies for parents and carers to follow, and information on getting further treatment and support, this book proves an essential resource for families who want to win the battle with anorexia nervosa.

June Alexander is a writer and journalist with a particular focus on eating disorders stemming from her personal battle with anorexia and subsequently bulimia, that lasted for 21 years. June is a strong supporter of the Maudsley family approach to treating anorexia nervosa, and is based in Victoria, Australia.

Daniel Le Grange is Professor of Psychiatry in the Department of Psychiatry, and Director of the Eating Disorders Program at the University of Chicago, Chicago, Illinois. He trained in family-based treatment for adolescent anorexia nervosa at the Maudsley Hospital in London, where he was a member of the team that developed the Maudsley Approach as a treatment for early-onset anorexia nervosa.

My Kid is Back is packed with practical, helpful and inspiring information. It gives parents a powerful message of hope – that recovery from an eating disorder is possible. Parents can feel overwhelmed when their child develops this most challenging illness. Knowing that there are ways they can help their child, and can play an active part in their recovery is so important.

Susan Ringwood, Chief Executive, Beat

The Maudsley Model of anorexia nervosa is one of the few evidence-based treatments for anorexia nervosa. In *My Kid is Back* June Alexander presents the narratives of families who have benefited from this approach when their young children have developed anorexia nervosa. This book will give hope to families who with help can provide the drive and energy to ensure that anorexia nervosa does not become too firmly entangled within the identity of the young person.

**Janet Treasure, Professor, South London and Maudsley
NHS Trust, and Director of the Eating Disorder Unit and
Professor of Psychiatry at Guys, Kings and St Thomas
Medical School, London**

Alexander and Le Grange have combined heart, history and healing in this thoughtful book. *My Kid is Back* should be required reading for any parent with the slightest suspicion that an eating disorder may be developing in their child. June Alexander's own testimonial should be a warning enough that families need to take action early and head on.

**Lynn S. Grefe, Chief Executive Officer, National Eating
Disorders Association (NEDA), USA**

My Kid is Back

Empowering Parents to Beat Anorexia Nervosa

*June Alexander with
Prof. Daniel Le Grange*

Routledge
Taylor & Francis Group

LONDON AND NEW YORK

First published in Australia by Melbourne University Press, 2009

First published in the UK in 2010 by Routledge
27 Church Lane, Hove, East Sussex BN3 2FA

Simultaneously published in the USA and Canada
by Routledge
270 Madison Avenue, New York, NY 10016

Routledge is an imprint of the Taylor & Francis Group, an Informa business

© 2010 Melbourne University Press

Typeset in New Century Schoolbook by
RefineCatch Limited, Bungay, Suffolk
Printed and bound in Great Britain by
TJ International Ltd, Padstow, Cornwall
Cover design by Andrew Ward

This publication has been produced with paper manufactured to strict
environmental standards and with pulp derived from sustainable
forests.

British Library Cataloguing in Publication Data
A catalogue record for this book is available from the British Library

Library of Congress Cataloging-in-Publication Data
Alexander, June, 1950-
My kid is back : empowering parents to beat anorexia nervosa /
June Alexander with Daniel Le Grange.
p. cm.
Includes bibliographical references and index.
1. Anorexia in children–Patients–Family relationships.   2. Anorexia in
adolescence–Patients–Family relationships.   3. Anorexia nervosa–Treatment.
I. Le Grange, Daniel.   II. Title.
RJ399.A6A44 2010
362.198'9285262–dc22
2009050200

ISBN: 978–0–415–58115–8 (pbk)

This book is for my children Shane, Rohan, Benjamin and Amanda.

—June Alexander

This book is for Babs, Tom and Zandré.

—Daniel Le Grange

Contents

Foreword

Doctor Ivan Eisler

Having a child suffering from anorexia nervosa is a bewildering and often very lonely experience. Parents wonder where they have gone wrong, blame themselves and, as time goes on, the eating problems seem to take over the whole family. Even when they find help, recovery is a long and difficult process, with no ready-made answers as to how they are going to get their child back to health. When June Alexander approached me to write a foreword to her book *My Kid is Back*, I was delighted. It sounded like a great project and I felt that many families I see, who struggle with how to help their child, would benefit greatly from reading about how other families have coped, what worked for them and, perhaps above all, that they would gain a sense of hope from these accounts. By reading this book they would know that even if it takes time, there is light at the end of the tunnel.

Historically, studies of families of people suffering from an eating disorder were primarily concerned with identifying the possible role of family factors in the development of the eating disorder. This was based on the belief that if we could identify 'underlying family causes' and treat them, the problem itself would disappear. Such beliefs were strongly reinforced by the work of Salvador Minuchin and his colleagues in Philadelphia more than thirty years ago, which showed that involving families in the treatment of adolescents suffering from anorexia nervosa led to remarkably good outcomes. Minuchin, one of the pioneering figures in the field of family therapy, was quite clear that to think of the family as the cause of anorexia was a mistake, but emphasised the importance of understanding the family context as a place in which the physiological and psychological factors interact over time. What more recent research has shown is that this process does not depend on there being a particular family constellation – in other words it can develop in a whole range of different types of family. Understanding the family context remains important, not because it gives us answers to *why* someone developed anorexia nervosa, but because we need to understand how the family gets caught up in the problem. We need to understand how the illness undermines the family's usual coping skills, and how it magnifies common problems or indeed normal variations in the way families function to the point where what they do may seem strange, bizarre and difficult to comprehend. Families do not cause eating disorders but they get caught up in the problems and get stuck. Family-based treatment is therefore not about changing families but about helping them to get unstuck; helping them to rediscover their strengths and how they can best use these to help their child.

After reading *My Kid is Back* I realised I was wrong to think that this is primarily a book for families trying to deal with anorexia nervosa. It is equally a book for clinicians and researchers who want to understand what it is like for the families. It is a remarkable book because it gives a voice to the families themselves, showing the different journeys they went through regarding both the developing anorexia and in re-establishing themselves and helping their child to recover. The stories are both painful and optimistic. They show remarkably well the often mundane nature of some of the factors that may be at the inception of the eating problem. They also show how often quite small things gradually build up to the point where everyone feels paralysed and unable to find a way out. The point where each family begins to rediscover their belief in themselves is testimony to the resilience that families have, and the reason why they should have a central role in the treatment of eating disorders.

Doctor Ivan Eisler is a Reader in Family Psychology and Family Therapy and Head of Section of Family Therapy at the Institute of Psychiatry, King's College London. He is also the head of the Child and Adolescent Eating Disorder Service at the Maudsley Hospital in London.

Acknowledgements

Many people have contributed to the creation and writing of this book. I thank Claire Vickery, founder and chairman of The Butterfly Foundation in Melbourne, for her encouragement and support.[1] On discussing the need to raise awareness of anorexia nervosa and 'tell the world' about the importance of prompt intervention with family-based treatment for children who develop the illness, Claire suggested I contact Professor Daniel Le Grange, Director of the Eating Disorders Program at the University of Chicago. Professor Le Grange and I met in October 2007 and *My Kid is Back* began to take shape. I thank Professor Le Grange for having faith and believing in me, and for being my collaborator on this book.

Two providers of the Maudsley Approach in Australia have been full of encouragement throughout the researching and writing of *My Kid is Back*. They are the family-based treatment teams at the Children's Hospital at Westmead, Sydney, and The Oak House in Melbourne. I acknowledge the support of these two teams in sourcing the ten case study families, in reading the families' stories and offering practitioner insights by way of footnotes within the family chapters.

Dr Michael Kohn FRACP FACPM and Dr Sloane Madden FRANZCP are co-directors and senior staff specialists with the Eating Disorder Service in the Department of Adolescent Medicine and Psychological Medicine at the Children's Hospital, Westmead. The Eating Disorder Family-based Treatment team leader is clinical specialist social worker, Andrew Wallis. Dr Paul Rhodes (Department of Psychological Medicine, University of Sydney) is a senior clinical psychologist, and Colleen Alford and Andrea Worth are senior social workers and family therapists.

The Oak House team, led by director Belinda Dalton, includes family therapist Vicki O'Dwyer, dietician Fiona Sutherland and psychologist Brooke Hunter.

From the bottom of my heart I thank the ten families who, motivated by a desire to help raise awareness of the seriousness of anorexia nervosa and ease the suffering of others, bravely and selflessly share their stories in *My Kid is Back*. Speaking from where this illness hits hardest, the family, your messages are the voice of this book.

I thank Mark and Katie Rogers, Gemma and Casey; Stephanie; Richard and Margaret; Cheryl, Nicholas, Rachel and Jonathan; Neil and Cathy Street, Pip, Doug and Alice; Kevin, Tanya and Carmen Paech; Tim and Bridget, Kelly and Nikki; Greg and Karen, Matthew, Lauren and Kristen; Duncan and Sally, Lachlan, James and Cameron; Eddie and Carolin, Rebecca, Juno and Billie.

To Dr Ivan Eisler, King's College London, a big 'thank you' for reading the manuscript, writing the Foreword, and explaining the situation in the United Kingdom (in Chapter 13). I thank Jane Cawley, who with Harriet Brown co-chairs Maudsley Parents,[2] for your encouragement and assistance.

Hazel Edwards, thank you for your mentoring and friendship; and Steve Cooper, thank you for being my 'anchor' and for reading and offering reflection on the manuscript, many times over.

Above all, I thank the team at Melbourne University Publishing, especially my publisher, Elisa Berg, for believing in the message of this book.

Introduction

> New opinions are always suspected, and usually opposed,
> without any other reason but because they are not already
> common.
>
> John Locke, English philosopher (1632–1704)

More than 125 years since anorexia nervosa was first defined,
it continues to be frequently misdiagnosed, underestimated
and misunderstood. The eating disorder, characterised by an
intense fear of gaining weight and becoming fat, has the
highest death rate of any psychiatric illness. *My Kid is Back*
offers hope to sufferers and their families and raises awareness of a family-based treatment, the Maudsley Approach,
which is producing promising evidence-based results.

Ten families courageously and candidly share their
experiences to illustrate how anorexia nervosa goes much
deeper than physical appearance – even after weight restoration the illness can linger in the mind, debilitating the sufferer. Their prime message is that early intervention with
family-based treatment can greatly reduce the severity of
anorexia nervosa in children and adolescents. The earlier a
child receives treatment, the greater the likelihood of fast
recovery and freedom to resume normal living. The best outcome is for those for whom intervention in their illness
occurs within six months.

Professor Daniel Le Grange explains it this way:

> If I were a dentist and noticed a tiny cavity in a child's
> tooth, would I tell the parent to take the child away and

return in six months? No, I would deal with it immediately and you would expect me to do so. I would clean and fill the cavity to prevent it becoming more of a problem, perhaps requiring a root canal. If a parent comes to me concerned that their child has lost 3 kilograms, I must take this seriously also. It is not normal for any child or teenager to suddenly lose weight, yet some health practitioners routinely tell worried parents, 'This is a phase. Come back in six months'. Usually, six months later, the illness is six months worse. A loss of weight is a sign that something's not right and needs to be checked immediately.

Parents constantly inspire Professor Le Grange: 'No one has as much commitment as the parents to hang in with their child'. Family-based treatment taps into the power of this loving commitment. Not all parents are suitable to take on the challenge of overcoming the illness that has overtaken their child, but for those who are, and succeed, their family unit is strengthened in many ways beyond that of beating the eating disorder.

Professor Le Grange's greatest inspiration occurs when parents, who twelve months earlier presented for assessment with a child 'looking like a skeleton with its life on hold or pushed back', enter his consulting rooms and say, 'I've got my kid back!'

As the voice of this book, parents raise compelling issues as they lift the lid on what living with anorexia is really like. Sufferers have an important voice, too. Bravely they describe the power and pain of this illness that slips into the brain and becomes part of one's sense of self. Together with their families, their wish is that increased understanding of anorexia nervosa will enable early recognition and intervention, so others do not suffer as deeply or as long.

That this book about family-based treatment has been written in Australia, far from its origin in England, is testimony to the willingness shown by teams of medical and allied health professionals around the world to adopt the family-based treatment method. However, there is more work to be done. Families in *My Kid is Back* describe their frustration at losing critical time in seeking help for their child. Despite visits to family doctors, other health providers and, in some cases, multiple hospital admissions, many families today learn about the Maudsley Approach only through their own desperate research.

For eating disorder therapy teams everywhere, this book's message is the same as for parents: unity is essential for family-based treatment to succeed in overpowering ano- rexia nervosa. Families must be united and empowered, ther- apy teams must be united in their commitment, and families and therapists must be committed to working together. After years of study and training, it can be a challenge for some therapists to see the parents as their most powerful ally in helping the child recover. But in fighting this illness egos must be set aside; so, too, any reluctance to alter or question long-held beliefs.

Anorexia nervosa has left many families with lifelong rel- ationship struggles in its wake, but the Maudsley Approach offers hope by reinstating fundamental family principles – by empowering parents, and supporting them and their children in their growth and development.

In fighting cancer, the oncologist is the leader; in fight- ing anorexia nervosa, each member of the family-based treat- ment team is on the same level in guiding and empowering the parents to help their child recover. *My Kid is Back* challenges the eating disorder community around the world to work as one in empowering parents through family-based treatment to fight childhood and adolescent anorexia nervosa.

Families who share their experiences in this book demon- strate abundantly the value of involving parents and siblings in the treatment of childhood anorexia nervosa. The power of family participation cannot be underestimated. My own life further emphasises this point. I developed anorexia ner- vosa shortly after my eleventh birthday, in 1962. The illness was unheard of in the dairy farm district where I was growing up – in the south-east corner of Australia.

My mindset then was the same as that experienced by children with the illness today. As I interviewed each of the children who share their experiences in this book, I felt an eerie connection as they related their thoughts and feelings – a replica of mine, in another place, another time, another century. If I needed proof that anorexia nervosa is a pervasive and insidious illness of the mind, this was it.

Anorexia nervosa can happen to any child, anywhere in the world – whether in a corner of Australia, Iceland or South Africa, in a rural district or in the middle of a big city like London or New York. It can happen to any child from any social status – wealthy or poor, it doesn't matter.

As the families in this book illustrate, recognising the symptoms of the illness is a challenge. Most have heard of it through the media, but not until the illness develops in a family member does the impact of the illness hit home. My parents and a sister, who was several years older than me, had not heard of anorexia nervosa. I had not heard of it either. This was the early 1960s after all. My parents took me to one doctor, when I was twelve, who advised them that I did 'not want to grow up' but that was the limit of any explanation. I was growing up at a time when there was a lack of awareness not only about eating disorders but about mental illness in general.

To my parents and sister I appeared difficult, selfish, self-centred, stubborn, moody and inflexible. My unsociable behaviour, together with my emaciation and insistence of running everywhere, was an embarrassment. My mother did not know my anxiety or depression was part of an illness, or that my self-centredness was due to fighting a battle within. She wanted me to behave 'like other girls in our district'. I wanted to be like them but didn't know how. I didn't know that I was suffering an illness, that my feelings of torment were not normal. If I tried to explain, I was told, 'You think about yourself too much' or 'Pull up your socks' – which I took as meaning I wasn't trying hard enough. As one of the teens interviewed for this book, Kelly, points out, the distinction between mental illness and not having mental illness is like a spectrum: 'Those who don't understand don't relate'. The illness can be divisive.

Sometimes family members may ignore or deny a loved one has a mental illness, because such acknowledgement compels them to address issues within themselves. But doing nothing allows the illness to worsen and exacerbates any family dysfunction. Seeking help as soon as symptoms appear is vital to minimise the suffering of every member of the family.

On entering my teenage years, my untreated anorexia nervosa evolved into bulimia nervosa. In many ways, my life became one big torment. I looked 'normal' but within my mind I was living two lives: one internally with my eating disorder and the other with the outside world. Feelings of isolation were immense. Literature and writing were my 'escapes'. At eighteen I began a career in journalism, and when I married a farmer at twenty, three of us walked down the aisle – my husband, my eating disorder and myself.

I tried to be 'normal' but my torment grew. At the age of twenty-eight I found the strength to confide in a family doctor. By now my illness had been untreated for seventeen years. For the next five years, I was misdiagnosed. I was thirty-three when referred to a Melbourne psychiatrist who understood my illness and my struggle. This was Professor Graham Burrows, and he remains a rock for me today. My undiagnosed and untreated eating disorder had set me on a roller-coaster path of chronic depression and anxiety, self-harm and broken relationships.

My long journey of recovery was about to begin. However, unlike the stories you will read in this book, my family did not understand what my journey was about. They could not understand that if I were sick, why did I take so long to recover? 'Your doctor must be no good', they would say, or 'You're not still seeing him, are you?'

Today I know such comments were born from a lack of awareness, but at the time they cut deep and hindered my recovery by feeding my illness, compounding my feelings of inadequateness and unworthiness. My self-confidence would crash to sub-zero, my anxiety would soar and my illness would thrive. Gradually, I learnt not to mention anything about my ongoing therapy and medical treatment to my parents or sister. Sadly, the effects of the illness had forged a rift that grew bigger and bigger between us.

Without my family's acknowledgement that I was really a caring, conscientious person, worthy of their love and approval, I floundered about, struggling to find a firm foot-hold on which to rebuild my sense of self. The little girl of eleven remained in my troubled mind and body, but needed help to escape from the prison of my illness. Months turned into years and years into decades.

A breakthrough occurred at age forty-seven, when I met Melbourne dietician and eating disorder therapist, Belinda Dalton. Belinda suggested that I try to separate my illness from my sense of self. By looking at myself in this way, I was able to start recognising what belonged to the real me and what belonged to my illness. This helped enormously in gradually piecing together my sense of who I was. This stage in my recovery took nine years. Sometimes I slipped and regressed but gradually and progressively I uncovered and rebuilt my identity, which my illness had marred.[1] After forty-five years of struggle the day came when was I free to shout to the world, 'I have recovered my soul! I have peace in my heart and my mind!' I'd got myself back.

Was my battle worthwhile? Yes.

The decades of emotional pain and torment have enhanced and increased my capacity to appreciate life, its beauty and its depth. Consider anorexia nervosa as the worst type of aggressive weed you can find in your garden, the park or the bush. The longer this weed goes untended, the stronger its roots take hold and the harder it is to 'weed out'. Natural growth is smothered and stunted. So it is in the fertile garden of the mind. Anorexia nervosa can spread rapidly if not 'culled' quickly and efficiently. This is why I believe that parents, working with family-based treatment therapists, are the most powerful 'tool' to take on the onerous task of overcoming the illness and setting the child free to flourish.

Without swift intervention, the anorexia nervosa may remain in the mind. A remnant of my illness lingers within me, and if it slips under my guard in a crisis, I seek help quickly to prevent or repair any mental, emotional or physical bruising. I am my own best friend. I am in charge of me.

To eating disorder sufferers – whether you are twelve, twenty-two, thirty-two, forty-two, fifty-two or older – please believe that your recovery is possible and is worth the fight. Don't give up. To families and friends of eating disorder sufferers I also emphasise, 'Don't give up'. This book aims to help you understand what an eating disorder is like and empower you in supporting your loved one.

Most importantly, the good news conveyed in this book is that children developing the illness today can avoid decades of debilitating suffering through prompt diagnosis and implementation of family-based treatment. I wish the Maudsley Approach had been available when I was eleven. Recovery from anorexia nervosa, as with other potentially chronic illnesses, requires a team effort. Without family support, the rebuilding of one's identity is more arduous; the reclaiming of a sense of self-worth and acceptance more difficult. If you don't have immediate family support, be open to accepting help from others who believe in you and who you know you can trust. My psychiatrist and therapist helped me reclaim my self-esteem. Their guidance over many years, together with the understanding and love of my four children, and the life-long friendship of their father and my best friends, has enabled my recovery and given me the strength to write this book.

Two years ago I resigned from my position as a newspaper editor to climb my 'literary Everest'. After decades in 'training', I felt ready: strong enough and resilient enough to confront and expose my eating disorder tormentor, in the only way I knew how – with words. I would share my story, with the wish that other children would not suffer so long. While researching for my memoir I learnt about family-based treatment and immediately thought, 'This is the answer! This is what I have dreamt of, and yearned for, through my long struggle'.

I don't want children to suffer from the effects of anorexia nervosa, as I did, into their adulthood. I want their personalities restored; I want them to be flourishing and embracing life, ensconced in their families' love and understanding. I don't want their illness to be tagging along, as mine did, when they leave home, enter relationships and embark on careers. This is why the family-based treatment is important in fighting anorexia nervosa. Besides helping the child recover, it bonds and helps families stay together. Nothing is more important.

In the first chapter of *My Kid is Back*, Professor Le Grange describes the illness and its effect on the sufferer and the family. He then proceeds to look at some earlier forms of family-based treatment for anorexia nervosa before turning specifically to the development of the Maudsley Approach, and looks at ongoing research in the field of treatment for anorexia nervosa.

In the following chapters, ten families provide graphic accounts of the destructive power of anorexic nervosa and, equally, the healing power of love. Where anonymity has been requested, other names for family members have been used. These brave and loving families, who live thousands of kilometres apart, invited me into their hearts and homes to share their stories because they know that anorexia nervosa can strike any family, anywhere. They offer empathy, hope and inspiration to others caught in the fight against this illness. Their message is simple and strong: early intervention with family-based treatment provides the best hope for recovery. Notes by the therapists who have guided these families on their recovery offer helpful insights and, again, the message is clear: the longer anorexia nervosa goes unchecked, the stronger its hold on the sufferer.

Chapter 12 lists symptoms that may signal a child is developing anorexia nervosa. In Chapter 13, guidance is provided for parents, wherever they live, in navigating their way to the best available help for their child. Health professionals are an essential part of the treatment team, and this chapter includes an Australian case study of introducing family-based treatment into both an established public hospital system and a private clinic. The Appendix presents a listing of treatment providers and support links for families in Australia, North America, the United Kingdom and New Zealand.

1

Family-based treatment of adolescent anorexia nervosa

The Maudsley Approach

Professor Daniel Le Grange

Anorexia nervosa is a serious disorder and affects the lives of many adolescents and their families in a profound way. It is usually first diagnosed in adolescence and affects as many as 2 per cent of young women and 1 per cent of males.[1] Anorexia nervosa is characterised by a fear of fatness that results in relentless attempts to lose weight, often to the point of severe malnutrition. Weight loss, in turn, often leads to a delay in the onset of puberty or the loss of menses in post-pubertal girls, also called amenorrhea.[2] Several major medical complications can develop if weight loss is not reversed, such as slow heart rate (bradycardia), swelling of the extremities (peripheral edema) and loss of bone density (osteoporosis).[3] In addition, physical development in terms of growth and fertility can be delayed,[4] and generalised and occasional regional atrophy of the brain[5] can occur. As a psychiatric disorder, anorexia nervosa often coexists with other psychiatric conditions such as poor social functioning,[6] low self-esteem[7] and high rates of co-morbid substance abuse, mood disorders and anxiety disorders.[8]

Even though anorexia nervosa was first recognised more than 125 years ago, this disorder still puzzles clinicians as much as it bewilders teens and their families. Our understanding of the medical complications of anorexia nervosa has advanced and has increased our ability to help patients restore weight in specialist in-patient settings. However, despite these successes, in-patient and day hospital treatments are disruptive to the adolescent, their social and educational life and their family. Moreover, relapse is common and weight restoration alone is not sufficient for recovery. In-patient treatment aside, outcomes in adolescent patients with anorexia nervosa receiving a variety of treatments are generally not optimistic. One study found that less than half of patients followed at least four years after the onset of illness are considered recovered (being within 15 per cent of ideal body weight), 25 per cent of patients remain seriously ill, while about 5 per cent have died.[9] Among chronically ill adults with anorexia nervosa, mortality rates as high as 20 per cent have been reported.[10]

Seeking the most appropriate treatment for one's teen with an eating disorder can be an overwhelming and emotionally draining process. In-patient or day hospital programs are costly and pose a potentially traumatic experience for both the adolescent and their parents. One promising alternative is the Maudsley Approach, a family-based treatment that aims to prevent hospitalisation and views families as a resource in restoring their adolescent's weight and putting them back on track with adolescent development. The Maudsley Approach is the only outpatient treatment for adolescent anorexia nervosa that has received relatively extensive research and clinical support. This approach considers parents an important part of the solution, and encourages them to be pro-active in confronting their child's illness. Siblings have an important role, too, as friends to their ill brother or sister. In all cases, the first important step is to seek help immediately when symptoms are noticed (see Chapter 12). Now, I will review some of the earlier accounts of family-based treatment for anorexia nervosa before turning specifically to the development of the Maudsley Approach.

First accounts of family work for adolescent anorexia nervosa

Salvador Minuchin, a child psychiatrist, and his colleagues at the Child Guidance Clinic in Philadelphia were among the first to include families in the treatment of anorexia nervosa in adolescents.[11] They treated more than fifty patients, mostly adolescents who had been ill for less than three years, and provided outcome data for family therapy in a follow-up of this cohort. While treatment was quite mixed – most patients initially received in-patient treatment and some individual therapy – the primary intervention was family therapy. These authors report that more than 80 per cent of patients were recovered at the time of follow-up. This study fell far short of the rigours of a tightly controlled treatment trial (for example, members of the treatment team conducted patient evaluations, there were no comparison treatment groups and follow-up varied greatly). However, while not claimed as a controlled clinical trial, the study deserves recognition for its significance in the treatment of anorexia nervosa. Based on this landmark study, as well as the high rates of treatment success achieved, Minuchin and his colleagues ultimately exerted considerable influence on ensuing treatment efforts for adolescents with anorexia nervosa. In particular, the underlying theoretical principles and clinical application of Minuchin's approach served as the foundation for the first controlled family-based treatment studies, which were pioneered at the Maudsley Hospital in London. It is this treatment that has come to be known as the 'Maudsley Approach'.

Development of the Maudsley Approach

Following the work of Minuchin and others, Dr Christopher Dare and Dr Ivan Eisler and their team of researchers and clinicians at the Institute of Psychiatry and the Maudsley Hospital in London, England, spent most of the 1980s developing a new and pragmatic type of family treatment. The Maudsley team regards families as a resource, and, as a result, this family-based treatment aims to support and empower parents to first address the starvation in their teen with anorexia nervosa in order to help put them back on track with adolescent development. This research team subsequently published several early and important articles documenting the treatment's success in its London-based studies.

In the mid 1980s, I joined this team. Through my training

at the Maudsley Hospital I developed a keen passion for this family treatment and its application to adolescents with anorexia nervosa and bulimia nervosa. I introduced the Maudsley Approach to my colleagues in the United States in 1994 when I trained at Stanford University. Through relationships established at Stanford, I teamed up with Professor James Lock to collaborate on studying the Maudsley Approach in clinical research trials for adolescents with eating disorders. As a result of our research, we have taken the initiative to develop a manual version of the Maudsley Approach for both anorexia nervosa and bulimia nervosa, and coined the phrase 'family-based treatment'. We have also been at the forefront of disseminating this approach to colleagues across North America, Europe, Australia and elsewhere. Our research, along with the ongoing efforts of the Maudsley team and a growing number of other talented researchers in the field, has been critical in revealing the potential for this treatment to alleviate the suffering of many young people with eating disorders and their families.

Family-based treatment: The Maudsley Approach

Family-based treatment and the Maudsley Approach are interchangeable terms to describe the treatment developed in London in the 1980s. Generally, this treatment can be construed as an intensive outpatient intervention where parents play an active and positive role in order to achieve at least three goals. These are, first, to help restore their teen's weight to a healthy level, given their adolescent's age and height; second, to hand the control over eating back to the adolescent insofar as it is age appropriate; and third, to encourage normal adolescent development through an in-depth review and discussion of these crucial developmental issues as they pertain to their child, especially given the degree to which the illness has interrupted this process.

Most traditional approaches to the treatment of anorexia nervosa advocate an individual approach where strict adherence to this perspective will engage only the teen in treatment. Such therapies might insist that the participation of parents, regardless of the format, is at best viewed as unnecessary and at worse seen as interference in the recovery process. Many proponents of such a treatment philosophy would go so far as to suggest that 'family problems' play a crucial part in the aetiology of the anorexia nervosa. There is little doubt that such a view probably adds to the parents' feelings of self-blame for their child's illness, which often hampers their efforts to care for their sick teen. Family-based treatment does not view families as pathological or consider that they should be blamed for the development of anorexia nervosa – mostly due to the lack of convincing evidence to support such a premise. In fact, family-based treatment considers the parents a resource and that mobilising these inherent strengths is essential to securing a positive outcome in treatment for anorexia nervosa.

Also, unlike more traditional forms of family therapy, family-based treatment does not view the eating disorder as an expression of family dysfunction. Instead, the eating disorder is seen as an illness much like any other medical illness and the family is regarded as part of the solution to the problem rather than a hindrance. This does not imply that families do not have problematic patterns of behaviour, but family-based treatment only deals with these patterns inasmuch as they may interfere with the parents' ability to eliminate the eating disordered symptoms and re-establish normal adolescent development.

Family-based treatment is a team approach and, in addition to the primary therapist and the parents, it is essential to work with a paediatrician who will serve as a consultant to the therapist and the parents and will oversee the medical stability of the adolescent. Eating disorders, and anorexia nervosa in particular, are life-threatening and a paediatrician will monitor the teen's health, provide nutritional information if needed, and guide the parents in terms of the appropriate time for the adolescent to return to normal activities (for example, gym class and sports teams).

The meaning of 'family' in the context of this treatment approach is quite broad and not strictly dictated by biology or law. The family engaged in the Maudsley Approach can be defined as narrowly as the affected teen's parent(s), or broadly to encompass step-parents, long-term significant others, siblings, grandparents, aunts, uncles or others. The therapist will expect to meet with everyone who lives with the individual with the eating disorder. In addition, people who are involved in caring for or feeding the individual, but who do not live with the individual with the eating disorder, will also be required to participate in the treatment. Enlisting the help of all caregivers is essential – for example, grandparents who watch their grandchild after school – and these care-givers are typically required to join a few sessions to learn more about the Maudsley Approach. Most important is to utilise such meetings to make sure that everyone is on 'the same page' with one another in the way that the disorder is viewed and treated. Siblings play an important role, but one that is different from that of their parents. Whereas parents' main focus, at least initially, is on weight restoration, siblings are encouraged not to get involved in the parents' efforts, but rather think of ways in which they can support their sibling outside mealtimes; for example, watching a movie together, playing computer games or just having a talk.

Family-based treatment always proceeds through three fairly clearly demarcated phases. Treatment is usually com-pleted within fifteen to twenty sessions over a period of about twelve months. Some families will complete treatment earlier, whereas others might require several more sessions stretching beyond one year.

Phase One: weight restoration

The first phase of treatment is primarily focused on weight restoration. In order to achieve this challenging goal, the therapist will first set out to highlight the many medical and psychological consequences associated with severe mal-nutrition in anorexia nervosa, such as hypothermia, changes in growth hormone, cardiac dysfunction, and cognitive and emotional changes. The therapist will assess the family's typical interaction pattern and eating habits, and assist the parents in their joint efforts to restore their teenager's weight. It is essential for the parents to be united in their efforts to help their child and the therapist will make every effort to keep the parents on such a united track. While the parents concentrate their efforts on weight restoration, at the same time the therapist will endeavour to align the patient with their siblings in support and activities that do not involve mealtimes. Very early on during this phase the therapist will conduct a family meal, eaten in their office but without the participation of the therapist. This meal serves at least two functions. First, it allows the therapist to observe the family's typical interaction patterns around eating, and second, it provides the therapist with an opportunity to assist the parents, in the moment, in their efforts to encourage the adolescent to eat more than the adolescent is prepared to.

The parents' task is both difficult and delicate and does not differ meaningfully in terms of the key principles and steps that would be followed by a competent in-patient nursing team. Sitting at the dinner table for as long as it takes for a child to eat a meal can be distressing, but the rewards are great. Parents should aim to consistently express their sympathy and understanding for their adolescent's predicament of being caught up in such a debilitating disorder, while at the same time being persistent in their unified expectation that adequate amounts of food should be consumed in order to assure weight gain. Phase One of treatment is mostly concerned with three goals: supporting and coaching the parents in their efforts towards weight restoration of their offspring; empathising with the adolescent given the fact that they are terribly caught up in their illness; and reaffirming their position within the sibling subsystem. Realignment of the patient with their siblings or peers is an effort to help the adolescent form stronger and more age-appropriate relationships, as opposed to being co-opted into a parental relationship.

One of the key tenets of the Maudsley Approach is externalising the illness from the adolescent. In practice, this means that these symptoms are mostly outside the adolescent's control and that the adolescent is therefore not to blame for the challenging eating disorder behaviours. Consequently, the role of the therapist is to exemplify to the parents an uncritical stance towards the adolescent, emphasising that at no point should this phase of treatment be interpreted as a 'green light' for parents to be critical of their child. In fact, this treatment underwrites very convincingly a non-critical stance, and the therapist will work hard to address any parental criticism or hostility towards the adolescent.

Phase Two: returning control over eating to the adolescent

The start of Phase Two of treatment is usually signalled when at least three specifically defined goals have been met. That is, the adolescent is now more accepting of their parents' demands for increased food intake, this relative acquiescence is accompanied by steady weight gain (that is, the adolescent is about 90 per cent of ideal body weight) and there is a tangible change in the mood of the family (that is, relief at having taken charge of the eating disorder).

Most of the work in this phase of treatment focuses on assisting the parents to help their child resume control over eating. The main task for the parents is to encourage the ongoing return of their child's physical health, but this process now continues mostly in a way that is in keeping with their teen's age and their parenting style. At the same time, this part of treatment serves to reassure the adolescent that the therapist is honouring their initial undertaking to the patient and their family – that supporting parents' control over weight gain was a temporary intervention. Eating disorder symptoms remain central in the discussions between the therapist and the family, although weight gain that is more independent from the parents, and with minimum tension, is encouraged.

Regular family relationship difficulties, in terms of day-to-day adolescent or parenting concerns that the family has had to put aside until this point in treatment, can now be brought forward for review. However, this discussion occurs only in relationship to the impact these issues have on the parents in their task of supporting ongoing weight gain. For example, the adolescent may want to join their friends at the mall for dinner and a movie, but because the parents are still unsure whether their child would eat sufficiently when they are without parental supervision, they would be expected to have dinner at home with their parents before joining their friends at the cinema.

Phase Three: establishing healthy adolescent identity

Once the adolescent is able to independently maintain their weight above 95 per cent of ideal body weight and self-starvation has mostly abated, the therapist will initiate the third phase of treatment. In this final part of treatment the focus shifts to the impact anorexia nervosa has had on the adolescent, especially in terms of their efforts to establish a healthy and independent adolescent identity. After a review of the main adolescent developmental tasks, the therapist will focus in more detail on issues such as supporting increased personal autonomy for the adolescent, the development of appropriate parental boundaries, and the need for the parents to reorganise their life together after their children's prospective departure. This discussion is tailored to accommodate the adolescent's age-developmental stage as well as the length of time that the eating disorder interrupted or delayed normal adolescent development. The length of time taken to complete the three phases will depend on many factors, the most vital of which is early recognition of symptoms and prompt intervention with family-based treatment. Generally, the more prompt the intervention, the more brief the treatment required for recovery. On average, most families receive about fifteen treatment sessions over a period of six to nine months.

Research into treatment for anorexia nervosa in adolescents

As discussed earlier, it was the work of Minuchin and his colleagues[12] that laid the foundation for the positive role that families can play in the treatment of their adolescent with anorexia nervosa. Since this large case series, several small case series also using family treatment for adolescent anorexia nervosa have been published.[13] These studies were modest in sample size but nevertheless further emphasise the value of the family's involvement in the treatment of adolescents with anorexia nervosa.

Controlled family treatment trials for anorexia nervosa: the Maudsley studies

A limited number of controlled clinical studies have been conducted to explore efficacious outpatient treatments for adolescents with anorexia nervosa.[14] This handful of treatment trials all investigated a family treatment and the results have been quite encouraging despite the lack of extensive data. It is also important to note that no other treatment for adolescent anorexia nervosa has received any consistent research support.

The first landmark study that built on Minuchin's work was conducted at the Maudsley Hospital in London.[15] This study randomly allocated eighty patients of all ages with anorexia nervosa or bulimia nervosa to one of two outpatient follow-up treatments following in-patient weight restoration (average stay about 10 weeks): either family treatment or individual supportive psychotherapy. Study patients were divided into four subgroups and one of these ($n = 21$) comprised young patients (mean age = 16.6 years) who became ill before the age of eighteen years and had been ill for less than three years. At the end of one year of outpatient treatment, this subgroup of adolescents had a significantly better outcome in family treatment as opposed to the individual treatment. A positive outcome was determined along several dimensions[16] but mostly indicating a return to normal weight and the start or resumption of menses. Good outcome was maintained when these patients were followed five years after their treatment was complete. Ninety per cent of those who were originally allocated to family treatment made a good outcome, while only 36 per cent of those who were in the individual therapy made a good outcome.

The family treatment that was utilised in this as well as subsequent Maudsley studies shared many similarities with Minuchin's work, although it also differed in important ways. Most significant, perhaps, was that the Maudsley team encouraged parents to persist in their efforts until the goal of weight restoration had been achieved. In the Maudsley Approach the parents 'stay with' weight concerns until this has been resolved. Consequently, more general adolescent and family issues are deferred until the parents have a better handle on the eating disorder behaviour.

This seminal work was followed by two studies from the Maudsley group in which Dr Eisler and I compared two different forms of family treatment for adolescent anorexia nervosa.[17] Methodology for both studies was similar in that the family treatment employed in the original Maudsley study (conjoint format) was compared with a separated format of this family treatment. In the latter the same therapist would meet with the adolescent and then with the parents, but not simultaneously. Both treatments were provided on an outpatient basis and subscribed to the same therapeutic goals. Most notably, patients in both studies did well and none in my study[18] and only 10 per cent of those in the Eisler study[19] required in-patient treatment during the course of the study. Admission to the in-patient unit was usually indicated when the adolescent's weight did not respond to the parents' efforts and/or the team physician determined that the teen was no longer medically stable for continuing outpatient management. Overall results for these two studies were similar, with both showing no differences in outcome for the two types of family treatment. About 70 per cent of patients were considered to have made a good (weight restored and menses started/returned) or intermediate outcome (weight restored but menses have not started/returned) at the end of treatment. In a five-year follow-up of the Eisler cohort,[20] patients in both types of family treatment did equally well, with 75 per cent of patients having made a good outcome, 15 per cent an intermediate outcome and 10 per cent a poor outcome (weight not restored and no menses).

Continuing the Maudsley Approach outside the United Kingdom

A significant advance since the first Maudsley studies has been the development of a treatment manual that accurately reflects the core procedures and interventions of the family treatment that had been implemented in the London studies.[21] This manualised format of the Maudsley Approach has come to be known as family-based treatment.

The first controlled study to use the family-based treatment manual was conducted by a group at Stanford University in California.[22] Adolescents (n = 86) aged twelve to eighteen years were randomly assigned to either a short-term family-based treatment (ten sessions over six months) or a longer-term family-based treatment (twenty sessions over twelve months). Findings at the end of treatment revealed no differences between the two groups. Examining the data more carefully, though, suggested that patients who scored high on obsessive-compulsive indices or came from single parent families did better if they were in longer-term family-based treatment. A four-year follow-up of these patients showed that more than 80 per cent of patients, irrespective of the length of the treatment they originally received, were weight restored and presented with no further weight and shape concerns.

At least four case series also have employed manualised family-based treatment. In the first of these, Professor Lock and I[23] describe the rationale and feasibility of developing a manual for the Maudsley Approach, and report on the acceptability of this treatment for the first nineteen adolescents with anorexia nervosa who were part of the randomised trial discussed earlier.[24] Favourable outcomes were reported for the majority of cases. These results also suggest that, through the use of this manual, a valuable treatment approach can now be tested more broadly in a variety of treatment studies.

In the second of these case series, my team and I[25] report pre- and post-treatment data for forty-five adolescents with anorexia nervosa. All patients received a course of family-based treatment and overall findings were favourable. Close to 90 per cent of cases were recovered or made significant improvements in this relatively short-term outpatient treatment (mean duration of treatment = 10 months; mean number of treatment sessions = 17). These findings led us to conclude that this series provides preliminary support for the feasibility of outpatient family-based treatment. Moreover, it underscores the beneficial impact of active parental involvement in the treatment of adolescents with anorexia nervosa. The third of these series to utilise family-based treatment was an open trial of twenty adolescents with anorexia nervosa. Loeb and colleagues[26] demonstrated high treatment retention rates and significant improvement in both eating disorder and general psychopathology of their patients. Finally, and in the only case series of family-based treatment for children with anorexia nervosa, Professor Lock and I demonstrated that this treatment is as effective for children with anorexia nervosa as it is for adolescents with anorexia nervosa.[27] Collectively, these studies demonstrate the efficacy of family-based treatment in that about two-thirds of adolescents with anorexia nervosa are recovered at the end of a course of treatment. Approximately 80 per cent are fully weight recovered at long-term follow-up (four to five years),[28] while similar improvements were noted in terms of psychological symptoms.

Research teams at the University of Chicago, Stanford University and Mt Sinai in New York have shown promising results for family-based treatment in their studies. Their findings are comparable to the positive outcomes that were initially established in the Maudsley studies in that most adolescents with anorexia nervosa require, on average, no more than twenty treatment sessions over the course of six to twelve months. Moreover, about 80 per cent of patients are fully weight restored and resumed menses at the conclusion of treatment.

Work based on the Maudsley Approach

Based on the Maudsley Approach, Robin and his colleagues[29] compared behavioural systems family therapy with ego-oriented individual treatment. Significant improvements in anorexia nervosa symptomatology were achieved at the end of treatment, with more than two-thirds of patients reaching target weight and 80 per cent regaining menses. These improvements continued: at one-year follow-up about three-quarters reached their target weight while 85 per cent started or resumed menses. There were, however, significant differences between the two treatments, in that patients in behavioural systems family therapy achieved greater weight gain and were more likely to have returned to normal menstrual functioning at the end of treatment compared with those in ego-oriented individual treatment. On the other hand, both treatments were similar in terms of improvements in eating attitudes, depression and self-reported eating-related family conflict. Contrary to expectation, neither group reported significant family-related conflict around eating, either before or after treatment.

Taken together, both treatments showed quite comparable improvements in eating attitudes and depression; however, behavioural systems family therapy produced more rapid symptomatic improvements.

Behavioural systems family therapy was modelled after the Maudsley Approach but differed in important albeit subtle ways. First, in behavioural systems family therapy, the adolescents were defined as 'out of control' and unable to take care of themselves. As a result, the parents were coached to implement a behavioural weight gain program. This differs slightly from the way in which the Maudsley Approach characterises the adolescent as 'overtaken by' the illness. To manage either definition of the adolescent's state of mind, both behavioural systems family therapy and the Maudsley Approach would encourage the parents to explore and, with the help of the therapist, find the optimal way to restore healthy weight in their adolescent with anorexia nervosa. Second, in behavioural systems family therapy the focus of treatment was broadened to include cognitions and challenges in 'family structure', but at the same time the parents were still in charge of the weight restoration process. In contrast, the Maudsley Approach typically would refrain from such 'distractions' until weight has been restored. While Phase One of behavioural systems family therapy and the Maudsley Approach present with these nuanced differences, Phases Two and Three are relatively indistinguishable between these two treatments. In Phase Two, both treatments would work towards returning control over eating to the adolescent when their target weight was achieved, while Phase Three would focus discussions on adolescent issues such as individuation, sexuality and career.

The current status of family-based treatment

Several recent developments have continued to move family-based treatment forward. Among these are multi-family day treatment[30] and the development of a treatment manual for adolescent bulimia nervosa. Turning first to multi-family day treatment, the Maudsley group has embarked on a more intensive version of family treatment appropriate for those who do not respond to the typical outpatient family-based treatment alone.[31] In conjunction with a group in Dresden, Germany, preliminary steps have been taken to develop an intensive program for adolescents with anorexia nervosa and their families.[32] Multi-family day treatment is similar to family-based treatment in that it aims to enable families to collectively uncover their own resources in order to restore their starving adolescent's weight. In doing so, families are encouraged to explore how the eating disorder and the family's interactional patterns have become intertwined, and how being so intertwined has made it problematic for them to get back on track with their family's normal developmental course. Multi-family day treatment is also quite different from family-based treatment in that the sharing of experiences among families is a collective process that takes place in a very intense way (meeting together for several consecutive days), which makes this a unique experience for families. Finally, the architects of multi-family day treatment would make the case that the importance of helping families find their own solutions is even more evident in this treatment than is typically the case in family-based treatment.[33]

Multi-family work is in a developmental stage and only preliminary findings are available. Both the London and Dresden groups have reported notable clinical improvements in symptomatic behaviours, which include weight gain with a return of menses and a reduction of binge eating and purging. A significant majority of adolescents (80 per cent) and most parents described working alongside other families in a day hospital setting as both 'helpful' and 'desirable'. In particular, parents reported that multi-family day treatment was helpful because of its collaborative nature and sharing of ideas with other families about how to cope with their common predicament.[34] In addition, this collective work environment served to keep drop-out rates low.

A clinician manual of family-based treatment for adolescents with bulimia nervosa[35] has been adapted from the version for anorexia nervosa. Until this manual was developed, treatment development for adolescents with bulimia nervosa was limited to a number of case series or case studies, although most of these studies involve the patient's parents in the treatment. Although anorexia nervosa and bulimia nervosa are distinct syndromes a substantial overlap in symptomatology is common, which makes it quite feasible that the efficacy of family-based treatment for adolescent anorexia nervosa could be extended to include adolescent bulimia nervosa.

Similar to family-based treatment for anorexia nervosa, family-based treatment for bulimia nervosa is an outpatient intervention that is usually conducted in twenty sessions over six months. As in all treatments flexibility is required: for some families a shorter course is sufficient while additional sessions may be necessary for others. Family-based treatment for bulimia nervosa proceeds through three phases. In Phase One of treatment, the parents are encouraged to help their teen put healthy eating habits in place and to curtail or take hold of binge eating and purging episodes. Quite distinct from family-based treatment for anorexia nervosa, normalising eating behaviours is a collaborative process between the parents and their teen. However, should this turn out to be a fruitless endeavour, parental authority is mobilised to manage the health crisis that the eating disorder poses. Outside of eating, the adolescent's autonomy in domains such as friendships and school is almost always kept intact at a level that is consistent with the patient's developmental status. In Phase Two, a return of full control over eating to the adolescent is managed only when acute symptoms have abated and regular eating patterns have been established. As family-based treatment for bulimia nervosa is more collaborative than its counterpart for anorexia nervosa, the line separating Phase One and Phase Two might be less distinct. Finally, Phase Three, in addressing termination issues, provides a brief review of normal adolescent development vis-à-vis the degree to which the eating disorder interrupted this process.

One of only two available controlled studies for adolescents with bulimia nervosa specifically tested the efficacy of family-based treatment for this population. My colleagues and I[36] randomly allocated forty-one adolescents to family-based treatment for bulimia nervosa and thirty-nine to supportive psychotherapy, and found significant differences between these two treatments. Almost 40 per cent of patients in family-based treatment for bulimia (39 per cent), compared with less than 20 per cent in supportive psychotherapy treatment, were free of binge eating and purging at the end of treatment. Although fewer patients were abstinent at six-month follow-up, this difference remained statistically in favour of family-based treatment (29.3 per cent versus 10.3 per cent). This study demonstrated that family-based treatment for bulimia showed a clinical and statistical advantage over supportive psychotherapy, and reductions in core bulimic symptoms were more acute for patients in family-based treatment as opposed to supportive psychotherapy.

In addition to a manual adapted to family-based treatment for bulimia nervosa,[37] this treatment has also been presented in a manual form for the prevention of anorexia nervosa in children and adolescents with clinically significant prodromal presentations[38] and for paediatric overweight.[39]

What these studies tell us

Almost all the studies involving adolescents with anorexia nervosa suggest that family-based treatment is an effective therapy for this patient population. It seems especially useful in preventing unnecessary hospitalisations and seems most efficacious in younger patients with a short duration of illness. About 60 per cent of patients who receive a course of family-based treatment reach a healthy weight by the end of treatment and a majority have started or resumed menstruation. At the four- to five-year mark post-treatment, well over 80 per cent of patients are fully recovered.[40] Therefore, based on current evidence, family-based treatment appears to be the treatment of choice for adolescent anorexia nervosa.

Family-based treatment encourages parents to take an active role in restoring their adolescent's weight and helping their teen return to a normal course of adolescent development. This family treatment has advantages over more 'routine' advice to parents, which involves them in a way that is supportive and understanding of their child but encourages them to step back from the eating problem. However, some aspects about the effectiveness of family-based treatment remain unanswered. Given our relatively limited data, it remains unclear how best to involve parents in treatment or how crucial their active involvement might be. For instance, it has been suggested that conjoint family-based treatment is more advantageous than this treatment in its separated form when addressing family and individual psychological issues.[41] On the other hand, conjoint family-based treatment might not always be the preferred way of involving families with high levels of criticism or hostility towards the teen with anorexia nervosa. Engaging critical families in treatment poses a unique challenge,[42] which may be further complicated when the family is seen together in session. It would appear that the challenge to engage such families might be related to the guilt and blame experienced by so many parents, which increases further because of criticisms or confrontations that occur during family sessions.[43] However, the manual for family-based treatment takes note of this potential dilemma and provides specific strategies for the therapist to alter parental criticism, which in turn enhances commitment to treatment.[44]

Taken together, there have been promising developments for family-based treatment in recent years. Perhaps most helpful of these has been the developments of treatment manuals for both anorexia nervosa[45] and bulimia nervosa.[46] Turning specifically to anorexia nervosa, the manual allows for the pioneering work of the Maudsley group to begin to be disseminated and replicated outside its site of origin. Family-based treatment for adolescent anorexia nervosa has been embraced with some enthusiasm, particularly in the United States and Australia. In addition to the treatment manuals, we also know more about the dose intensity in family-based treatment that would facilitate maximum benefit from this intervention. Contrary to conventional belief that subscribes to long-term treatment, most young patients can benefit from relatively brief outpatient family-based treatment.[47] In the end, the true efficacy of family-based treatment can be established only through rigorously conducted and well-powered randomised controlled trials.

Conclusion

During the past thirty years, family-based treatment has gradually been established as perhaps the most prominent outpatient treatment of adolescent anorexia nervosa. In contrast to some other treatment methods, parents participating in family-based treatment are viewed as a resource and as part of the solution. As such, they are assigned an active role in treatment and recovery.

Family-based treatment assumes that no one knows and cares for their children as well as parents do, and while the parents may be struggling with how best to deal with their starving child's illness, almost all parents have the skills to help their child. The therapist's task is to empower the parents and help them rediscover their footing so they can do what parents do so well – take care of their children. We now have the benefit of three long-term outcome studies indicating that more than 80 per cent of patients participating in family-based treatment are fully recovered at a four- to five-year follow-up.

However, larger randomised controlled trials are required to establish the true significance of the role of the family in anorexia nervosa treatment. Family-based treatment holds great promise for most adolescents who have been ill for a relatively short period of time, and it can assist the adolescent in their recovery and ultimately prevent hospitalisation. These goals can be achieved only if parents are regarded as a resource and therefore invited to play an active role in treatment and recovery. Several critical advances have been made to enable clinicians in many parts of the world to learn about this treatment and how best to implement it in clinical practice. Detailed manuals for anorexia nervosa and bulimia nervosa are available, and they clearly spell out how parents should be involved in this treatment. A parent handbook that reinforces the positive role that parents can play in their child's recovery accompanies these treatment manuals.[48]

PART 1

Family case studies

2

Chloe

Thirteen-year-old Chloe felt so scared when hospitalised that she became convinced she must not swallow her saliva in case it contained calories. Her solution was to store her saliva in plastic bags and hide them in her bedside drawers. She couldn't let herself cry because she was afraid she might swallow the salt in her tears, and that the salt, like her saliva, might contain some food value. She stuffed jelly in her underwear and poured her glasses of milk into her shoes to dispose of when alone. This tactic was not discovered for weeks.

Just getting Chloe into hospital was a challenge of Goliath proportions. On one admission, her parents Lynette and Charles arrived at the hospital entrance carrying their daughter from the car because she refused to walk: she was screaming, scratching and biting.

'We had to literally drag Chloe into the hospital', Lynette said. 'I was holding her legs and Charles her hands. People were looking at us. The staff had to call security; she was placed in a six-bed ward and, after the door was locked so she couldn't run away, she wrecked everything she could in the room. Another day she jumped out of the car when I was driving down the highway taking her to the children's hospital. We had to arrange for an ambulance to transport her, and Charles travelled with her. We wouldn't have got her there in our car. Chloe's illness was making her do crazy and dangerous things.'

Anorexia loves to play games: *Alice in Wonderland*-type games where rules, if any, can change in the blink of an eye. Chloe's illness seemed to be particularly creative. As I entered the front door of her family home for our planned interview, Chloe was overcome with an urge to escape out the back. On being warmly welcomed by the rest of her family, I looked around with a smile and asked 'And where is Chloe?'

'Chloe has done a runner', parents Lynette and Charles chorused.

'Oh no!' I thought. I'd been forewarned that some sufferers of anorexia, depending on their stage of recovery, might feel unable to speak with me. I was prepared for this, but for an interviewee to run away was an unforeseen challenge. I'd been outfoxed. Our interview, I thought, surely would need to go on hold while a search was mounted for Chloe, but Lynette and Charles were amazingly calm, suggesting we proceed without her. 'Chloe often runs away', they said, 'and comes home when she feels ready'.

Offering to make a cup of coffee, Lynette and Charles sat at a large timber table in their family room and, with their four younger children aged three to fourteen years coming and going, began to share their journey with anorexia nervosa with me. When I departed several hours later there was still no sign of Chloe, and her parents, outwardly at least, remained unperturbed. I later learnt Chloe did come home, as her parents had suggested she would, when she was ready.

The following month I arranged to call Lynette, a fulltime mother, to follow up our interview. It was a Sunday morning and a young female voice answered the phone. On introducing myself, I asked if Lynette was at home. 'I'm Chloe', a polite young voice said, 'and my mother's out shopping just now'. My mind raced, wondering 'can I hang on to Chloe or will she drop the phone and run away again?' Determined not to let the illness win a second time, and almost holding my breath for fear I might frighten Chloe away, I talked quickly and openly, and soon relaxed as Chloe settled down for an hour-long chat.

Chloe was in fifth grade, aged ten, living in a provincial town of 100 000 people, when she developed anorexia nervosa:

> I don't remember how it happened. I just stopped eating. I always did a lot of exercising, not because I had to but

because I enjoyed it. Sometimes I would feel angry and playing sport helped me to feel better. I swam, played netball and water polo and went running. I had plenty of stamina.

Chloe's anorexia took hold suddenly and aggressively, robbing the already tiny girl of her childhood in a matter of days. Striking at Christmas, this was one festive season Lynette and Charles would never forget. They had packed their four young children and belongings in the car for a 350 kilometre drive to visit relatives for several days. On the way Lynette offered their children some peppermint sweets to help pass the time. The sweets were Chloe's favourite but she said 'No', she didn't want any. 'That's odd, something's not right', Lynette thought.

That was the first inkling that Lynette had that something unusual was happening to Chloe. On arrival at the grandparents' house and after unpacking, Lynette walked with her mother, daughter and several nieces and nephews to the local convenience store. She planned to buy a few groceries and, because the weather was hot, an ice-cream for each of the children. Again, Chloe declined what she had always regarded as a treat. Lynette also noticed that her daughter's mood had altered the moment she had been offered the ice-cream – she had become withdrawn and distant.

Lynette felt more worried as Chloe became increasingly and uncharacteristically prone to crying and being unsociable. She had noticed mood swings before but until now Lynette had thought her lovely sweet daughter was entering puberty and her volatile temperament was related to early adolescence. Chloe's refusal to eat favourite foods, however, had occurred 'overnight' and didn't fit this analysis. Teenagers were known for being grumpy one minute and in a party mood the next, but not for denying themselves their favourite treats.

Lynette voiced her fears to her mother and the following week, when the family returned home, took Chloe to see their family doctor. He suggested that Chloe write a journal for a month to keep track of her food and mood patterns. But she went downhill so fast her mother returned her to see the doctor in two weeks. This time Chloe was referred to a paediatrician and within four weeks was hospitalised with a very low heart rate. It was there that her illness was diagnosed.

'Charles works in the medical profession as an oncologist, but we had no idea what was happening, or why, to our daughter', Lynette said. 'When told Chloe had developed anorexia nervosa we were beside ourselves with worry, wondering where we had gone wrong as there was no history of eating disorders in our family.'

Chloe's anorexia was voracious. She slipped from naturally petite to extremely thin within days. The paediatrician referred the family immediately to a psychologist and family therapist. The next three years were a struggle and, despite the best efforts of her caring parents and medical team, a climax came when Chloe went away from home for two days with her water polo team. Her illness made the most of the moment, striking with a heightened vengeance. She ate nothing the entire two days and returned home dangerously sick.

The illness was on the rampage. Chloe's behaviour was increasingly embarrassing in public and Charles and Lynette were of necessity becoming socially isolated to shield themselves from misunderstandings of family, friends and strangers while trying to cope with her.

Being aggressive, Chloe's illness often erupted into physical violence. Without warning she would punch, bite and kick her parents. Her tiny size belied her strength: she pulled towel racks from the bathroom wall, smashed furniture, broke windows and many dinner plates shattered when hurled against walls or on the floor. Running away developed as an option. So far, Chloe had returned home when she felt 'ready', but once she disappeared for an entire day and her worried parents had to call the police.

The illness could be frightening and terrifying. At times Chloe became hysterical, smashing her dolls and toys. Hospitalisation helped keep her alive but did little for her mind, and she thoroughly tested and outgrew the local health system. The doctors and nurses did not know how to treat her. They did their best but their care was failing Chloe. The local hospital was not set up to manage childhood eating disorders, and Chloe's hugely disruptive behaviour stretched the medical staff beyond their capabilities.

At first, when admitted to the local hospital, Chloe was placed in a general children's ward:

> I was the only child with anorexia in this ward that was filled with kids with broken arms and legs. There was no special menu for me and I felt the doctor didn't understand me. Neither did the nurses, who had only general training. Dad assures me they meant well, but they were no match for my illness.
>
> My mother would try to help by bringing in homemade food that she knew I liked, but the nurses were easy to fool. They were supposed to sit and watch while I ate my meals but they often didn't do so. When they remembered to look at me, I would pretend to eat. They would give me a bag of nuts as a compulsory snack. I would hide the bag and they never bothered to check. This happened many times. They would give me an energy drink and I would wait until they had gone, and pour it down the bathroom sink. Sometimes the nurses would go out of my room and come back to ask if I had eaten everything and I would say 'yes'.

The lack of vigilance led to the nurses being surprised when they put Chloe on the scales and saw she had lost weight. Chloe would feel upset because the nurses assumed her weight loss was due to exercising and purging when the real reason was that they had not been watching her eat. The nurses, lacking understanding of Chloe's illness, would exert punishment by not letting her out of bed even to have a shower.

At thirteen, Chloe was admitted to the state children's hospital for the first time. She had been declined admittance to a private eating disorder clinic due to her extreme low weight requiring medical intervention, and didn't want to go to the big hospital as she didn't like change and would be 350 kilometres from her home town. She had no choice about this, however. During the next six months she was admitted to the state hospital three times. Each time the doctors and nurses did their best but, despite their extra resources and training, they were no match for the aggressiveness of Chloe's illness. According to Lynette, 'The only way to stop her harming herself or destroying property was to lock her up, really, and we didn't want to do that, or let anyone else do that. She was already terrified'.

On Chloe's first admission to the state hospital no bed was available in the adolescent ward, so she was placed in another room with chronically ill young children. Some were dying. She didn't mind being there as the children were a distraction and she enjoyed helping them draw and colour picture books.

> When I was transferred to the adolescent ward I hated it. For the first time, I was with other kids who had eating disorders. I would look at them and they would look at me. I felt they were continually comparing me with them, and that they would not like me if they thought I was thinner than them. They had little habits and I felt uncomfortable. I could see they didn't look nice, being so thin. Dad said we were 'mirrors to ourselves' but I couldn't see that reflected in myself. We ate meals together and this was okay. We would get off our beds and eat in a large room in front of a television. I liked doing this, as the TV programs were a welcome distraction. Some girls were on nasogastric tubes. After a while I got used to it. A psychiatrist tried to talk to me but I hated her.

Nurses at the state hospital set a target weight for Chloe and her illness played the game, allowing her to reach the magic amount so she could go home. There was a dietician, a special menu and the nurses were more vigilant. If Chloe lost weight, she was fed more food rather than face punishments such as being confined to bed. All the time she would think, 'I will do what I have to do to get out and then I'll lose weight again'. When she was in hospital, her parents visited once or twice a week but were not allowed to stay while she was eating. This suited Chloe's illness, as this meant there was no threat to its control.

The stress on Lynette and Charles was enormous. An

ambulance trip was required when Chloe, between hospital admissions, became so dangerously thin it was considered the safest way of keeping her alive on the three-and-a-half hour trip back to the state hospital. This time she was bedridden for more than a month. Despite needing to travel a long distance, Lynette and Charles were allowed only two hours for a visit with their daughter, and Charles was often allowed much less. He found this a particularly harrowing time:

> I could take more than four hours to drive to the hospital due to peak-hour traffic. And then as soon as I entered Chloe's room, she would become very upset and angry. She would shout and scream and yell obscenities at me. Her illness did not want me there and staff would come running. They discouraged me from being there at all. I was lucky to get five minutes with my daughter before the nurses would ask me to leave.

Feeling helpless and upset, Charles would have no option but to get in his car and drive home again. To drive for seven hours for five minutes with a daughter who told him she hated him was difficult to deal with. Emotionally, Charles felt devastated.

Stamina was a major trait of Chloe's illness. Channelled into aggressive and violent behaviour, it tested the stress levels of not only her parents but also the many health providers who tried to help her. For four years, Chloe's illness had led to admissions in both local and state hospitals, and her illness had outwitted the medical staff at each one.

This pattern of periodic hospitalisation continued until Chloe was at death's door. With both local and state hospital systems unable to assist, doctors decided the next best option would be to admit her to a psychiatric hospital, more than 500 kilometres from her home, and refuse family contact for some time. Such a suggestion pierced Lynette's heart. 'I couldn't bear the thought of my daughter being locked up, and separated from me, so far from home', Lynette said. 'I told Chloe's doctors, "No, I won't allow this, there must be another way".'

Lynette intensified her own search for answers. It was

then she heard about the Maudsley Approach, and made inquiries. The Oak House, a private eating disorder clinic in the same city as the children's hospital where Chloe had had repeated admissions, was offering an outpatient service in this family-based treatment. Lynette and Charles contacted the clinic immediately, arranging an assessment. They were accepted.

'Chloe's doctors laughed and joked when I told them what we were going to do – that we were going to undertake family-based treatment', Lynette said. 'One doctor implied that we were definitely going down the wrong track, and that Chloe wouldn't stand a chance. But we did it anyway.'

Initially the anorexia raged afresh, and Charles and Lynette often wondered if the day would ever come when they would get even a small part of their eldest child back, and when they would get their own lives back. Fighting Chloe's illness required intense concentration every minute of every day, but, guided by the family-based treatment therapist, Charles and Lynette committed themselves to the task. Applying the Maudsley Approach, they began insisting Chloe pick up her food in front of them and they would not budge, or let her budge, until she ate it. This was the last thing Chloe wanted.

The house was her battleground. Her illness reaching new heights of destruction and torment, she had to sleep on a mattress on the floor with no furniture in her bedroom. Anything more, such as a bed-frame, and she would wreck it.

Her mealtimes required much planning and preparation, but, as Lynette said, not only with food:

We had to lock all the doors and windows to our home, or Chloe would escape. At the worst times, we had to isolate our younger children to keep them safe because Chloe would hurl things around. One time our toddler was running by and a dinner plate narrowly missed her head. We know Chloe would not deliberately hurt her little sister but we had to take steps to prevent the risk of her illness doing so. This meant our little children could be separated from their sister for most of the day because by the time Chloe ate her breakfast it would be time to start her midday meal. And the children could hear – the whole street could hear – Chloe's screaming and shouting.

In her first twelve months on the program, and for the first time in more than four years, Chloe reached and maintained a consistent healthy weight and completed a full year of school. Chloe has now remained in Phase One for more than two years:

> I don't know if this is necessarily a good thing for me. It is good in that I have not been readmitted to hospital since starting family-based treatment, but I have become dependent on my parents to the point where I feel scared to be without them for even one meal. If I am left alone I am afraid my illness will grab me and tighten its hold.[1]

Now sixteen, Chloe counts her dependency on her parents as a problem but acknowledges that she has come a long way in fighting her illness. Every two weeks the family does a seven-hour round trip of more than 650 kilometres to attend a session at The Oak House, the only private family-based treatment clinic in their state. Although her parents continue to supervise her meals, she has matured and has a greater understanding of her illness. After several years of being in and out of hospital, with her weight so low she could not participate in any normal life activities, Chloe has resumed swimming with a squad once a week, plays netball and tennis, and walks to the homes of friends for a visit.

Lynette and Charles, while grateful for all advances, big and small, know that for Chloe a normal teenage lifestyle is some way off. Charles said that while he and Lynette had felt no sense of connection with staff at the state hospital, there was an immediate feeling of encouragement, support and hope at The Oak House: 'This was a turning point for us. Chloe was so sick before starting this treatment that she was reptilian and her pulse was dangerously low.'

For the first eighteen months, Chloe would sleep all the way to the therapy session and all the way home, and remain silent during the consultation. Lynette and Charles could have been forgiven for wondering if anything the therapists were saying was seeping through the strong wall established by the illness – a wall so solid it would not allow Chloe to speak. Bit by bit, however, a line of communication was forged and now Chloe chats with her therapist for up to thirty minutes each session.

The understanding approach presented by the family-based treatment therapist was a huge relief. The effort required to get others to understand that Chloe was not simply behaving badly but was in the grip of a deadly illness had often reduced Lynette and Charles to despair. As Charles explained, a lack of understanding among extended family, friends and medical circles had been hard to cope with:

> You get a lot of crappy advice from people who don't understand the illness. You don't ask for such advice but parents and friends say things without thinking. Like, one parent said, 'Give Chloe to me for a month and I'll get her to eat'. So far we have been advised to have Chloe try hypnosis, crystals, faith healers and herbalists. All such remedies are most likely to be fantastic in certain situations, but not when someone is dying.

'People would say things that would cause us to stop and think that we must be to blame in some way', Lynette said, 'and we would wonder if Chloe's illness was due to our genetics. We would look at ourselves and ask, "What have we done wrong?" ' To avoid hearing unwanted, unhelpful advice from people who did not understand their daughter's illness, Charles and Lynette have tended to become socially isolated from their local community. Unfortunately, as Lynette explained, this has sometimes meant extra hardship for them and their younger children:

> An understanding lady said to me the other day, 'Why didn't you call me on the phone? I would have looked after your younger children while you were feeding Chloe'. But you only have so much energy and it is difficult asking for help when you fear others are unable to appreciate your situation. These feelings are made worse when ignorant people take delight in engaging in malicious gossip.

Sometimes people ask how Chloe is, and I know they are being patronising. I feel they are enjoying my pain. This illness has made not only Chloe but also her dad and I very sensitive. Even when well-meaning people ask how we are coping and if Chloe is progressing, they can inadvertently say words we may find hurtful so we avoid discussing our situation. At times we have had to take our phone off the hook and, yes, we've lost friends.

Lynette and Charles are trying to keep their family functioning for their four younger children and, as they live several hundred kilometres from other family members, they cope without their support. This is probably just as well; if their parents did visit, they would be more a burden than a help because they don't understand what is involved in fighting the illness.

Charles has given up expecting any emotional support from, or trying to explain the illness to, his family: 'I would call my mother and leave the phone on loudspeaker while I made a coffee, and come back to the phone and she would be still talking about all she had been doing during the week', he said.

As Lynette explained, she and Charles are sustained by love:

> We feel sad that our child has been ill for six years. We know the violence and the bruises she has inflicted are not really her. Every day I feel like giving up; every day I wonder, 'How much longer?' But every day I know I must keep going, because I love Chloe. We've learnt to put all our energy into our family, our children, because they are our priority. Charles and I are so lucky we are still together. The family-based treatment and counselling has helped. Without it, anorexia would be winning. It still has a hold on Chloe but is nowhere near as powerful as it was.

Thankfully, today, with her weight at a healthy level and stable, Chloe's frightening episodes have eased. However, although she looks 'normal', people don't understand that her mind is still recovering, so Charles and Lynette respond to any comments with 'Yes, she looks well, but she is not 100 per cent yet'. In year 11 at school and seventeen next birthday, Chloe recently tried taking her own lunch to school and eating without supervision, but lost 3 kilograms in two weeks. So her mother resumed the supervision and was relieved to find Chloe was peacefully compliant. 'Without our family-based treatment, there would have been a huge outburst', Lynette said.

> Life is much better than it was and we look forward to every little improvement. For Chloe to remind me it is mealtime would be wonderful, but we have to fetch her for every meal. Otherwise she won't eat and she won't make any comment. She will never say, 'I'm hungry'. Even if she missed a meal and it was time for the next one she would say, 'I'm not hungry'.

Eating is not Chloe's only struggle; her illness hampers her concentration when studying, too. She doesn't like to start anything at which she cannot confidently excel, as the thought of achieving anything less than 100 per cent is unacceptable and unbearable. If she attained a success rate of 99 per cent, Chloe's illness would magnify the missing 1 per cent a thousand times or more and she would feel dreadfully guilty. This self-imposed standard of excellence was a huge weight to bear, Lynette said, and if Chloe considered that there was any risk she would not attain a perfect score in tests and exams, she preferred not to try at all. Her life was acutely black and white; usually the black or nothing option was easier, being less stressful and less painful to deal with. When Chloe attempted to achieve some white, some light, in her life, her illness would try to sabotage her, preventing her from making the best choices.

Right now Lynette and Charles want to plan a family holiday. They are asking themselves if they have enough energy, if they are adventurous enough, or if they are too afraid. Their trepidation is due to Chloe's illness turning previous holidays into nightmares. The most recent holiday was to a big theme park on the coast, interstate. They were looking forward to catching up with an old friend over dinner one night, but when they shared these plans with Chloe, she reacted fearfully, becoming withdrawn, teary and flatly refused to attend. This was unusual behaviour, even for Chloe's illness, and she was unable to express why she felt afraid. Chloe then 'fell into an incredible state', Lynette said.

We were afraid she would jump off the balcony of our high-rise holiday apartment. We had to cancel our special dinner. Instead we went somewhere else to eat and Chloe was perfectly fine. The incident, however, ruined our holiday because just once in a while we would like to do something that is normal.

Lately, the therapist has been gently encouraging Lynette to take her younger children on outings, leaving Chloe with Charles for a few hours, at least. In a major achievement, Lynette watched her 8- and 10-year-old sons compete at a swimming carnival without concerning herself that she had to be home to supervise Chloe's lunch. 'Our other children have been missing out on one-to-one time for years and this big step forward is working out happily for everyone. We have to be careful because, as Chloe said, she does not like change and her anxiety can erupt into sudden violence.'

The family-based treatment therapist is encouraging Lynette and Charles to increase variety, not only by taking the family on outings, but also by branching out at home, mixing routines and allowing themselves more time alone with their other children and themselves. This is because the anorexia nervosa is very comfortable with the same thing. For recovery to occur, it must be challenged. With Chloe's illness so volatile, progress is of necessity slow, but sure.

Overcoming, or at least working around, Chloe's rigid dietary habits is a constant challenge, as Charles noted:

Taking care of Chloe is more work than looking after our three year old. Not only because of the focus on food, but because she is not able to do normal activities that teenagers can be expected to do, like setting the table. She does not like to be reminded of anything to do with food, so our 14-year-old son does more to help in the kitchen.

While participating in her family's life is a struggle for Chloe, the seven-member household these days has achieved a relative calmness. At first, Charles and Lynette would be black and blue with bruises after their weekly visit to the therapist. Today, outbursts are rare. Lynette gave a recent example when Chloe didn't want to eat all of her meal and Charles told her, 'If you don't eat it all we will have to take your iPod', and Chloe's response was to attempt to bite him. That behaviour occurred daily for five years but has subsided in the past twelve months, so life is more relaxed.

Our fear is we can't bear the thought of regression. Chloe's illness seems entrenched and she has missed much of her childhood and teenage years – such years should be the best of your life. We feel sad because our other children have missed out, too, but we work hard at keeping everyone reasonably happy. Living with a child consumed by anorexia nervosa is unrelenting, but we are better parents for the experience.

The illness, Charles said, has helped the family simplify their life:

Materialism is less important now; family is everything. Our three younger children don't remember Chloe any other way and we tell them she has an eating disorder, to explain her behaviour. Her closest sibling, a brother, initially picked up her mannerisms as the two of them had a close relationship. She tricked him into doing things, such as going on long and inappropriate walks. He was eight at the time but now he is fourteen we can explain more to him.[2]

As for the future, Charles is optimistic about Chloe's recovery, saying she has progressed a long way since the days he feared her illness could cause an early death. At one stage he had contemplated this fear, envisioning a white casket and vowing he would plan a happy funeral for his beautiful girl. His eyes fill with tears as he recalls this low moment. Lynette has always thought positively because it is unbearable for her to think any other way.

Since starting the family-based treatment Lynette and Charles have felt less isolated, knowing they are not alone and that others understand. They know to concentrate on the moment at hand, the next mouthful, the next meal, each and every day. Eight months after I knocked on the front door of her home, Chloe confides that she rarely feels an urge to run away any more but remains uncomfortable with herself. Lynette believes that her daughter is at a crossroad – between moving forward and being entrenched with her illness.

Chloe has had no admissions to hospital for eighteen months, but anorexia nervosa continues to affect her, as Lynette explained:

> Its bizarre thoughts trap her. Hopefully a breakthrough will occur soon, something will click over in her mind and she will realise she is okay. Otherwise she won't have choices because her illness prevents her from thinking about what she would like to do with her life. She is very bright and we want her to be independent. We want her to have adventures and fun. We wish for her to find something to be comfortable with in life.

The breakthrough that Lynette hopes for may occur at any moment and, when it does, Chloe will be free to rediscover her true self. A growing sense of self-awareness will help her recognise and repel the negative thoughts that sap her happiness and belong to her illness. Instances of refusing to participate in her school's annual debutante ball or in the annual class photograph, because she does not feel worthy, will be in the past.

For now though, Chloe maintains her struggle every moment of the day. 'I've been at what they call a safe weight for a year', she said, 'and I feel annoyed when people say, "You look better, so you must be better" '. She knows she must maintain the fight to liberate her mind from her illness.

'I would like to be free like my friends', Chloe said. She can manage to go to the movies with them now, and looks forward to when she can defy her illness sufficiently to go out socially without her parents and eat a snack and sip a drink. For Chloe these simple pastimes and joys, which others take for granted, will be heroic accomplishments.

3

Matthew

'I wish I was a puff of wind so I could blow away', Matthew murmured as he drew his legs into his frail body curled under the crisp, white hospital sheets. His voice dropping, he whispered to his mother, 'I can't do this any more'. Anorexia nervosa had so completely taken over his mind and body that he wanted to die. His mother did not doubt him; she could see the illness was draining him of life. This was the lowest moment in 11-year-old Matthew's struggle. His parents, April and Ted, desperately searched for a way to gain control over the horrid illness that was consuming their son. They didn't want to let Matthew go. There had to be an answer.

Ted and April have three sons – Andrew, Kyle and Matthew, the youngest. They'd never dreamed that anorexia would affect their family. The illness had crept slowly into their lives over a few months, coinciding with news that due to a change in Ted's employment the family would be relocating from a popular tourist city on the coast to an inland country town.

At first they thought Matthew's rapid weight loss must be part of a growth spurt because 'surely 10-year-old boys don't get eating disorders?' But yes, they do, and now a year later Matthew's tiny body lay curled in a foetal position on the hospital bed. April and Ted had no idea how their nightmare with anorexia nervosa had started or when it would end. April sought refuge by writing in her diary, something she had not been able to bring herself to do during the first months of Matthew's illness. 'It is hard to keep a diary when your heart is breaking and you feel you can't take one more day living with this monster that has taken over your previously happy, gorgeous child', she wrote.

Matthew had been a typical chubby little boy, full of laughter and happiness, and a delightful companion to his two older brothers. This was a factor that saddened April the most – anorexia had devoured Matthew's personality and replaced it with a sad, anxious, dispirited child who looked in the mirror, sucking in his face and drawing in his stomach to see how many ribs would stick out.

The nightmare had accelerated when Matthew became obsessed with exercising and increasingly fussy about what he would eat. He developed a self-loathing, which deepened each time he looked in the mirror, checking his fat. 'I'm a hippopotamus!' he shrieked in horror one day as he looked into the mirror and tugged his cheeks with his hands. Matthew had a big, round beautiful face, complete with dimples, but to him it appeared fat and ugly.

As Matthew's illness took hold he went from being an outgoing, bubbly natured boy to a boy who lay on a sofa in the family room, weak and sad. He finally refused to eat or drink anything. Within days of moving to the country town, Matthew could barely walk due to stomach cramps and dehydration. He was admitted to the local hospital for the first time shortly after starting classes at his new primary school.

In hospital, Matthew was introduced to a regime of dietary plans. If he ate his meals, he would be rewarded with privileges, and if he didn't eat his meals, he would be punished. Punishments included restricted visiting hours and confinement to bed, neither of which Matthew wanted. Particularly, he missed his family. Gradually, during the next six weeks, he regained weight and returned home. He slowly returned to school but with a strict food menu and weigh-ins. If his weight dropped below a healthy range he would have to return to hospital.

April, uncertain of how best to help her son fight his illness and keep him out of hospital, was pleading for counselling but the specialist guidance they needed was not available where they lived. All she had was a menu, and she thought that was nowhere near enough to fight an illness of the mind. Matthew managed a term at school, but his will was slowly disintegrating as the anorexia took over again.

Thinking a holiday might offer encouragement, April and Ted packed their bags and took their boys to a favourite tourist destination, but their hopes were quickly dashed. Matthew's illness raged afresh and he was eating less at every meal. The holiday was cut short and Matthew was readmitted to hospital, and this time a nasogastric tube was inserted. By now Matthew was so weary he told his mother he was ready to surrender the last thread of his tormented life.

Desperate, April lay on the bed beside him. Big tears rolled down her cheeks as she told him her heart was breaking and she could not let this insidious disease take her little boy from her. Feeling powerless and with her voice her only weapon, she drew on her deepest self to find words that would connect with and inspire her ailing son. Trying to give an analogy with which he could identify, April pleaded for him to find the strength within himself somehow, just like the heroes in his favourite movies:

What if Frodo Baggins had just given up and not bothered trying to return the ring to Mount Doom? Matthew, God has put you here on earth for a purpose and would not like to see you waste away your life, your unique gifts, your talent and your beautiful personality that is silently disappearing from us.

In saying this, April felt something of a fraud as she did not have a strong Christian faith, but intuitively believed this ploy might evade the illness and get through to her weakened son. Unable to think of anything more to say, she left him that night feeling gut-wrenchingly sad. The following morning she wept with relief when Matthew rang from his hospital bed and said he had thought about what she had said. He would try to get better! Another day of the battle with anorexia had begun.

April recorded in her diary, 'One day at a time. We want our Matthew back. I will do anything to see his dimples again'.

Why had this happened to Matthew? April and Ted didn't know. They had already been at breaking point before Matthew had begun losing weight due to their son Kyle's struggles with a serious obsessive-compulsive disorder. Was the illness something to do with their genetics, biology and environmental circumstances?

April scolded herself for thinking like this. She had to keep going. Britain's wartime Prime Minister, Winston Churchill, had said, 'If you are going through hell, keep going'. She repeated these words often. And a therapist had said, 'Never, ever give up'. But April wondered how much time she and Ted had to save their little boy. They needed expert help but did not know where to find it.

They did not want the dislocation and exhaustion of travel that they had already endured with Kyle, travelling hundreds of kilometres for medical appointments. They did not want continual readmissions to their local hospital, which provided the best treatment it could based on traditional schools of thought, but at the same time did not want Matthew admitted to a specialist anorexia unit of predominantly teenage girls hundreds of kilometres away in a major hospital. 'He was still our innocent little boy and what he didn't know about anorexia already, we didn't want him to find out from the teenage experts', April said.

Now thirteen, Matthew recalled how, towards the end of fifth grade, his life began to change: 'I decided I had been eating quite a lot and was feeling fat, so I began to go for a little jog to help me feel on top of things'.

Matthew remembered small but significant events that heralded the onset of his illness. A friend had celebrated a birthday by bringing a cake to school to share with the class, but when slices were passed around the normally cake-loving Matthew said he didn't want any. He was on a get-thin mission, progressively eating less and jogging more. His jogs became hour long and he cut his meals back to one a day. But this wasn't enough, so he added cycling to his exercise routine.

Looking in a full-length mirror while on a weekend visit to his grandparents Matthew felt disgusted, deciding he was fat, horribly fat – he had lost touch with reality. When the family returned home on the Sunday night Matthew did not want any dinner, saying to his mother, 'I'm so fat I do not think I will eat any more'.

By now the summer school holidays had started and Matthew was to stay with an aunt and uncle for a week while his parents supervised the family's move to the country. Normally Matthew enjoyed visiting his relatives, but this time he was on guard. His fears were realised when his aunt, forewarned that he was being 'difficult' at mealtimes, sat him down and said, 'You must stop being so stubborn, Matthew, and eat your meals. You know your parents have enough worries without you behaving like this. You know how much this is upsetting your mother'.

Matthew always had been an agreeable little boy who liked to please others. He did not like upsetting his mother and had been worrying about her long before his aunt began her lecture. By now, however, thoughts associated with his illness were overpowering those for his mother. He politely listened to his aunt, saying nothing but thinking, 'I don't care what you say, I'm not going to eat'.

The family was reunited the following week, but the house they had moved into seemed dark. Matthew needed light. He felt scared and shut himself in his room. He missed his dad, whose new job required him to be away from home for a few days, and the thought of attending a new school increased his anxiety. Above all, he felt ugly. He would not know any children at the new school. He would have to make new friends and was afraid of being laughed at and called 'fat'. Trying to ignore crippling physical pains from prolonged hunger, Matthew clung to the belief that losing fat was the key to making everything in his world seem manageable. And the key to that, Matthew thought, was to exercise more and eat less.

'I'm in total control. I can keep doing this', Matthew thought, and found any excuse to exercise. He cycled more every day and ran more and more. He hated sitting still and at school was known as Forrest Gump. He had no idea who Forrest Gump was, but the other children thought of the name because he ran everywhere, just as Forrest did in the movie. He did not always want to exercise, but felt compelled to, even when feeling sick. Lack of food was making him light-headed and, realising he had to eat something, he sucked on ice cubes made from plain water.

With her other son, Kyle, and to a lesser extent, Andrew, suffering obsessive-compulsive disorders, April had hoped Matthew would have a trouble-free childhood. When he began to question the fat content of foods and was becoming finicky with his meals, she tried to tell herself that this was a phase that would pass once they settled into their new home. However, instead of passing, it intensified. With a new school year about to start, April took Matthew to a family doctor who, on observing he was seriously underweight, referred him to a paediatrician. Matthew began classes at school but threw his lunch into the bin and, within two days, was admitted to the local hospital suffering crippling hunger pains and dehydration.

Unfortunately, the hospital's medical approach was not the full answer for Matthew's illness. Away from his family, without support from his parents, his anorexia worsened. Matthew was aware of the doctors' and nurses' intentions: they wanted him to gain weight. He also was aware that their approach would fail:

> The medical staff make you gain weight, but your mind stays the same. It was like they were playing a game. They thought they could fool me and win, but I knew what they were up to. I would think, 'You can make me gain weight but when I get out of here I will lose it again'.

Sometimes the hospital staff unwittingly fed Matthew's illness and supplied him with new strategies. A nurse, wondering why he was taking a long time to gain weight, asked, 'You don't stick your finger down your throat, do you?'

Matthew played the adults' game, gaining 5 kilograms, and they let him go home. Within five months he was back again, this time weighing 1 kilogram less than at his initial admission. At home, worried that people would not like him because he was 'fat', Matthew had determinedly refused to eat:

A boy at my first school had been fat and he wasn't liked, and this bothered me because I wanted to be liked. When they admitted me to hospital for the second time, I thought, 'Oh, this is happening again. They will do the same thing to me as they did before. They think they can fatten me up and everything will be alright, but I know it won't be: last time I gave in, this time I won't'.

True to his word, Matthew refused to eat anything. The medical staff did their best to coax him to get well, but the nurses were forced to insert a nasogastric tube that became his food lifeline. Today, whenever Matthew feels sad, the traumatic experience of having the tube inserted comes back to haunt him:

They wouldn't leave me alone in my room and followed me to the toilet, but the shower was my opportunity. Someone had dropped a syringe on the floor, and I picked it up and hid it. When I showered, I'd syphon the content of my tubal sac out with the syringe and squirt it down the plughole. I was able to avoid a lot of food intake for several weeks until, one day, I dropped the syringe on the shower floor and the nurse, who was waiting outside, asked me to explain the noise. She did a good job to catch me and seized my syringe.

The nurses didn't want Matthew to see his weight but he would distract them and get a quick look. 'I wouldn't like what I saw and would renew my efforts to cut my food intake', Matthew said. 'I felt sad and was starting to think I would be in hospital forever. They had different levels of rewards and restrictions. It got really hard for me, especially when I was deprived of family time.' When the nurses and doctors were not happy with Matthew – usually for not gaining weight – he lost 'privileges'. Initially, visits by his parents would be reduced to one a day, and then his weekend leave from hospital would be cancelled with his parents allowed to visit for two hours, then only one hour a day.

The hospital policy of isolating Matthew and allowing visits as a 'reward' if he ate his meals and gained weight was hurting every member of his family. April felt upset because she knew Matthew wanted and needed his family around him. Left alone, the illness increasingly dominated his thoughts. He was in hospital this second time for seven weeks, and couldn't see the point of being there.

The only person Matthew found helpful during this time was a volunteer play therapist who visited him in hospital. She had suffered anorexia and understood how he was feeling. 'This therapist said I had to fight my illness. She wrote affirmations on small pieces of paper and gave them to me to read for strength when I was alone', Matthew said. 'The trouble was the nursing staff discouraged her from spending time with me as they said she was a bad influence. Without her understanding, I would have been in hospital a lot longer.'

Matthew went home several centimetres taller and only 500 grams heavier. His parents were despairing. They had been hoping to gain help for Matthew locally as their financial resources were already stretched. By now, however, they were at crisis point, and on hearing of the Maudsley Approach, which sounded more caring than the local hospital's isolationist program, they decided to travel 450 kilometres to a large city-based hospital, the Children's Hospital at Westmead, to find out more about it.

April phoned for an assessment appointment. She and Ted were a little apprehensive as they had visited the same hospital many times during Kyle's treatment and had seen patients with anorexia in the adolescent ward. 'We didn't want Matthew to be in that environment as he was only twelve', April said. When told the hospital offered an outpatient program, they felt overjoyed at finding a way of helping Matthew in the comfort of their own home.

By now, nine months had passed since Matthew's first hospitalisation due to precariously low weight. As they drove their family to the hospital, Ted and April listened to the news on the car radio. None of it seemed related to their life; it felt surreal, their world revolving around a mission to rescue their son from anorexia. Nothing else mattered. At the hospital, the family-based therapy team was compassionate and, acknowledging the family already had endured a lot

of dislocation, confirmed they would work with Matthew
as an outpatient. The family-based treatment would start
within a few weeks. For the first two weeks the family would
need to attend the hospital every day to develop relationships with the medical team and learn how the treatment
worked. Accommodation for this short time was arranged
with relatives who lived in the city.

On meeting the team of high-powered people – psychiatrist, psychologist, paediatrician, dietician and social
workers – April's initial thought was that she and Ted were
lucky to have access to so many well-qualified people. She
felt sure they would cure Matthew's illness. 'We were prepared to do whatever it took', April said. 'When the therapist
heading the team offered video conferencing every second
week, we thought "What a godsend".'

But April and Ted were in for a shock. They thought they
would be able to relax a little now that Matthew was in good
hands, but instead were told they would be doing the work!
'What the team said was such a turnaround on all that we
had been told before', April said. 'It was a revelation for
Ted and I to be told that we would be confronting the illness.
We were told that "today is the first day in your son's
recovery".'

April felt confused and angry as the therapist explained
why, of all the people in the world, she and Ted were the two
most likely to help their son recover. The reason, the therapist said, was because they knew him better than anyone else,
loved him more than anyone else, and were with him more
than anyone else. Initially, Matthew would require constant
devotion and vigilance, twenty-four hours a day, every day, to
recover. He could do this if his parents were committed to
helping him. All they needed was empowerment and guidance from the family-based treatment team to get him over
the line. On hearing this, April 'felt angry at the amount of
time wasted on other methods. I wanted to know that if the
solution was that simple and straightforward, why hadn't we
been told before? Everything we had been told had been
turned on its head'.

On learning that she and Ted would be responsible for
getting Matthew to eat, April wondered how the method

could work when their entreating had not worked before. There had to be more to it; there had to be a catch. Then she thought, 'This cannot possibly work, because surely the therapy team first needs to deal with the thoughts in Matthew's head'. She had no idea how they would persuade him to eat. Previously when he refused a meal they had been discouraged from making a fuss, because the evidence would be revealed at the weekly weigh-in and Matthew would have to suffer the consequences. Now, they were being told that the secret to Matthew getting better was to make a big fuss, to be insistent. It was a revelation.

The therapist explained that if Matthew had cancer, he would be treated with chemotherapy. Because he had anorexia nervosa, he would be treated with food. The therapist was not interested in analysing the family or looking for someone to blame. This was a big relief, too, because Ted and April often had wondered if they were doing something wrong with their child rearing. But this therapy team was reassuring them that 'no family is perfect' and they would not be pulled apart and analysed as before. Their family was being acknowledged and accepted for what it was, and the therapist was ready to support it.

There was no question: Matthew would have to eat, and would need his parents' help to do so. 'We thought we had used up our energy with helping our son Kyle and his obsessive-compulsive disorder', April said, 'but now we had to fight anorexia for Matthew. This fight would be crucial; a matter of life and death'.

The therapist assured April and Ted that family-based treatment would empower them, but warned, 'You won't be able to give an inch'. The parents struggled during those first few weeks. April would become distressed, overwhelmed and tearful. Over and over, she could not believe the remedy really was simple. She looked for a catch but could find none. Gradually she began to see the strategy made sense – good common sense. She and Ted were to sit with Matthew until he ate each meal and snack, however long that might take; they were to encourage him and persist, but not give up. The therapist was empowering them to confront the anorexia and seize back the control that it had snatched from them and their son. They had fed their child when he was a baby; of course they could do it again.

As for a special hospital menu, something April and Ted had been accustomed to receiving from the previous medical teams, they were told there was none because it would 'feed' the anorexia control. Matthew was to eat what the rest of his family were eating – normal homemade meals, ice-creams and occasional fast foods. Matthew, listening to the adults discussing his treatment, vowed silently to himself, 'This won't work. I won't let it'. His vow was tested that very day when he was told to sit at a table with his parents in the therapist's consulting room. None of them was to leave the table until Matthew had one sip of lemonade and a teaspoon of ice-cream. 'I was determined not to eat or drink anything', Matthew said, 'but my parents wouldn't budge'. An hour and forty minutes later, Matthew was able to leave the table having swallowed the sip of lemonade and eaten the teaspoon of ice-cream. This small win was a major breakthrough for parents and son.

The therapist, present while the confrontation with Matthew's illness took place, explained to the parents how their love and support would strengthen Matthew's will in fighting his illness. It was Matthew's illness, not Matthew, that was resisting recovery efforts.

Matthew was listening, too. While he thought 'this therapist guy kinda makes sense', he felt anxious on hearing he would have to eat a chocolate chip biscuit within the coming week. Despite his fears, having his mother and father challenge his illness was making him feel a little happier that he had to sit there, because deep down a little, hidden and much-starved part of him did want to eat. Eventually, Matthew decided he might as well do what his parents wanted him to do – eat the mouthful of ice-cream and sip the lemonade – and get the agony over quickly. So began the dismantling of the illness's rigid control. It wouldn't be easy. April and Ted would draw on every ounce of stamina to cope with the intensity of battling the illness at every meal.

On day two of Matthew's family-based treatment, the family went to a large shopping centre and decided to eat lunch in the busy and noisy food court. Matthew, much to his dismay, was told to eat a small punnet of frozen yoghurt. His illness baulked at this. He refused to eat and ran away, disappearing in the throng of shoppers. April and Ted took more than thirty minutes to find him. By the time they returned to the table in the food court, the yoghurt had melted. 'We had to report a failure on that one', April said.

> We realised that expecting Matthew to eat a meal in front of others, in a shopping centre so soon in his recovery, was too frightening for him. At home, however, he surprised us when we introduced foods as challenges. While at first he took ninety minutes to eat a tiny tub of ice-cream, a few months later he was licking the bowl clean and asking for more.

The illness initially sowed seeds of doubt in Matthew who thought, 'If I get better, my doctor will think I am weak'.

However, within a few days, amazing changes began to happen. The unrelenting persistence from his parents at every meal and snack time was connecting more strongly with Matthew and increasingly bypassing his illness. When the two-week session was completed at the hospital, Matthew and his family returned home and continued to communicate with the family-based therapy team via video conferencing.

At about the same time Matthew's compulsion to exercise, a characteristic since the earliest days of his illness, began to lessen. For instance, every day he had been 'secretly' doing 400 jumps – he called them 'Toyota jumps', jumping into the air and hitting the backs of his legs with his heels – usually in his bedroom. Sometimes this was a big challenge as he felt weak, but although the calves in his legs would ache, he had to keep going until he had counted 400. After a few weeks of his mother and father insisting he eat every meal, the urge to complete his daily exercise routine began to abate, as did associated feelings of guilt. 'At first I made it easier for myself by hanging on to a bar above my head and pulling myself up with my arms when I kicked', Matthew said. 'Then I needed to do only 300 jumps, then 200, and, suddenly, my urge to do any at all stopped.'

Matthew's sense of self, restoring quickly, was trouncing his illness. His weight rose progressively, and within four months of starting treatment April heard words that were music to her ears when one day he came home from school and called, 'Hey, Mum, I'm hungry!'

By now Matthew was in year 7 at school and had gained 7 kilograms. April, who had put her career on hold during the illness, felt she was also getting her life back when Matthew began to take his own lunch to school. She felt wonderful, no longer having to eat lunch in a classroom with her 12-year-old child. Having his mother beside him while he ate lunch had not fazed Matthew and although April did not mind either, she knew it was not normal. His year coordinator was supportive, taking over April's role for a while and sitting with him while he ate his meal. Weekly checks revealed no weight loss and soon Matthew was eating without supervision. The coordinator also checked on his exercising and found this was not excessive.

Following the family-based treatment introduction, Matthew required no further hospital admissions and, in twelve months, gained 12 kilograms and grew 7 centimetres in height. The threads of his personality were well on the way to being mended and the dimples in his cheeks reappeared. April and Ted could smile again and say, 'We've got our kid back'.

As April explained, a year after completing the therapy program, Matthew was continuing to thrive:

He is doing well with his studies in year 8. His school marks have gone through the roof. He is conscientious and his healthy diet allows him to concentrate on his studies. He is enjoying sport, too. For a while, he was dubious about running or getting back on his bicycle, in case he felt driven to do more, and more, but he is running and cycling and is free of these obsessive thoughts.

His performance in 1500-metre and cross-country races had gained him selection in long-distance events at the regional athletic titles.

To have Matthew back and to see him enjoying life to the

full was beyond April's wildest dreams. Wonderful things continued to happen. She put a bag of chocolate biscuits in the refrigerator and Matthew ate the lot! April said she was grateful for the family-based treatment, and hoped that it could be available to all families of anorexic children:

> We lost valuable time, allowing the illness to extend its hold, while searching for the right treatment. To learn through the family-based treatment that we, the parents, had to maintain control was a major revelation. To not have a chasm created between our child and us, and to have an encouragement rather than a punishment regimen, was a huge turnaround. Prior to starting family-based treatment, doctors had been basing decisions on what they knew, on what they had been taught years before, but Matthew was getting worse. They seemed to be trying to make him feel they had some control over his illness, when he knew absolutely that they didn't.

Matthew's experience has given him insight and maturity beyond his years. He wants people to understand that anorexia nervosa is life threatening:

> What anorexia does to you is totally horrible. Every second you live is misery. You feel like you are working for your illness twenty-four hours a day, seven days a week; it is always there; you can't get away from it alone.
>
> When I first heard about family-based treatment, I thought, 'You can't do this to me', but then when I got to a certain stage, I started to think 'this is okay'. As I gained weight I felt better. Deep down I hoped the treatment would work, but for a while my illness thought it could cope and beat it. I was only eleven and am very grateful to my parents for persevering. Without them, I would have struggled to recover, because this illness was stronger than my will.
>
> Anorexia 'just happens'. You certainly don't ask for it. I can tell you that it is full of pain and misery. However, if someone had said that to me before I became anorexic, my illness wouldn't have listened. So mothers and fathers

must be alert. I am so glad to have my parents and caring teachers. You need at least the equivalent of a caring mother and father because they need to be on board 100 per cent of the time to help you recover. I say this because during my recovery I looked for any chance to feed my illness rather than me – like, at school when someone wasn't keeping watch, I would tip the chicken out of my sandwich.

Matthew feels 'totally normal and happy now'. This eloquent and thoughtful teenager doesn't give his illness a chance. If he's having a bad day, he tells his mother and she supports him until the moment passes. Far from wishing his life could blow away in the wind, Matthew is thriving on youthful ambition.

4

Kelly

One family doctor tried to shock me; he didn't understand I wasn't doing this out of choice. He told me I was tearing my family apart, my parents would divorce, my sister would become depressed and I would cause the family finances to be used up. He really laid on the guilt trip and I took it all to heart. I knew I was shallow and ugly inside and out. I was screwing around a lot of people's lives and was helpless to do anything about it. Hatred is too weak a word to describe how I felt about myself. I don't wish this illness on anyone.

Kelly, fourteen, had a problem – she had developed anorexia nervosa but she didn't think she was sick. To make matters worse, her doctor didn't know how to help. Almost three years would pass before Kelly would be able to describe her helplessness while in the grip of her illness:

> For a long time I was thoroughly convinced everyone but me was totally deluded. I was stuck in a time capsule, looking out and I felt trapped. I couldn't see how I could get out. I couldn't bear to have other people look at me or watch me eat. I hadn't cracked a joke or been to a party for two years.

Kelly's happy early childhood was filled with a love of the outdoors and books. She played soccer and netball, did surf lifesaving and competitive swimming, and later on took up long-distance running. Her favourite books focused on the human condition – Harper Lee's *To Kill a Mockingbird* had been a favourite since she turned ten or eleven.

Kelly enjoyed time with her girlfriends, describing herself as shy and self-conscious, though not chronically so – 'not extroverted but not reclusive'. Conscientious but not a perfectionist, Kelly enjoyed school and achieved high marks with little effort. Until the end of grade 8, she said, her childhood had been 'very normal'.

> I don't think anyone could have guessed I would develop an eating disorder, and I didn't really understand what one was. I thought that eating disorders were diseases exclusively for glamorous people or narcissists. I'd never been interested in fad diets or wanted to be a model. When kids in grade 7 called me 'fat' I became more self-conscious and food-conscious and then, by chance, began to compete in cross-country running.

Kelly was also increasingly scientifically minded. Several members of her family were doctors and she had a basic understanding of what could go wrong with a body, but had limited understanding of mental illness. 'I'd heard only about schizophrenics, and that was in the context of comic situations in movie scripts.'

She celebrated her fourteenth birthday when her family went to Borneo for five weeks at the end of grade 8. Kelly was already slim but had heard of people losing weight on vacation in developing countries and thought she would like to do this. 'I felt driven by an impulse, a general feeling that this was what I should do. I minimised my serving sizes and secretly made myself sick several times', Kelly explained. 'One of my friends was naturally very light and I would think, "What would Sally eat?" and allow myself that much. So my illness crept in.'

On returning home from Borneo, Kelly began avoiding desserts and foods containing fats, preferring fruit and vegetables. She began year 9 and stepped up her involvement in sport, especially netball. She played in as many as five teams and was selected in the regional schoolgirls' team that played at state level. She also trained with a squad for cross-country running. She had never been overweight but people were now commenting on how fit and athletic she was looking and she was clocking personal best times with her running. Kelly's exercise program did not seem obsessive to her parents, Tim and Bridget. 'We thought she was just "doing sport" ', Tim said. 'Weighing ourselves was not part of the family routine but, in hindsight, we could see that despite growing taller Kelly was not putting on weight and may have even lost a little.'

Tim and Bridget soon noticed Kelly was eating less, and nowhere near enough to compensate for her high level of activity. Hassling and nagging her to eat more food was having no effect, so they took her to a dietician. This would be the first of three.

This first dietician failed to recognise the symptoms of a dangerous illness and merely recommended a focus on healthy foods. Shortly after, Kelly went away to compete in a netball championship and came home 2 kilograms lighter. This didn't ring an alarm bell with the dietician, but it did with Tim and Bridget. 'That was our first attempt to get help', Tim said, 'and we thought "this is wrong, we have to do something more" '. They took Kelly to a family doctor, who didn't diagnose her illness. A second family doctor, however, recognised symptoms of depression and an eating disorder. He began treating her and referred her to another dietician who set up a diet plan that required Kelly to select from a number of choices for each meal and snack. This was just prior to the cross-country titles when Kelly was training hard. Subsequent visits to the dietician revealed she was still not consuming enough to compensate for her activity.

The diet plan had encouraged Kelly to think more about food – unfortunately not about eating enough, but eating less. 'Until then, I hadn't been measuring my food, but now, if I were meant to have one-and-a-half cups of rice, I would measure less. That was probably when I started to calculate amounts and count calories.'

Bridget and Tim soon realised that Kelly was unable to stick to to the dietician's plan. 'Making the choices got harder and harder for her', Bridget said. 'The dietician started reducing the choices but Kelly was finding it impossible to eat enough.' Kelly, who by now had been struggling with the first stages of anorexia for more than six months, managed to hold herself together for the state schoolgirls' cross-country championship. The race was run over 4 kilometres and she came sixth, a big improvement on her thirty-eighth position the year before.

She was hugely relieved the event was over because her sole purpose in eating had been to provide fuel for her running. Now she didn't have to do that any more, but another event was coming up. Although only fourteen, Kelly had been offered a role in an adult play being presented by a local dramatic society.

The rehearsals, over about six weeks, were held in the evening and often finished late. Two weeks prior to opening night, Bridget and Tim could see that Kelly's energy was waning fast – she was becoming waif-like – and asked the play's director to arrange for her role to be shared 'just in case'. Kelly was barely getting through her rehearsals, and was struggling at school. Tim asked her if she realised that she needed to eat to keep living and she replied, 'the air is okay for me'.

Kelly was also purging. 'I would eat dinner before going to rehearsal, and purge my meal there', she said. She was going downhill fast and her parents feared she might be unable to complete the play's two-week season.

Bridget obtained an emergency appointment with a paediatrician. He began joint management of Kelly's case with the family doctor and suggested she may need to enter hospital; however, she managed to cope until the play had finished. Kelly resisted going to hospital and her parents did not want her to go there either. 'We worried that the nurses, who hadn't known Kelly before she became sick, wouldn't understand that her behaviour didn't really belong to her', Bridget said.

When her running season finished, Kelly had thought, 'Good, now I can stop eating'. When the play season ended, she thought, 'Even better, now I can stop everything; now I can pull out of life'. If she had had one last wish it would have been to play in her team's netball grand final, but she was beyond being able to participate. Her weight crashed. She had to pull out of school, unable to complete year 9.

By this stage Kelly's weight loss was life threatening and

she was incapable of eating enough to save herself. Her doctors decided to add to her diet a nutritious supplement given through a tube fitted through her nose and directly down into her stomach, called a nasogastric tube. To avoid a hospital admission the doctors agreed that Bridget and Tim could try this at home. Over the next five months with the aid of tube feeding, Kelly's physical decline halted and her weight slowly increased, but it was an ordeal for her:

> The tube was awful. It scraped my throat when it was inserted and irritated my nostril. The weeks following its insertion were the most physically painful of my life, and the fact that I continued to 'eat' through the night when everyone else was sleeping caused me deep emotional upset. During the day I was eating small supplementary meals; the tube was attached full-time and I used syringes on the tube to drain my stomach contents whenever I could.

Bridget said that Kelly never stopped eating completely:

> She nearly pulled the tube out some nights, but we would say, 'If you can't accept it here, you will be in hospital' and each time that was just enough to persuade her to leave it in. Tim and I took turns sleeping in her room with her. The feed sac would empty at about 3 a.m., and we had to flush the tube and clean the equipment. It was like having a newborn child again, but without the joy. We gradually increased her meal size and dropped what was in the tube. We now know we did this too slowly. Five months is too long for the tube.

Kelly developed a strange relationship with the tube: 'I found it easier to go out with it than without it. People would stare but I thought this was okay because the tube symbolised that I had been denied the right not to consume food'. Kelly was being fed without her permission and this, she believed, was why she was not only 'fat' but also 'the fattest person in the world'.

As soon as the tube was removed, Kelly became socially

withdrawn and didn't want to go out at all. 'Logically you would think it would have been the other way around', Bridget said.

By the time the tube feeding stopped Kelly had gained about 12 kilograms and was able, with supervision, to eat enough to maintain her weight – but she remained deeply disturbed, as Tim recalled:

> With this medical team we had re-fed Kelly until she was out of physical danger. I don't think the doctors felt further weight gain would help her mind. They eased the pressure when she was out of physical danger but she needed more weight for her mind to recover. We should have pushed re-feeding a lot further, but at that time we didn't know.

Different therapists came and went. A woman who had developed anorexia as a child and again in her twenties, and was now a counsellor, helped Tim and Bridget in trying to understand Kelly's thought pattern; but although they were seeing the counsellor up to four times a week, she could not connect with Kelly. They ceased seeing the counsellor and were referred to an occupational therapist who specialised in clients with mental disorders. They also changed doctors to one with a special interest in mental health, and he suggested using a different drug therapy and trying to normalise Kelly's eating behaviour. None of this helped. In desperation, Tim and Bridget took Kelly successively to a hypnotherapist and two different acupuncturists, again to no avail.

Kelly remained extremely distressed, frightened and angry. 'She would lose control around meal times, trips to the doctor and whenever changes were made to her daily routine', Tim said. At times her physical violence was so extreme that it took both parents to restrain her. In one outburst, she pulled the bookcase over in her bedroom, threw treasured keepsakes on the floor and smashed a glass-top table.

For Bridget, 'They were just things, and none of that upset us. But Tim found the physical attacks on me hard to accept'. Kelly's behaviour was frightening, sometimes toying with suicidal impulses. She would put plastic bags over her head, and threaten to put objects in electrical sockets. She used neckties as nooses. She self-harmed, scratching the skin from her belly and arms, banging her head, and cutting and burning herself. She would climb out her upstairs bedroom window and stand on a narrow ledge. On one occasion, Bridget had to close her eyes and hope, as there was no room on the ledge for two. Eventually Kelly came back inside. 'When she got into a rage, she seemed to lose connection with reality; her sense of self disappeared completely', Bridget said.

Coping with the illness had become a full-time job. Running his business from home, Tim was on hand, and Bridget had put her business on hold. 'We took turns watching Kelly closely to keep her safe, but learned that when she was upset our intervention would often makes things worse. It was a balancing act', Bridget said. Tim and Bridget arranged home schooling for Kelly for year 10 and into year 11. Kelly explained:

> I could do the school work, particularly the subjects that were hard like maths, because I only felt worthy of doing things that were difficult or boring. I didn't allow myself to read, as I loved it. I wouldn't see my friends and, if they visited me, I made sure I didn't have a good time – this meant they didn't either and so they visited me less.
>
> I cut out everything I liked – I wouldn't let myself look at my favourite TV shows and couldn't choose a movie. We got a puppy. I had always loved animals and I wouldn't allow myself to pat or talk to it. I was a horrible person. I found nothing to smile or laugh about and wouldn't let myself even if I had the inclination. I didn't laugh in more than two years.
>
> Mum and Dad made me play the guitar after each evening meal; I had enjoyed playing it before my illness but now I hated it for its connection to food. I thought if I did the same exercise over and over they would stop insisting, but I was wrong.

Compared with other challenges, the guitar upset was

minor. Kelly had moments of near insanity, after which she would have no recollection:

> Apparently I would brandish knives or say to my parents that I was glad one of their friends had died of breast cancer and may they die soon, too. At times my parents may have felt safer placing me in an institution, but they thought the nurses would not understand that I was really a nice person, and that I was not meaning to behave this way, so they stuck with me. But they weren't perfect. Sometimes they would overreact – shouting and restraining me physically. I am sure I goaded them, especially Dad, when hurting my mother or myself.

On one occasion, Bridget, pushed to extremes, sat on the floor sobbing in front of Kelly. 'I realised this was not good because I was adding to her guilt', Bridget said, 'but it is hard when someone is shouting "I hate you" and "You are the bastards making me fat". I was so frightened for her'.

Early on in her illness Kelly would get 'wilder and wilder' and Bridget and Tim could see in her eyes they were not dealing with a rational person any more. The human was stripped away: eyes glazed, manic grin. 'Then she would collapse in a heap and she would "return" ', Tim said. Holding on to memories of their beautiful daughter, Tim and Bridget were determined to get her back. They read that parents were to blame and thought 'that is bullshit'. Kelly had been healthy and switched on throughout her childhood and they knew her enormous potential. No one could convince them that they had caused the anorexic symptoms in their daughter.

Bridget and Tim strongly believed that they had to keep Kelly eating. It was her lifeline, as Tim related:

> We told her constantly that we loved her too much to let her starve. She was so terrified of eating that it was no use saying things like, 'If you don't eat you can't watch television or use the computer' – she didn't care about those things any more. We found we had only one trump card, and that had to be played at nearly every meal. The trump was that she had to eat and if she refused

she would go to a hospital where strangers would feed her. Knowing that she had no choice was the only way that she could eat.

Bridget and Tim coped by accepting Kelly's behaviour – the self-hatred, the rages and antisocial and irrational behaviours – as symptoms of her disease. As Bridget explained, she and her husband came up with a string of analogies to reinforce this thinking:

> If Kelly had been diagnosed with leukaemia, she would have had distressing symptoms which we would never imagine to be 'her choice', nor would we allow them to get in the way of diagnosis and treatment. It helped us to put the disease in the same context – right up there where it should be. With leukaemia, a parent might drop out of the workforce to become a carer and so on, and it was the same with anorexia.

Reinforcing this view, one doctor with a special line in mental health but with no experience in eating disorders suggested, as with schizophrenia, that Tim and Bridget try to separate their child from her illness. By now Kelly had been suffering anorexia nervosa for a year, and taking this new view helped reinforce their conviction that it was counterproductive to see Kelly's behaviour as anything but a symptom.

A different doctor, driven to the point of exasperation in his consulting room, sternly lectured Kelly on what she was doing to her parents and threatened to call the police because of the disruption she was causing in his office.[1] His use of guilt as a tool to get Kelly to cooperate had no effect, but his words caused Kelly such overwhelming pain that to this day she cannot abide the thought of him. According to Tim, 'The doctor's reaction illustrates the huge ignorance about this illness'.

Twelve months after the play and almost two years after Kelly began losing weight, a breakthrough occurred. A child psychiatrist, who had trained in the Maudsley Approach at the Children's Hospital, Westmead, took a temporary posting in town. After meeting Kelly he told Bridget and Tim that he recommended family-based treatment, also known as 'Maudsley'. They had read about the treatment and, on meeting the doctor for an assessment, instantly felt they could have faith in him. He said words that they would remember forever: 'I can help you'. When Bridget sought reassurance and asked 'Will this treatment work?', he said 'Yes, every chance'. This was the first time any practitioner had been positive about Kelly's prognosis.

Within six months of starting family-based treatment, Kelly would reach her healthy body weight and achieve good physical health. Six weeks after reaching this weight, her psychiatric symptoms would begin to disappear spontaneously and during the ensuing five months her mental health would return to normal.

But initially, faced with this new doctor, Kelly bucked:

I was terrified of any change, not only related to food.
I even had my own special spoon. Apart from my special
chair at the dining table, I would sit in only one chair in
each room of the house and if people visited and sat in my
chair I would stand rather than sit on another. I could tell
my chair by the scuff marks on the legs, and the marks on
the seat covers.

If her mother rearranged the chairs when washing the floors, Kelly would be furious. The order had to be maintained in an effort to subdue her anxiety.

For two years, Kelly insisted on wearing only two pairs of old, baggy tracksuit pants and two long-sleeved cotton tops. 'They were already old before she became ill and they became threadbare and developed holes', Bridget said. 'Kelly felt she didn't deserve anything nice to wear. She wore those same clothes everywhere – around the house, to the doctors, and out walking.' Bridget found this behaviour difficult to accept, as it was illogical. It wasn't related to food, but was obsessive and compulsive.

Kelly had reached the stage where taking one step out of her set routine could seem catastrophic. Early in her treatment a doctor had suggested walking would help strengthen her bones and be uplifting for the family, so mother, father and the two daughters would go on an evening walk. This rapidly became part of Kelly's rigid routine – she would insist on the same route, at the same speed, every night. Tim said:

> We took our two dogs with us on their leads. One night, the dog Kelly was leading desperately wanted to stop for a wee, but Kelly couldn't stop and pulled him along.
> We didn't know what was going on with her then and we argued about the distance and the pace. It wasn't a very happy family walk.

'We would have to go around the same side of every tree', Bridget recalled. 'Kelly felt she had to take exactly the same steps.'

Now this new doctor who had recommended the Maudsley Approach was posing a threat to Kelly's delicate but rigid sense of control, and he became her enemy number one. Kelly said:

> He was definitely someone I would not talk to. There we were, in his consulting room, and he was saying that my treatment would start with a family meal in that very room and I thought 'You have another thing coming'. There was no way I would eat new and unmeasured foods in a new environment with new people watching me eat. And I didn't.

Kelly wouldn't eat in front of others, and would eat only at home when sitting on her particular chair at its particular place at the table. She ate only certain foods and each had to be measured and weighed. Her daily diet comprised one of three different types of calorie-controlled dinners from the supermarket, a specially made sandwich for lunch, and measured muesli for breakfast. Twelve cashews had to be selected, weighed, chopped up and placed on the muesli. Kelly would then extract each piece of bran from the rest of the muesli and eat it separately.

According to Bridget, 'Kelly wasn't staying at home

because she loved us, but because she was terrified of any change. We were the devil she knew. She didn't know what others would make her eat and this fearful thought was enough to make her eat for us'.

While Kelly had gained 12 kilograms before starting the family-based treatment, the doctor suggested another 10 kilograms would make a big difference in her recovery, both physically and mentally. Bridget and Tim liked the directive of 'Step in now, get the weight up and help your child get better'. The doctor emphasised Kelly's illness was not their fault and, although they had never felt it was, his words were reassuring.

'The "no-blame" for parents is a strong part of family-based treatment. Another part is that you can keep your desperately ill child at home – for us the nearest hospital offering any form of specialised treatment was 1500 kilometres away', Bridget said.

I wished the doctors who treated Kelly with traditional methods during the first eighteen months could have seen the changes in her as a result of re-feeding to a genuinely healthy weight. The big difference with family-based treatment is that you treat food as medicine – you cure the starvation first and then deal with anything else. With traditional therapy, a psychological line is taken, food isn't pushed, and the child is expected to choose to get well.[2] The critical link between good nutrition, weight gain and mental health is undervalued.

Book readings were a vital aid in Kelly's recovery.

Leo Tolstoy's *War and Peace* was apt for what was happening in our lives. Reading was a good distraction that kept us all sane and stopped us getting too frustrated while waiting for Kelly to eat. We had read to the children when they were little and now we re-read favourites by Jane Austen and other classics we hadn't got around to.

Bridget and Tim read out loud during every meal, sometimes for an hour or so, until the meal was finished. They devoured books by John Steinbeck and read the twenty books in the Aubrey–Maturin series by Patrick O'Brian. Kelly couldn't allow herself to choose a book so they selected ones they liked and thought Kelly would like as well. 'I hated the reading because it coincided with every meal', Kelly said. 'But it distracted my parents from my meal, so that was good.'[3]

Kelly's mental outlook began to change rapidly about six weeks after gaining the extra 10 kilograms and reaching her ideal weight. 'Some children begin to recover their sense of self as soon as their weight increases', Bridget said, 'but this didn't happen with Kelly. She had gained 22 kilograms and still had total anorexic thinking. We were worried but our doctor said "just give it time" '.

Following the first sign of improvement – 'a half-smile like that of the *Mona Lisa*' – Tim and Bridget were buoyed. 'This was the first sign that cracks were appearing in the illness, that the bad stuff was starting to fall away. Gradually her obsessive-compulsive behaviour began to ease', Bridget said.

Many more wonderful breakthroughs began to occur. An invitation to a family wedding arrived and Bridget took Kelly and her other daughter Nikki shopping for something new to wear. 'To my amazement Kelly was happy to try on clothes and chose a bright red dress', Bridget said. 'This was the first time she had wanted any item of new clothing in two years. I was so happy I bought both Kelly and Nikki two dresses each!'

Kelly's food control was the last thing to be overcome and, although she did not eat at the wedding reception, she coped well with attending the big social event. Family pictures were taken, but while Kelly was happy to be photographed she became very upset when the pictures were developed:

I thought I looked terrible. This was a backlash of the truth that I had done it, that I had gone out in public. I felt a huge upsurge of guilt. I felt very self-conscious and nervous and couldn't let the pictures be seen by anyone. I was completely illogical and became quickly upset. It was one of the last times I did this. I can look at the pictures today – I look young and you can see that I have just come out of the end of something.

The gaps between the bad times were widening but this, Bridget said, was 'a bad time'.

The family's persistence and determination not to give into the illness eventually won through. 'The change in my relationship with food', Kelly described, 'was like the lifting of a veil from my mind'. It occurred three months after her *Mona Lisa* smile and 'was not a gradual lift, but a jerk'. At the time, Kelly was on a trip with her family to watch Nikki play field hockey in a town 400 kilometres from home:

> I had taken the kitchen scales, measuring cup and my special food, but watching the others buy their lunch at a cafeteria I realised suddenly that 'Everyone is doing this, why can't I?' The precise moment that thought entered I felt elated and, riding that high, instead of going through my usual routine, I bought a sandwich! It had egg and mayonnaise filling. When I held the sandwich, I didn't feel as comfortable – I felt incriminated – but fought back feelings of panic and ate the lot. Two years had passed since I'd allowed myself to eat anything like this! Not only that, I ate it in this public place, full of people. This was a huge step forward. Until then, I might have exchanged one small slice of tomato for a gherkin, but now I had eaten a sandwich, like everyone else!

To this day, Bridget has difficulty describing how extraordinary and wonderful she felt to see Kelly eat that sandwich. 'Tim and I were overcome with surprise, and after that, Kelly improved rapidly. For the first time she really understood that she had been sick and became determined to get well.'

Soon, Kelly was thinking about things other than food, teenage things like having her nose and belly button pierced. Six months after reaching her 'healthy weight', with most of her psychiatric symptoms resolved, Kelly returned to school. She had been absent for two years and, while her friends knew she had had anorexia, they 'really had no idea of my experience'. Suddenly her home, which for several years had seemed a prison, became a haven:

> Trivially, the first thing I noticed at school was that the boys' voices were deeper. I didn't recognise the boys unless face-to-face; and the ways in which boys and girls interacted had completely changed. They were more aware of their sexuality, and they swore more, words I'd not heard before. Sexually and socially, I was naïve because I had missed the important teenage development years between fourteen and sixteen-and-a-half, yet I'd been to places some of them may never go. In the matter of inner perspective I was years beyond them.

During a lunchbreak one day a girl noticed scars on Kelly's legs, where she had burnt and cut herself.

> I explained how I'd come by them truthfully. My friends were shocked and to their credit they did not draw back. But they could not understand that I had chosen to hurt myself and that I had almost enjoyed it because the distraction of physical pain was minute compared with my mental pain.

From then, Kelly began to have many happy 'firsts', like eating her first piece of liquorice in two years, and her first sleep over with friends. One of the biggest happy events was Kelly's seventeenth birthday six months after eating the egg sandwich, when her school friends organised a surprise party at the beach. 'I almost fainted, I couldn't believe that all these people had given up a Friday night, a football night, to celebrate the fact that I existed', Kelly said.

The next day, Kelly attended the funeral of a male friend's parent and could feel his pain. 'I could see that the depth of my fear about changing my clothes compared with my friend's deep grief over his dad's death', she said. 'I realised I had been as upset over eating a piece of lettuce as my friend was at losing a parent. I was horrified.'

This insight helped Kelly gain a perspective as to how

others saw her illness. She knew people couldn't understand that her level of pain and grief had been that deep, day after day, month after month, year after year. Now, Kelly was looking at the world with fresh eyes. She began to enjoy the guitar again – because she was free to enjoy it.

Anorexia is an illness and therefore is separate, but
it is also mental and is part of you. For the first time
I could understand I had been sick and had an illness.
I never had a 'voice' in my head; my illness thoughts
were my thoughts, my sick brain. When you are coming
out of this illness, it is like losing part of yourself. It is
a real conundrum. Sometimes the illness will dominate,
and you have bad days or weeks. Sometimes, when
having a relapse, I would make myself sick three times
a day.

Initially, Kelly felt hugely anxious at the depth of the emotional void left by her illness but

it filled gradually and I don't know how full it is normally,
but I am happy. Sometimes I overflow: when I go to
movies and watch my friends laugh and cry, when my
baby cousin takes off along the beach just because she's
alive, when my sister makes me laugh. I love batting the
big issues around with my friends – the flaws in religions,
whether life has a meaning, how our perceptions are
shaped, and what comes after death. Philosophy is the
asking of the questions, not the arrival at an absolute
answer. I love being with people.

Kelly's illness had some unexpected outcomes. Tim and Bridget's attitude towards people with a mental illness or an addiction changed. 'We are more aware of the difficulties facing people who, through no fault of their own, have an illness in their mind', Bridget said.

Kelly's sister, Nikki, now a tall and athletic sixteen year old, was twelve when Kelly developed anorexia. She enjoyed the book readings, and coped with her sister's illness by drawing on the reserves of a well-grounded personality and immersing herself completely into competitive swimming, surf lifesaving and hockey. Nikki tried to ignore what was happening and pretend that it was not real, but sometimes had difficulty sleeping because of the fighting:

> I had no idea Kelly was so sick until we began family-based treatment, and then I freaked out. I remember we also watched movies as a distraction, and used an egg timer to help control the mealtimes. We began with ninety minutes and would reduce five minutes at a time. We went through quite a few egg timers!

While ill, Kelly said she lived in the same family as her sister but that was all:

> Nikki wasn't making me eat so I did not feel unkindly towards her, but I resented that she could exercise and I couldn't. I would take up to three hours to eat a piece of toast and she would be outside playing or going to sport. Now my illness no longer dominates, we have resumed a normal sisterly relationship.

Throughout the long illness, Nikki and Kelly tended to pass like 'ships in the night', Tim said. But Nikki must have retained some level of awareness because only days after Bridget and Tim detected the first fleeting *Mona Lisa* smile – which suggested their hidden daughter may some day soon reappear – Tim was amazed to see Nikki and Kelly having a play wrestle in one of the bedrooms and bounding on the bed. This indicated to Tim that Nikki's instincts, too, had told her things were changing for her sister.

Until Kelly became ill, Bridget thought anorexia happened to children from unhappy homes or who were abused. One doctor, early on, had assured Bridget and Tim that Kelly could not have anorexia because 'You don't have the right family profile'. As Bridget commented:

> Little seems to be taught about anorexia in medical training. Also some doctors and nurses don't want to deal with the animosity and huge level of commitment that

comes with the illness. They find it difficult dealing with patients who don't understand that they are ill and who see treatment as torture. There is no other illness like it.

Eating disorders occur in all types of families – dysfunctional families and functional families, as Bridget noted:

Latest research suggests that some people are genetically susceptible to these illnesses – like diabetes or cancer they can crop up in all sorts of families. I don't know what triggers anorexia but with family-based treatment you don't dwell on the past: you get on with the re-feeding. I wonder if traditional therapies, where causes are sought and blame is attributed, may, in some cases, do more harm than good. If a psychiatrist had sat down with Kelly when she was ill she would have reported that we were obsessively controlling parents and that she hated us and we hated her; she doesn't think that now but certainly did so then. She had many distorted thoughts, which she didn't have before getting sick and has not had since.

Fighting anorexia was full on, Bridget said, but, as with children with cancer, parents could do 'amazing things when push came to shove'. When a child is diagnosed with anorexia, food is the first priority, and other problems should be sorted after that.

Bridget has three wishes:

- to see the Maudsley Approach taught in medical school so that new doctors understand the illness and the importance of early intervention;
- for clinicians to see the remarkable transformation, as occurred with Kelly, achieved by weight restoration through the family-based treatment; and,
- to see family-based treatment widely available to enable early diagnosis and prompt treatment – so parents can be told 'your child has an eating disorder, and this is what we can do to help with family-based treatment'.

On reflection, Bridget and Tim acknowledge the work of

all the doctors and therapists who saw Kelly, but feel as though they lost a lot of precious time. As Bridget recalled:

> At crucial times several practitioners could be said to have saved her life, and all had her best interests at heart. However, we feel that early intervention with family-based treatment could have shortened Kelly's ordeal considerably. It also could have saved her from the most extreme symptoms, and the worst experiences which we believe were due to her extended period at a body weight well below optimal.

Bridget said that increased public awareness of anorexia nervosa was another challenge:

> The public perception of anorexia nervosa is way off the mark. Mine was, too, before my daughter became ill. This illness is not a choice and it's not about being thin and vain. It's a biologically based mental illness, which can make kids very, very sick. This hatred of oneself – there is nothing about this in magazines. Readers are presented with a distorted view.

Kelly agreed, saying anorexia was so misunderstood it was like 'a magazine illness'. 'Every week, magazines seem to run a story about a celebrity developing anorexia. But they don't show an understanding of the illness.'

In the final phase of her family-based treatment Kelly had weekly sessions with a psychologist to help her come to terms with her illness and adjust back to teenage life. Her father, Tim, thinks this was helpful but in hindsight wonders whether family counselling at an earlier stage would have helped Kelly recover faster:

> At a rational level, Kelly could acknowledge 'Oh yes, my parents helped me get through this', but I believe she had some difficulty separating us from the emotions of that time. For two years, we were sort of in Kelly's face, watching her eat, taking her to the doctor, managing her behaviour in our own inexpert way – we were the ones

doing all of these 'terrible' things. It took a little time but our relationship with Kelly is great now.

Bridget continues to feel very grateful for and amazed by Kelly's recovery. 'Nowadays, when sitting down for a family meal, I sometimes pinch myself, and ask "did all that really happen?" '[4]

Tim and Bridget believe that full recovery from anorexia is possible but they encourage Kelly, now she has been shown to be susceptible to anorexia, to take steps to proof herself against a relapse. This means keeping up a full and balanced diet and not skipping meals, particularly when she's stressed and tired.

Kelly does not believe she would be alive today without family-based treatment:

At the state I was in, I don't think I would have hung on to life. Without my parents, I would not have made the five to seven years that is the average recovery period with old treatment methods. I would have passively killed myself through starvation or actively committed suicide. The acuteness was terrifying.

I want people to know about mental illness and anorexia. These days, by the time students leave school they know how to perform CPR (cardiopulmonary resuscitation) but cannot recognise the signs of mental illness, which is far more prevalent among their peers than heart attacks.

When people ask me why I was out of school for two years, I want to say more than 'I just had anorexia'. I want to say 'I was severely depressed, I was delusional about my body, I was flooded with suicidal thoughts and locked into obsessive-compulsive and psychotic-like behaviours', because otherwise they'll just slip me into their pre-conceived, magazine-fuelled image of a shallow girl who wanted to be thin.

Anorexia, Kelly said, is not a superficial illness: 'I don't want people to brush it off or diminish it. I want them to know enough so they can recognise it in other people. I think the distinction between mental illness and not having a mental illness is like a spectrum. Those who don't understand can't relate'.

Now eighteen, Kelly lives with Bridget and Tim, Nikki and two big, friendly dogs in a coastal city of 150 000 people. She has completed high school and is taking a year to work and catch up on life before starting university studies.

Kelly has had to come to terms with the painful knowledge that two years have been 'stolen' from her life:

Those years have a shadow quality now. I can understand the depth of the void and remember the pain and overwhelming despair, but I cannot feel them. It is not very tangible but the threat remains. I have relapsed several times. Not much, but enough for it to be physically and emotionally draining. I know every meal has to have a balance of proteins, fats and carbohydrates, but sometimes I look for a soup or salad containing the least amount of calories, and I feel guilty if I eat something greasy.

Today, Kelly said, she can appreciate that what her family-based treatment doctor did was great. 'I thank him, and almost all the health professionals who treated me, even those who my parents thought were a waste of time; the fact they tried, I commend them for that.'

Kelly wishes that anorexia didn't exist but 'if that's not possible, that people will understand the illness; that doctors will understand it; and that recovery can be guaranteed for all children'. She maintains a healthy weight and her bright and positive personality is restored. Kelly is revelling in the dawn of her new light, her freedom.

5

Kristen

Anorexia slowly crept up on me. It has taken two years of my life, and continues to torment me. I don't know exactly when it made its debut, but it came without warning and with a mission. Shocking both my family and me, it became the start of a challenging and exhausting journey. At first I was scared. I didn't know what was happening: things began to mean nothing to me; life felt a burden and sometimes I wished to fall asleep and not wake up. The anorexia engulfed me, consuming my every effort and thought, causing me to push away the people and things I love. I became nasty, disobedient, deceitful, abusive and selfish. I started to isolate myself from my family, my friends, the activities I once enjoyed, and, most of all, God.

Kristen had been suffering from anorexia nervosa for two years when, at fifteen, she wrote and delivered the above words to her church congregation as part of her baptismal testimony. Her mind and body ravaged by the illness, she amazingly found the courage to stand in front of the church congregation and read her testimony. Struggling to remain composed, the frail girl read bravely on, her clear voice wavering and eventually choking with the challenge. Her mother, Karen, stepped up to the podium and embraced her, giving her the strength to continue. There was not a dry eye in the church when Kristen completed her testimony. While her mother helped her back to her seat, the worship leader stumbled with emotion as he acknowledged the fragile girl's effort. The church congregation had known Kristen was not well but, until hearing her baptismal testimony, had little understanding of the depth of her suffering.

The people listened in awe as Kristen told how she was placed in hospital a long way from home and had begun to question her faith and herself: 'Was it my fault? I must have done something wrong!' Or 'Am I a bad person, a bad Christian, and is God punishing me because I deserve it?'

After three weeks Kristen was allowed home and things seemed okay, but anorexia had given only a sample of what was to come. The illness continued to engulf her: 'I spent weeks in and out of hospitals, with my self-hatred continuing to build and my family struggling to cope. Nothing changed, no matter how long I spent in hospital or with doctors, counsellors or dieticians'. But now, thanks to the 'amazing support and perseverance' of her family, Kristen's prayers had been answered and a new direction was being taken – this time with a family-based treatment program:

> By being baptised, I do not expect things to be suddenly different, but I believe that by living a God-focused life, those things in my life that are wrong will fall away and become insignificant. I pray that God will use me for His will and that good will come out of my illness for the benefit of others.

Kristen expressed her inner struggle in poetry. She began her testimony with a poem written at fifteen, when her illness was sabotaging not only her relationship with her family, but also her relationship with God:

> I've turned away and gone my way, a way I knew was wrong.
> I've been living in the darkness, hiding from the sun.
> For nothing I can say or do, can change the things I've done.
> No longer do I follow, no longer do I smile.
> I bear the load of all my sin, and walk the longer mile.
> Though deep inside I know you, I've slowly slipped away.
> Your light has left my window, and my sins have blocked your way.

My candle has extinguished, and the wells have all gone
  dry.
The door of my heart is closing, as I throw the key away.
As I enter into darkness, where I fear I will remain,
I call out to my Master a cry of grief and pain.
As my voice echoes in the shadows, you turn your face
  away.
Then silently you whisper, this is where you'll stay.

Kristen concluded her testimony with another poem:

Life has become a tug of war, of which I cannot fight.
An ever-going battle through all my days and nights.
The truth has become so faint now, I can barely hear its
  plea,
As lies begin to fill the place, it always used to be.
My thoughts are now of evil, of selfishness and grief.
Where love and peace and happiness, were once a part
  of me.
Now I find myself alone, to this battle I've surrendered,
All good has been replaced, with shamefulness and
  sorrow.
No light shines on my face, only tears flow from my eyes
And every day ahead of me seems to be another lie.
The battle still continues, I can hear it from within
Though evil maybe leading, I know that truth will win.

Today Kristen is seventeen. The youngest of Greg and
Karen's three children, she was thirteen when she developed
anorexia. She lives with her parents, brother and sister in a
rural town with a population of 100 000. Her dad works for the
government, her mum works part-time in after-school care.

Kristen's battle surfaced when she was a happy girl who
embraced the outdoors and enjoyed cross-country running at
school. She was not overweight, had never been a big eater,
ate little junk food and was not concerned about her body
image, but she did want to improve her personal best running
times. One way to do this, she decided, would be to lose a
little weight so she would have less to carry:

I thought, 'If I am thinner, I will run faster'. I don't think there was any trigger to this thought except one day at school we had a 'beep test', where I was weighed and ran for a fitness assessment, and I became determined to improve my times. I just started to cut back my food and I kind of had my own set of rules, which got bigger and bigger. First I got rid of all takeaways. No more fish and chips, hamburgers, chocolate, sweets, sauces, gravy or cream. My mother didn't seem to mind so long as I still ate healthy foods.

Kristen stepped up her exercise at the same time. Her cross-country times were improving; she ran until she was exhausted and then would run some more. 'We have about an acre in our backyard and I ran in the dark at night, and in the morning before my parents got up', Kristen said. 'I did this until they started catching on to it.' The crunch came at Easter on a visit to her grandparents – when her grandmother, who hadn't seen her for few months, said to Karen, 'Kristen looks like she has lost weight'. 'Then my mother started to keep watch on me', Kristen said. 'She had a set of scales in her bathroom, and she hid them after she saw me weighing myself several times a day. I searched for them and couldn't understand why she hid them.'

Karen's concern grew when Kristen's sports teacher called to say that measurements of weight and height taken in a second beep test had revealed a marked weight loss. The sports teacher confronted Kristen and asked if she was okay. Kristen broke down, feeling scared at her 'secret' being revealed, and said, 'I think I know what is wrong – I think I have anorexia'.

'My teacher was comforting', Kristen said. 'He rang my mother and asked her to come to the school. He told her about another girl who had suffered the illness and offered to put her mother in touch with my mother and that was helpful.'

Until now, her father, Greg, hadn't realised Kristen was struggling. Karen was at home, and saw the children more, he said. He had noticed Kristen was always running, but said that as a parent, 'to see your child want to exercise is great'.

We had begun to think she was becoming a little obsessive about her cross-country training, running laps around our backyard, but we didn't know that was only part of it – we didn't know she was exercising behind closed doors, so her illness was out of control before we knew about it.

A visit to the family doctor in the nearby city, a ten-minute drive from home, confirmed Kristen's diagnosis. The doctor weighed her and said, 'This doesn't look good'. He said he would ask staff at a nearby eating disorder clinic to contact Karen. However, six weeks went by and Karen heard nothing.

During this time Karen began to search for other health professionals to help as Kristen's illness was raging and she was determined to keep running. An important cross-country race was coming up and Kristen dearly wanted to compete. Unfortunately, her parents, concerned about her weight loss, forced her to withdraw, but she determinedly kept running whenever possible. She ran from class to class and 'sometimes kids would pick on me', Kristen said. Between classes she ran around the oval or kicked a ball with the boys, doing anything to keep on the move. Her concerned and insightful school principal suggested to Karen that Kristen would require a team approach to get well – including a nutritionist, psychiatrist and paediatrician.

With Kristen's weight continuing to plummet, Karen stepped up her efforts to find help:

I rang our family doctor and he apologised. He said he hadn't realised how seriously ill Kristen had become, or that we had not heard from the clinic. Eventually, we found the clinic did exist, but catered only for sufferers who were aged eighteen or older. At fourteen, Kristen did not qualify.

Discovering there was an eating disorder clinic close by that was unavailable because of Kristen's age compounded the family's struggle to find help. She needed help immediately.

Her family doctor ordered a blood test and arranged an

appointment at an adolescent clinic in the state capital the next day. Both Karen and Greg accompanied her to the clinic, a two-hour car journey from home. The blood test had sparked alarm. Kristen was so thin and sick she was admitted in the emergency section to the nearby state children's hospital. By now her punishing exercise regime included hundreds of sit-ups after every meal, school lunchtime being the only time out. Sitting on her bedroom floor, Kristen counted the sit-ups in 500 lots. She also did star jumps, push-ups and pedalled the exercise bike: 'I would get home from school and ride the bike as fast as I could until my mother got home from work. I would aim to pedal a certain number of kilometres before she came through the door'.

Her illness, in driving her to extremes, was endangering her life, and now here she was in a strange hospital far from her country home. Kristen's refusal to consume not only food but also liquid, including water, had led to severe dehydration. Discovering this, the emergency medical team had inserted a nasogastric tube and pumped in six units of fluid. By the time her medical status was stabilised, all beds had been filled in the adolescent ward, so she was placed in the baby and toddler ward. Kristen was there for two weeks and felt lonely:

> The babies had their mothers and I couldn't understand why my mother couldn't be with me, and I was scared. I had to wait for a bed in the adolescent ward because they had only a set number of beds for children with anorexia, and we had to be in separate rooms. I was moved into a room with three other children and I was the only one with anorexia. I was there for another week.

In this restricted environment, Kristen kept up her punishing exercises. 'This was a challenge but I found ways to do them', Kristen said. She did her sit-ups from her bed.

> The nursing staff gave me privileges if I ate my meals and did what they said. At first I had to stay in bed, then I was allowed in a wheelchair and then allowed to walk. The

nurses didn't know that I would jump up and down on the spot and do push-ups when I went to the toilet.

Sessions with a female psychologist at the hospital were fostering a sense of trust. 'She understood how I was feeling', Kristen said. 'But basically I just wanted to go home and decided "I will do what they want".' By gaining sufficient weight, Kristen was allowed to go home providing appointments had been organised with a paediatrician, dietician and counsellor in her home town. The counsellor was arranged through the government's child and adolescent mental health service. But Kristen was not happy:

> I loathed this next psychiatrist. She asked the same questions every time and I didn't feel we would get anywhere. So I gave her the same answers every time. I don't think I was open to her and only saw her a few times. After that, I saw a case counsellor weekly who tried very hard to get through to me and who then reported to the psychiatrist.

The psychiatrist had recommended that Kristen take medication to treat her depression and, although unhappy about this, Karen agreed: 'The paediatrician believed the medication would help and Kristen obviously did need something to ease her depression and help her sleep'. By now Kristen had tried to self-harm several times. She had been discovered when about to drink a poisonous liquid in hospital, and at home had run away to avoid a meal. Karen recalled a harrowing moment:

> One evening Kristen took off and, knowing her state of mind, I was very worried. We live 6 kilometres from her school; she ran there and on to her grandmother's house and our pastor's house, but neither her grandmother nor the pastor was home. It was getting dark and we were about to contact the police when she rang from a convenience store. She had no money but the store owner let her make the call.

The medication, Karen said, seemed to reduce anxious behaviour like this. However, several months later it appeared to be losing its effectiveness and was gradually withdrawn. As this occurred, Karen noticed that Kristen became more anxious and more easily upset, and balancing this behaviour against the side effects of taking the medication was difficult. On one visit to hospital, Karen found Kristen lying on her bed, dopey, tired and sick, saying 'You had better go home, I don't want visitors'. Karen asked the staff why her daughter was so 'zonked out' and learnt they had tried a new medication to which Kristen was found to be allergic. Another medication, supposed to calm Kristen as well as help her to eat, had no effect.

Kristen began to yo-yo back and forth between hospital and home. At home, besides looking after the rest of the family, Karen was busy taking her sick daughter for weekly appointments with the paediatrician, the counsellor and the dietician, knowing all the time that if her weight fell below a certain level she would have to return to hospital. The psychiatrist, paediatrician and counsellor told Karen and Greg not to be 'food police'. 'They told us not to pressure Kristen in encouraging her to eat', Karen said.

The medical team was hoping she would get through the illness of her own accord. Karen and Greg would say 'this isn't working', and the doctors would say 'you have to give it time'. This was despite Kristen requiring multiple hospital admissions, and nasogastric tube feeding. Her dietician had more rapport with her, but by now her illness had too much hold for a trust to form.[1]

Kristen was fifteen, and Karen was frustrated. She couldn't understand why her daughter was losing weight even when eating her meals. Then she realised Kristen was purging. 'I caught her cutting tops off empty plastic milk bottles so she could vomit into them in her bedroom', Karen said. It all seemed natural to Kristen – her parents wouldn't let her exercise to work off the food she ate so she came up with another solution. School sport had been banned long ago. 'We seemed to be getting nowhere and I was angry', Karen said. 'Despite their best efforts, Kristen's counsellor had been unable to "break through" and assist with her mental state.'

Eighteen months after her initial family doctor consult-ation, on the advice of her paediatrician, counsellor and psychiatrist, Kristen was discharged from the local hospital where she was on a repeat admission and sent to the ado-lescent unit of a large hospital, which was a two-hour drive from home. Greg and Karen expected her to spend up to two weeks there while waiting for a bed at the state hospital in the same city. They had agreed to Kristen's admission on the understanding she would start a psychiatric assessment and treatment program to address mental health, behavioural and family difficulties. Greg said that what happened next was a nightmare:

The first night at this large hospital was dreadful. Kristen was extremely distraught and was placed under suicide watch. We didn't like leaving her there. The small window to her second-floor barren room overlooked the hospital parking lot and gateway. As we walked out we looked back and saw her tearful face pressed against the windowpane. Our hearts were too heavy with worry to drive home that night.

Greg and Karen felt anguish in knowing Kristen needed help, but didn't know what more they could do. They booked into a nearby motel and returned to the hospital the next morning, where they were met with a negative report – Kristen had refused to eat. This was hardly surprisingly, for the little girl had been left alone with her illness all night:

The nurses told me to help myself to food in the hospital cafeteria. They didn't care if I ate nothing, or if I smashed my head against the wall. I liked to draw during my hospital admissions to help pass the time, but these nurses confiscated my pencils saying I would hurt myself. I was alone in this room for two days and two nights. Containing only a bed, it was stone cold, and its stark walls and bleak setting made me want to die.

Concerned at the effect of this latest 'treatment' on Kris-ten, Greg and Karen received no comfort from those in charge. They wanted to take Kristen home straightaway, but were advised that she was too sick to travel. At their insistence the medical staff obtained early admission for Kristen in the adolescent ward at the state hospital, but there was more disappointment. It was just after Christmas and the special program there would not start for another five weeks. Kristen's illness flourished in this uncertain environment. In the first week after leaving her home town, Kristen's food consumption tallied two sandwiches:

> The nurses were nice but didn't keep a close watch on me so I didn't eat or drink. After a few days they tried to encourage me, but I would eat only set foods. Eventually a dietician tried to compromise and my mother brought some of my set foods from home, including strawberries, wholemeal bread, ham and cheese. I was allowed to help fix my meals, like my breakfast cereal, which had to be prepared in a certain way, with a certain amount of milk.

This care, however, failed to halt the anorexia. Kristen's health continued to weaken. Her parents, back home in their country town, received a call saying Kristen was being moved to the paediatric ward as her weight was too low, and they needed Karen's assistance to pacify Kristen while they 'inserted a nasogastric tube'. By the time Karen arrived at the hospital two hours later, the staff had coaxed Kristen into allowing the tube's insertion. Other girls with anorexia were in her new ward. 'I thought how unwell they looked', Kristen said, 'but I couldn't see that in myself. I wanted to help them, but I was too much the same'.

When Kristen's weight rose above the critical level, she was returned to the adolescent unit. By now she had been transferred between the adolescent and paediatric wards several times, usually for forty-eight hours at a time. The medical staff would stabilise her, she would slip back, they would stabilise her, and she would slip back. This is how it went. 'There was no program, no plan to help Kristen overcome the cause of her illness', Karen said. Kristen disliked the tube intensely and fought every insertion. One day she reached her tolerance limit. The tube still inserted, she packed her bag and was leaving 'but the hospital staff caught me before I got out the front door', Kristen said. 'They made sure the ward door was locked after that.'

During Kristen's many hospital admissions, Karen had researched for further help. She had visited her local public library and borrowed all the books she could find on eating disorders. Something new had to be tried. Karen and Greg followed up a recommended internet site and read about The Oak House, the private eating disorder clinic, a two-and-a-half-hour drive from home, that offered family-based treatment. The website related a few girls' journeys and Kristen seemed typical of them. Karen and Greg visited the private clinic and arranged for an assessment as soon as Kristen's medical status stabilised – discharged after five weeks at the state hospital, her weight had again dropped dangerously low, requiring yet another admission to the local hospital. Greg felt they were at last getting somewhere:

When we met the family-based treatment team we noticed an immediate contrast with our previous experiences. For the first time, the focus was on the illness and this was encouraging. It made sense that for Kristen to fight her illness, she first had to be at a healthy and stable weight so the team could work with her mind. In contrast to earlier advice, now we were told to insist that she eat her meals. We had to be food police after all. We also noticed the team environment; everyone was working together and telling Karen and I that we had to take control.

Kristen was uncertain about her parents' new tactic. After all, two years had passed since the family doctor had confirmed she had developed anorexia and no one had been able to help her. 'Here we go again', she thought. However, the team at the family-based treatment clinic looked very determined, as if they knew the ways of this illness, and Karen and Greg, if not Kristen, felt hopeful of a positive outcome. This was the first time their daughter had been in the care of a team solely dedicated to treating eating disorders.

Karen and Greg were pleased they could follow the

treatment program in their own home. With their other two children, Lauren and Matthew, still at home, the family would be less disrupted with Kristen at home as well. Besides, Kristen already had been admitted to hospital eight or more times, and shown no improvement.

On learning a concentrated effort would be required to challenge the illness, Greg committed himself to the battle that lay ahead. He arranged to take one day off work each week to attend the therapy sessions, and rearranged his work hours so he could help at lunchtimes.

Since starting family-based treatment, Kristen has required no further hospitalisation. She has been attending school full-time and, despite moments of self-doubt, is doing well in year 11. Attendance at the family-based therapy session every second Tuesday means she misses a favourite subject, but her teacher is supportive in helping her catch up.

Kristen's goal is to take up studies in performing arts, majoring in psychology, and her dream is to establish a practice with the Maudsley Approach so that she can help others. 'I like making people laugh, especially through drama; when I'm on stage I can be anyone I want to be', Kristen said.

Every little step forward in conquering the thoughts that belong to her illness requires an enormous amount of courage. She takes a morning snack and lunch to school alone, and her therapist is encouraging her to increase her food variety. Adding a new ingredient to her sandwich is scary, but she knows it is a 'normal' thing to do.

An exciting outcome in reaching a healthy body weight has been the green light for resuming her less strenuous sports. Long-distance running is a little way off, but 'I am getting back into team sports', Kristen said. 'My mother is a bit scared that my bones might break easily, but she understands that playing sport will strengthen them. This winter I'm playing competitive youth girls' football.' As a safeguard, on medical advice, Kristen takes calcium tablets and has a bone scan annually.

A strong Christian faith has sustained Greg and Karen during the tough times. Their faith, shared by their children, has played a big role in the family's fight against Kristen's anorexia. When her daughter's illness was diagnosed, Karen was reluctant to go public, but Greg, who was secretary of his local church, said, 'Our church family needs to know and we need its members to pray for us'. For many members of the church community, this would be their first experience in learning what it was like to suffer from anorexia. As Greg explained, Kristen was not happy for others to know about her illness,

> but support was immediate. I don't know how we would have managed without our faith to draw on. Although we've had some difficult times, I always believed there would be some positive outcomes, and that we would come out stronger in the end, and I still believe this. We have stayed united as a family and within our church. A few women in the church came forward and told Karen of other people they knew who had suffered with the illness. Sharing our struggle has enabled others to share as well, and we have supported each other. Fighting anorexia is character building; you can let your challenges overwhelm you or get on with overcoming them and become stronger for it. In the re-feeding stage we almost had fisticuffs to get Kristen to eat, and she would later apologise for this. I knew that it was her illness, not her, that was giving us a hard time.[2]

A month after her baptism and starting family-based therapy, Kristen made and presented a framed certificate to Karen and Greg, describing them as her 'heroes' and thanking them for their unrelenting effort in helping her to fight her anorexia. The cherished gift hangs on the wall in their bedroom. In the precious moments she managed to separate her sense of self from the anorexia, Kristen was creating little mementoes that would remain a touching reminder of her journey.

Kristen's Christian faith remains very important to her:

> I believe if not for God in my life I would not be here today. He has always been there for me, even in hospital, and in my Bible I have found verses that are helpful in my

struggle. My greatest challenge now is to learn to do things on my own. I can't always have the support of my family with me, but at the moment I fear that when everybody thinks my illness is gone, and I am alone, it might sneak back. It might take hold and, if I let go, no one may care about me any more. I am very much afraid of being alone.

Kristen draws on her Bible for comfort and strength. She shared several of her favourite passages, including Romans 7, verses 15–22, which provides insight into the anguish of living with a mental illness. It reads in part:

I do not understand what I do – for what I want to do I do not do, but what I hate to do . . . I have the desire to do what is good, but I cannot carry it out . . . Now if I do not what I want to do, it is no longer I who do it, but it is sin living in me that does it. So I find this law at work: when I want to do good, evil is right there with me . . . but I see another law at work in members of my body, waging war against the law of my mind.

Kristen finds these verses 'pretty amazing. They help me understand that even though I try really hard the illness sometimes continues to take over and I can't control it. It is scary but at this stage in my recovery I am able to kind of fight back'.

With support from her family-based treatment therapist and her family, Kristen feels safe in taking part in church youth services. But social events, where food is served and shared, remain a little frightening.

I like to have someone on hand that understands. Sometimes people offer me food because they think I am better now, and I need someone there who can say 'no' for me.

We had a church luncheon where my mother brought a packed lunch for me from home and I felt everyone was staring at me, expecting me to partake of the same lunch as them. I felt so anxious, I asked my mother to take me

home. At times like this I want to be left alone. I know God
wants me to have others in my life and yet, when I can't
cope, I feel I don't deserve help. Reading the Bible and
other inspirational books is a comfort.

Misunderstandings add to the challenge of coping with
the illness. Because Kristen no longer looks like she has
anorexia, 'some well-intentioned people create difficult
moments when they say, "You look well" or "You have put a
bit of weight on" '. Karen hastens to tell them, 'Kristen is
still struggling mentally inside, so please avoid commenting on her appearance'. 'I know such remarks really hurt
her', Karen said. 'I tell her that they mean she is looking healthy, and she is slowly learning to walk away and
treat such comments for what they are – well meant but
misinformed.'

At home, Glen and Karen try not to pressure Kristen
when her illness does not allow her to sit still for long –
making study and the completion of homework difficult –
but at times her siblings have felt frustrated. Matthew was
nineteen and Lauren sixteen when Kristen was diagnosed
with anorexia. Lauren was studying her final two years at
high school, and the disruption added pressure:

Kristen was really sick, and in and out of hospital. I felt a
bit angry at her, for always taking up our mother's time,
and felt scared as I knew little about her illness. I felt
frustrated when Kristen would be asked eight times to sit
down to dinner. I just wanted her to be normal and sit
down like the rest of us. She would run up and down on the
brick pavement outside my bedroom window, and this
really annoyed me when trying to study. I had heard a
little about anorexia in school and started reading books
my mother brought home. This knowledge helped me with
a year 11 assignment on mental health – I wrote about
anorexia and got a good mark.

Lauren saw a counsellor during year 12 as she didn't like
to put her problems on others and would only tell her friends
'little bits'. Sometimes she would cry herself to sleep and

worried 'the worst' would happen. 'The biggest scare was when Kristen asked us to let her die and I found her in her bedroom at home with a dressing gown cord around her neck', Lauren said. 'I ran and got Dad.'

Lauren has found the family-based treatment sessions helpful in understanding anorexia:

> The biggest thing I have learnt is how big this illness is, how much of your life it takes over – your concentration, your memory, your physical self, bones and muscles; you push everyone away and it isolates you. It is not something you can go and have surgery for, and it is not about behaviour – it is a disease. People with anorexia can't help what they are doing. When Kristen would get really angry and upset, I'd try to remember that. It was hard enough for us, let alone anyone else, to understand she was being somewhat controlled by a voice.

To see Kristen smile, Lauren said, was 'a wonderful breakthrough'. For a long time her smile wasn't there. 'This illness is about a lot more than "not eating", it is huge', Lauren said. The truth was that anorexia manifested itself through food, using it as the medium through which to manipulate and torment its victim – sometimes for a long time after a healthy body weight had been achieved.

During the most recent school term holiday, Kristen, who has now achieved a healthy weight, pushed her illness further aside. For the first time since developing anorexia, she went out with friends for an evening meal and then to the movies. She strives to be 'Kristen' when with her friends, pushing her illness to the back of her mind. Her next step, she said, will be coping with other people who know about her illness. This will be more 'scary' as she feels these people look for signs that her illness 'is still there'.

'It's easier with friends my own age as they accept me as I am. They visited me in the hospital and know about my illness', Kristen said. 'I am able to enjoy their company more now and look forward to surprising them by saying "yes!" when invited to stay at their house for a meal. So far I have always declined but I am planning to say "yes" very soon.'

The thought of making her friends happy is helping Kristen
to quell her tormenting thoughts – what will a friend's parent serve for the meal? Will she be strong enough to eat it?
Or will her anorexic thoughts make her feel guilty? Suggestions on how to resolve such issues would unravel at the next
family-based treatment session.

Now that she is able to take such rewarding steps in
recovery, Kristen looks forward to these sessions. 'We have a
good chat', Kristen said. 'Last time I spoke for fifty minutes
with our therapist and my parents only got ten minutes!'
That Kristen is able to share her feelings augurs well for her
completing the family-based treatment and proceeding to
realise her life dreams and goals.

Early in her recovery journey, Kristen wrote the following poem to her mother:

> I just want you to know how much it means, to have a
>   Mum like you on my team.
> When times get tough, and I start to feel I've had
>   enough.
> I think about what lies ahead, and what I'd miss if I were
>   dead.
> I know God's with me, He has a plan, so all I have to do is
>   hold His hand.
> So remember, Mum, times will be tough and when you
>   feel you've had enough,
> Just look to God and you will see, just how much you
>   mean to ME![3]

6

Hayley

Elfin-like and lively, 5-year-old Hayley lived with her parents Kathryn and Evan and baby sister Daisy in an outer suburb of a large coastal city. She had completed kindergarten and was about to start primary school. Her bedroom was full of dolls and soft toys, some almost as big as herself. Her life was full of pinks and purples, cuddles and laughter, softness and love. Then one day, when her mother was out shopping and her dad was mowing the lawn, her small world went horribly black.

The boy who lived across the street had come over to play. Some years older than Hayley, he had formed a friendship with her and the two often played together. This day, however, his play included sexual 'interference' in her bedroom. Hayley's father did not hear her screams above the lawn mower's roar and the boy warned her to be quiet. 'You will get in trouble if you tell your parents', he said.

Kathryn returned home thirty minutes later to find Hayley in tears. She had always encouraged her daughter to share any concerns and, despite the boy's parting threat, Hayley managed to tell her mother what had happened. Kathryn comforted her little girl and then ran across the road to confront the boy and his parents. They were preparing for a big family party and did not appreciate her interruption. 'I did my nut at the father', Kathryn said. Doctors were called and Hayley was counselled. It turned out the incident was not the first. Too upset to stay in the house where their daughter had been molested, and wishing to avoid further contact with their neighbours,

Kathryn and Evan sold their house and moved to a new location.

Now sixteen, Hayley has difficulty recalling the childhood trauma that sparked a six-year struggle by her parents to find help for her. Kathryn's memory remains painfully clear, not only of the event but also of what came afterwards. 'Nobody would believe me', Kathryn said, of attempts to get help for her daughter. 'Almost immediately, from the age of five, Hayley suffered serious problems but she was eleven before someone would take me seriously. I was always told that she had a behavioural problem rather than a mental illness.'

Hayley became progressively more anxious and nervous. When she was six years old a paediatrician chastised Kathryn for being an overreactive mother and said that she and Evan should be stronger and exercise more discipline with Hayley. He said 'there are sick people out there', referring to his crowded waiting room, and implied that Kathryn was wasting his time. By the time she was eight years old, Hayley had virtually stopped eating and had begun to insist on carrying a plastic bag whenever she left the house. The bag had a purpose: she would worry so much when going out that she would be physically sick, after which she would feel calmer and be fine. Doctors expressed concern at her low weight but repeatedly said 'do not worry', and offered no diagnosis.

At ten, Hayley entered a darker period, withdrawing further into herself. By now her plastic bag was her constant companion, and this included going to school. Kathryn began to notice a worrying pattern – Hayley would feel sick, 'throw up' and start shaking every time she set off to her girlfriend's house around the corner. The two girls walked the short distance to school together. On investigating, Kathryn learnt that an older child in the friend's family was bullying Hayley at school. This explained why Hayley had been coming home from school recently with glue in her hair and bruises on her arms.

Determined to pursue the matter further, Kathryn met with the school principal, who offered support. Eventually the family with the child 'bully' moved away, but unfortunately this also meant Hayley lost her best friend. In response to her increasing anxiety, Hayley became moody and began to self-harm by pulling out her eyelashes, and hair by the handfuls. This continued for months. Many people attributed her behaviour to 'spoilt brat syndrome'. Friends and health professionals alike would suggest that Hayley was putting Kathryn through hell and back, and the mother was letting the child get away with it.

A turning point came when Hayley was eleven and in sixth grade. Kathryn noticed she was not touching her school lunches. Hayley did not try to hide the fact, saying she 'just was not hungry' or 'did not have time to eat'. Kathryn, finding the sixth grade teacher a trustworthy and caring person, confided in her before Hayley departed with the class on a school camp. The teacher promised to keep an eye on Hayley, especially at mealtimes. On returning home the teacher called and said Hayley had serious problems. 'At last someone was agreeing with me!' Kathryn said.

Steps were taken to have Hayley assessed by mental health staff within the school system. But nothing happened in a hurry – the attitude was that she would surely grow out of her problem. Apart from Hayley's parents, no one was taking the little girl's distress seriously. She was admitted to the local hospital one night as the family doctor thought her bad stomach pains could be due to her appendix, but, on further examination, the doctor realised how thin she was and that her pains were due to hunger. When told some counselling was being organised through the school, the doctor said he would leave it at that. Hayley recalled when the doctor thought she had appendicitis: 'I was not eating and I had to eat a whole tin of spaghetti for the pain to go away. Eating the spaghetti took three hours; I could not eat quickly because my stomach had shrunk so much'.

The counsellor offered Kathryn and Evan hope at first, but soon concluded that they would benefit from undertaking a behaviour course, saying 'this will fix Hayley's anxiety'. The counsellor's philosophy was that 'fixing the behaviour will fix the anxiety, which in turn will fix the eating disorder'. 'We enrolled for the course', Kathryn said, 'but halfway through we could see it was not addressing our problems with Hayley. Months were passing by and she was slipping further from us. She was dying'.

Another counsellor suggested an alternative course, this time for 'cool kids'. They tried this, too, but quickly realised that being 'cool' was not enough to help Hayley. Kathryn did not know where else to turn. Her sick child, who was continuing to self-harm, said voices in her head were telling her not to eat. When out of control she would say, 'I want to die so that I can go to a better place'.

Hayley doesn't remember going all day without eating, but recalled regularly skipping breakfast and lunch:

> I would binge eat in the afternoon and Dad would come home from work and find no food. This was before I started family-based treatment and I was still getting thin. I would eat ice-cream, potato chips and drink lemonade, but made sure I was doing more exercise than eating. I was playing too much sport – netball, touch football and school sport; I was on the run all the time. I forced myself to do it. I struggled and everyone could see it, but until I started family-based treatment, nobody stopped me.

Kathryn, meanwhile, was ready to snap. Besides meeting dead ends with doctors and counsellors, she was receiving little support from her family. Her mother was in denial and so was Evan. He had no idea how to help and had established a habit of escaping to the local pub to chat with his mates as often as he could after his day's work. This seemed the best way to avoid the stress at home. Feeling helpless and desperate, Kathryn said to him, 'If Hayley dies because you will not face reality, I'll take Daisy and you will not see us again'.

As news of the family's plight spread to extended family members, a cousin blessed with an assertive nature offered to help Kathryn find a solution. She said she would engage 'a bulldozer', if necessary, to knock down brick walls of medical indifference in seeking help for Hayley. 'Otherwise she will die', the cousin flatly said, as she got busy with her research. By now Hayley was twelve and dangerously emaciated.

Through a network of friends the cousin tracked down the family-based treatment called the Maudsley Approach, offered at the Children's Hospital at Westmead, a ninety-minute drive from Hayley's home. This form of treatment was news to Kathryn and Evan. An appointment for an assessment was made. Seven years after her torment began, little Hayley was about to begin her recovery.

Kathryn and Evan felt overwhelmed when the family-based treatment team acknowledged Hayley had more than a behavioural problem. The couple had feared they would be told they were 'going on about nothing' yet again. They felt crushed when told their daughter had been suffering anorexia for a long time, but joyous when the therapists said they could treat her illness. To have her concerns affirmed after a seven-year battle made Kathryn feel like racing home and telling local health providers, especially the education department's mental health counsellor who had refused to provide a referral to the hospital. Kathryn had begged for the referral but had been told 'do not dare tell me how to do my job'. Desperate, she had gone to her local family doctor, who could see Hayley was very sick. Lacking the skills to help her, he immediately provided the referral. The doctor had tried to help previously, but nothing had worked and, like Kathryn, he hadn't heard about the Maudsley Approach. It was worth a try.

Kathryn's cousin, rather than Evan, accompanied her to the initial assessment. This was because Kathryn had felt very let down by Evan's preference to spend time at the pub rather than home. Evan was genuinely remorseful for not having shown much support or interest to date, Kathryn said, 'but at that point I had to do it alone. Unless you are there, no one understands'.

When told she would be participating in family-based treatment, Hayley was not happy. Two days after the family's first trip to the assessment team, she was threatening to suicide and was admitted to hospital. She remained there for two months. She did not need to have a nasogastric tube inserted – the medical staff gave her the choice of that or a nutritious milkshake. She chose the shake and gradually gained weight.

'At first I did not like being in hospital, and I said to my parents for the first two weeks "if you loved me you would take me away" ', Hayley said. Driven by her illness, she tore her clothes apart in protest at being challenged. 'She ripped them up', Kathryn said, 'so I needed to go out and buy new ones. I also bought a new quilt for her bed so it looked less hospital-like, and she could feel less anxious by knowing she could have the same quilt when she came home'.

The initial outbursts subsided as Hayley adapted to the hospital's therapy routine:

> The discipline helped me. We had to eat at a table and a nurse would sit with us, and we had a certain time limit in which to complete our meal. When we had finished we could leave the table. We did this for three meals plus two snacks every day. If we were watching TV, we would have to stop and eat, but the sooner we ate the sooner we could get back to it.

Hayley was one of six girls in the ward with anorexia. 'When I arrived, the other anorexic patients were supportive, and I was supportive to others who arrived after me. We were fighting the illness together; we understood and helped each other. We had a pool table and cable TV, and we could have a sleep-over every night!' By the end of the first month, Hayley was starting to relax and enjoy her stay so much she did not want to go home! Her family was visiting her every day and she suggested that they did not need to come so often.

Nonetheless, Evan and Kathryn continued to visit Hayley in hospital every day. They were so pleased to see her making progress. Kathryn took her younger daughter Daisy with her on the three-hour round trip, and the hospital gave Evan permission to see Hayley out of normal visiting hours because he was working at night. As Hayley gained weight and her physical health improved, she was sent home on day trips and weekends. 'That's when we started the first stage of the family-based treatment program', Kathryn said. Hayley was eased into the program and, when her health was sufficiently restored, she came home full-time.

At home, Hayley's improvement continued, and she gained 2 kilograms in the first month. However, her illness, which had become entrenched, was not giving up without a fight.

Sometimes without warning she would refuse to eat, saying 'You do not love me. If you loved me you would not make me eat this'. When that had no effect she would tell her parents they were wasting their time and cry, 'I am never going to get better. I will always have this [illness]'. If Kathryn and Evan did not give her precisely what she wanted for dinner, she would abuse them and yell, 'If I do not eat I will die and that will be your fault. I hate you!' She would try to pick a fight and storm off from the dinner table.[1]

Hayley's fixation on food affected everyone in the family. Often Kathryn would be standing at the pantry door, checking to see what she needed to buy at the supermarket to restock, when she would sense Hayley had 'sneaked up' and was watching her from behind. 'Her behaviour was unnatural and it frightened me', Kathryn said. 'Every time someone went to the pantry or the fridge, she wanted to know what food we were taking out.'

Food was not the only thing that fed Hayley's anxiety. The problem, nine times out of ten, was not worth worrying about, Kathryn said, but Hayley would 'freak out' and be unable to handle it. Buying a different brand of shampoo because it was a supermarket 'special' that week would be insignificant to the rest of the family but monumental to Hayley. The thought of using a different brand could explode her anxiety level. Or it could have been the purchase of a new T-shirt. Most children would be excited about wearing a new top to show their friends, but the mere thought made Hayley fret. Any change was stressful for her and could drive her to self-harm.

With the support of the therapy team, Kathryn and Evan persisted in helping their daughter strengthen her sense of self so that her anxiety gradually eased. Evan took his turn at taking Hayley's lunch to school. The re-feeding made sense to Evan and he was 'really good at it', Kathryn said. He would park the car in the school car park and sit with Hayley while she ate. 'I felt strange', Evan said, 'but if this is what it would take for Hayley to get well then I was happy to do it. I became an expert in high-energy foods and knew exactly where to find them on the supermarket shelves'. Muesli bars were best, Evan said, but some days Hayley refused to eat them. She insisted on cooked pasta – it had to be freshly cooked, and delivered to her warm. That was not all – the pasta had to be a certain brand, as did the tomato-based sauce, and had to be measured precisely before mixing.[2]

Family-based treatment helped Evan to re-establish his place in the family:

> In some ways life was easier for me before we began family-based treatment because once we accepted the challenge of confronting Hayley's illness, there could be no backing down. I'm a shift worker and I had to learn to fit Hayley's needs around my work hours. I could not slip off to the pub and be in denial any more! My mates are mostly tradesmen, and the pub is our meeting place. In some ways I probably went there too often, and at the wrong time, to get away from the stress at home.
>
>   Before, it was easier for me to stay out of the way because it was all too hard. I did not understand; I did not know what to say or do, and probably had my blinkers on. I had been thin as a teenager and was a late developer and thought Hayley would be the same. But the difference was I was eating and she did not eat – starting by refusing breakfast – and she would get sick with anxiety, and got headaches. I learnt to look outside the square. You can't always think your kid is like they are because of genetics. Hayley will always be slight but throughout her primary school years she was undernourished. Unfortunately, until we found family-based treatment, our efforts to get help kept 'hitting walls'.

Once Evan knew what he and Kathryn were up against he was able to fight full-heartedly to get his daughter back: 'Kathryn and I began working as a team, with a united front, and Hayley knew there was no point pitting us one against the other. Hayley would say "It's not fair now, you two against me" '.[3]

Within fifteen months of leaving hospital, Hayley had completed the three-phase program. She had gained more than 10 kilograms and grown 15 centimetres. 'After all those early years of discouragement and dismissals from doctors, the turnaround in Hayley's health after starting family-based treatment was truly amazing', Kathryn said.

Today, another nine months on, Hayley is in year 10 at school and is an 'A' student. She has required no further hospital admissions. She remains small for her age, but, with a big grin, she said that besides beginning to menstruate, she has gained another 4 kilograms and grown several more centimetres. She is continuing to rebuild her sense of self and place in her family. If she feels tormented, she says to her mother, 'I'm having a setback'. Unless Hayley shares that she is having a difficult day, Kathryn doesn't ask about her feelings. 'You can't ask too many questions otherwise she shuts down and withdraws.'

Having reached and maintained a safe weight, Hayley has resumed playing sport. She enjoys playing competition soccer, but this, Kathryn said, is a privilege and Hayley knows that if at any time she loses 'too much' weight she will lose the right to play. 'I'm feeling more me', Hayley said. 'I feel like I've got half of my life back. I like being able to play sport and I've been able to keep up some friendships from my two-month stay in hospital.'[4]

Hayley said that suffering from anorexia nervosa was horrible.

> You lose everything. I lost all my sport, I lost my freedom, I had to be watched 24/7 and could not do anything. When I was not in hospital, I was stuck at home, too sick to go to school, and I lost some precious years of my life. I would struggle with my moods and get angry. It would just happen and I would take it out on people. I do not do that any more.

Having been denied the freedom to enjoy her childhood, Hayley is embracing her teenage years. Besides her studies and sport, she works twelve to twenty hours a week in a takeaway food shop, and her employer has praised her attitude and performance. She continues to deal with some obsessive-compulsive disorder habits, which Kathryn lists as including having her hair done a certain way and washing it on certain days, wearing the same clothes, eating certain

foods, such as spaghetti and stroganoff, and an insistence
on watching certain teenage television programs. Some of
these habits could be said to be quite normal for her age
group!

She eats anything she wants and said, 'I always go back
for more'. Hayley enjoys talking about food and happily lists a
typical day's menu: breakfast – a slice of toast; morning tea –
a packet of potato crisps or popcorn; lunch – dry biscuits with
butter and a little spread; afternoon tea – cake, iceblocks,
chips or pasties; dinner – meat or chicken with vegetables
and pasta, rice or chips, and sometimes ice-cream for dessert;
and supper – a banana, grapes or watermelon. 'I've a favourite takeaway, too', Hayley quipped. 'Hot chips with gravy
and salt!' Her diet is perhaps not a nutritionist's dream, but
Hayley remains lively and easily accounts for the carbohydrates – her meals are regular and she is enjoying them.

This is all a big relief to Kathryn, who has told Hayley
'we have been through so much with your disease I do not
have energy to deal with a normal teenager's tantrums'.
During her long search for help, Kathryn's confidence as a
mother fell dangerously low at times:

> I was grateful when we got to the bottom of Hayley's
> problems, but felt angry when I thought of all the money
> we had spent, and of precious time wasted because health
> professionals wouldn't think outside their set way of
> thinking. I was angry, too, because they doubted me as
> a mother.

Support did not come from closer to home either. Kathryn felt her mother basically blamed her for Hayley's problems. She claimed Kathryn favoured Daisy and was too
'hard' on Hayley. The manipulative illness promoted this
misconception.

Kathryn would be beside herself with frustration when
the family was about to leave home for a visit, as Hayley
would be ill and would need another outfit:

> I would clean her up, and we would get in the car and she
> would argue the whole way because she had not wanted

to leave the house. When we reached our destination, she would act okay, but by then I would be feeling aggressive towards her because of what she had just put me through. This happened when we were going anywhere.

   In front of my mother Hayley would eat, and so my mother would think there was nothing wrong with her. Then Hayley would binge, and go and throw it up. My mother did not see this and had no understanding. Even at the hospital when we had to do the 'tough love' thing and make Hayley remain at the table until she ate her meal, my mother would tell me that I shouldn't be doing this, I should be showing Hayley that I love her. My mother did not understand the need to be tough on the illness, not on Hayley as a person.

The illness had driven a wedge between a mother's and a grandmother's love. Hayley's inward struggle was too difficult for Kathryn's mother to understand. Kathryn's father did not understand either but, Kathryn said, 'he did not butt in'. Her parents' response was awkward at a time when she needed support and could not find it:

   I literally had nobody but my cousin to confide in. I tried talking to my friends but they did not understand, with one saying Hayley 'needed a good kick up the arse'. Seriously, I do not know how I am not in the loony bin. Luckily my employer was helpful and offered me counselling and helped me with time off. People would ask 'How is Hayley going?' and it was difficult finding the right answer. One woman would ask about Daisy, and I would say, 'It is Hayley who is sick', and she would say, 'I know, but how is Daisy coping?'

Kathryn often felt like everyone was trying to make her feel guilty.

Daisy, now eleven, has coped well with the upheavals caused by Hayley's illness. Encouraged by her parents, she has focused on her own development and especially enjoys singing and acting classes. Having grown up with her sister's illness, she is relieved that the 'food fights' have subsided: 'I would want to say, "Hayley, please just eat!" Our family life is heaps better now'.

Today Hayley requires no supervision in helping herself to breakfast and in eating her lunch at school. This independence enables Kathryn and Evan to get on with their lives, and the family generally sits together around the kitchen table for their evening meal. This is when Kathryn and Evan catch up most on their daughters' activities.

Kathryn urges parents to take action if they notice their child is getting too tired, is losing weight or their moods are changing: 'Go to your local doctor, get information and check if the symptoms indicate an illness is developing'. She doesn't recommend keeping scales in the house as they offer encouragement to anyone with anorexic tendencies. 'We wait for our six-monthly hospital appointments and weigh Hayley there', Kathryn said.

Kathryn wants increased awareness and understanding of anorexia nervosa in the school system. When Hayley was admitted to hospital, her teachers knew of her illness and held a special assembly to inform her classmates. Kathryn was disappointed when not invited along: 'I could have explained the illness and treatment to the children and answered their questions, as the teachers could not do so. The teachers did not know what Hayley's recovery program would entail, and at one stage they weighed her during a class session. I was upset'.

Recently, Daisy brought a consent form home from her primary school for her parents to sign. The form related to an upcoming visit by a 'childhood obesity team', which wanted to weigh each child to see if they were in a healthy weight range. Kathryn saw red. She not only refused permission in writing but also called and warned school staff that putting children on the scales could encourage the development of anorexia. Kathryn said 'if they put Daisy on the scales, I would sue the education department. Many parents complained. The people making decisions to put children on scales are not thinking about their health. They risk causing more damage than doing good'.

Reflecting, Kathryn said that if the illness had to happen, she is glad it happened while Hayley was under parental supervision.

> If she had been over eighteen, she probably would be dead by now because she wouldn't have helped herself. We feel very sad she lost her childhood but are grateful she is still here. Life is a lot better, a lot quieter now. There's no more anxiety before going out. But we can tell if Hayley hasn't had her medication, which is ongoing due to her long-term problems. Sometimes she tries to pretend she has taken her medication when she hasn't, and I feel annoyed that she will not accept responsibility. I can be sound asleep, and I wake up and think 'Oh my God', and I have to get her up and make sure she has had her pills. It is tiring, checking all the time.

Since Hayley's completion of family-based treatment Kathryn has opened her own business – a long-held dream come true. 'Hayley's experience has taught each of us that life is too short and we must live our dreams to the full. Life is good. We have got our daughter back', she said. And Kathryn has her life back, too.

7

Claire

Concerned about their daughter's weight loss, Jennifer and Michael took Claire to their family doctor. He gave a swift appraisal. 'Don't worry', he said, 'Claire's not heading for serious trouble. Whatever you do, don't make her eat'. Believing their doctor knew best, Jennifer and Michael went home and heeded his advice. If they forgot for a moment and became overly encouraging at meal times, Claire reminded them of the doctor's instruction. She continued to lose weight but again the doctor said, 'Don't pressure her; don't insist that she eat'. This doctor unwittingly was giving Claire's illness permission to grow and take control of her life.

Discovering a child has an eating disorder is difficult enough, but Jennifer is blind. Therefore it was not visible signs, like weight loss, that fuelled her suspicions. Her daughter Claire was fifteen and starting year 10 at high school when Jennifer began noticing changes in her behaviour. Claire was getting up later in the mornings and saying she had no time to eat breakfast before rushing to school. Instead of taking her usual sandwich, Claire began insisting on rice cakes without anything on them for her school lunch and, when the family was about to sit down for the evening meal, she would say she was not hungry or arrange to be elsewhere.

Individually, the changes were subtle and easy to miss and Claire's dad, Michael, was oblivious to all until Jennifer mentioned them. He agreed Claire didn't seem her normal happy self and could see that she was losing weight, but wondered if this was a teenage phase. However, a phone call from the school counsellor, prompted by Claire's concerned friends, confirmed Jennifer's suspicions. There was a problem. On consulting with Claire, the counsellor called again to suggest the problem was an eating disorder.

Jennifer and Michael, who lived in a large inland city with Claire and their son Rhys, thirteen, had begun to think Claire was developing a borderline eating disorder, but felt shocked when the counsellor voiced their fears. They did not think that the disorder might be anorexia nervosa as they associated that illness with someone who was skeletal and Claire, while thin, didn't match that image. However, encouraged by the counsellor, they sought medical advice.

This was easier said than done. For six months, Jennifer and Michael hit 'brick walls'. First, they took Claire to see the local family doctor, who advised that they shouldn't make Claire eat. Adhering to their doctor's advice, Jennifer and Michael went home and didn't insist that Claire eat her meals. In this environment, anorexia had everything going for it. Concerned at Claire's continued weight loss, Jennifer and Michael took her back to their doctor. This time, although observing an emerging self-image problem with Claire calling herself fat when she was thin, the doctor again said, 'Don't pressure her; don't insist that she eat'.

Encouraging the parents to think logically, the doctor said surely they could see that parental pressure would make Claire stressed and more determined not to eat. Michael and Jennifer felt compelled to believe him. They didn't know he was inadvertently giving the anorexia permission to grow and take over Claire's life; that instead of challenging the illness, he was supporting it.

Standing by helplessly and allowing their daughter to starve became increasingly difficult for Michael and Jennifer. Before her illness, Claire had been openly affectionate and loving with them. Now she was withdrawing. However, the doctor dismissed this and other concerns as 'normal' teenage behaviour, and Michael and Jennifer began to wonder if they were overreactive parents.

Eventually the family doctor referred Claire to a psychologist regarding her self-image problem, but Michael and Jennifer were excluded and received no feedback. In a bid for more assistance, Jennifer contacted the state child and adolescent mental health service, which arranged for another psychologist to meet with the family for an assessment. This led to a suggestion that Claire would not thrive in a one-to-one situation and a recommendation that she join a discussion group for adolescent girls who were experiencing 'issues of adolescence'. The group was not specifically for girls with eating-related problems and, again, Jennifer and Michael received no feedback.

The parents felt the professional inference was that Claire needed help because she had been overcontrolled and was in need of independence. But apart from letting Claire do what she wanted to do at mealtimes, no one was telling Michael and Jennifer how to help her. A dietician tried to educate Claire about nutrition. She related well to her but Jennifer said, 'Claire simply was not able to act on the information she was given. The disordered thinking caused by anorexia nervosa cannot be overcome by logic and reason alone'.

A paediatrician assured the parents that Claire was not 'medically compromised'. 'She is physically healthy', he said. 'If her weight drops to a level where that is not the case, we will admit her to hospital.'[1] While taking the medical line, the paediatrician was also supportive of the family, Jennifer said.

We felt some relief in learning that Claire's weight would not be allowed to spiral downwards indefinitely. The paediatrician acknowledged that an eating disorder was a serious psychological illness and encouraged our search for effective support and intervention. He continued to monitor Claire's physical health after we heard about and began family-based treatment, and strongly affirmed the Maudsley Approach as a good therapeutic fit for our family.

For now, though, Jennifer and Michael remained confused. Claire managed to stay above the borderline weight that would have led to hospitalisation and this kept confirming to them that their family doctor was correct – they were imagining a problem. The doctor's opinion challenged their parental intuition, and they didn't know his view was common – that symptoms of anorexia were often not acknowledged until the situation was drastic. The long-established practice was that a child would have to be very thin before symptoms of the illness would be taken seriously. Some parents would take their child to their family doctor two, three or more times before managing to obtain a referral to an eating disorder specialist. Michael and Jennifer tried to refrain from expressing concern because their doctor warned them not to 'make an issue out of it or it will become one'.

As they stumbled around, not knowing where to seek the right help, Jennifer and Michael wondered if they were overanxious and if ignoring the eating disorder was the key to controlling it. Until now, the only time Michael had heard of anorexia was in the 1980s when American pop star Karen Carpenter died from the illness at the age of thirty-two. He had never dreamt of his daughter having the illness decades later. Meanwhile, Jennifer, who was trained in social welfare, was increasingly frustrated with medical advice.

Six months had passed when a newsletter email from Claire's dietician became a turning point in acknowledgment of her illness. A local eating disorder support group had been established for families and although doubting that they qualified, Jennifer and Michael attended a meeting. 'We were still labouring under the misconception that an eating disorder is primarily about food and weight', Jennifer said. On joining the support group, however, Claire's parents learnt her illness was more serious than clinicians had led them to believe. They had been conditioned to think that Claire was not as sick as other children, and that she needed to be sicker, and thinner, to be taken seriously, as Jennifer explained:

Claire was still eating small amounts of food – she was not flatly refusing to eat. This was why we felt she was on the verge of having an eating disorder, but that her condition was borderline. Speaking with other parents helped us to clarify that the behaviours we were observing were in fact part of the illness. For the first time we were made aware of the anorexia's constant, negative impact on Claire's thoughts.

Jennifer said she and Michael went from thinking Claire had a borderline illness to understanding they were caught up in a life and death battle:

> We had a general notion that an illness is progressive, and you reach a certain level where help is required. Like the common cold, you put up with it and recover or you get sicker and need medical intervention; we didn't know at what point we should take Claire's eating disorder seriously.

Prior to her illness, Claire had been outgoing, chatty and laughed a lot. She was fun to be with, amiable and social, going out with friends and inviting friends into the family home. Now the fun and laughter had vanished. There was a lot of crying and shouting, and Claire had withdrawn from her parents. She would be either silent or would shout at them, 'What do you care, what would you know?' As her illness became entrenched, Michael and Jennifer remained confused by conflicting advice, wondering if they were responsible for her illness; wondering if they should step back or step in. At times, Claire could still show a compassionate concern for others but most of her personality had disappeared into the clutches of anorexia.

Outside the family home, Claire tried to hide her illness. She kept a part-time job in a fast-food outlet and, physical appearance aside, appeared her normal self. The contrast in behaviour inside and outside the home compounded her parents' confusion. 'We felt as though we were overreacting', Jennifer said. 'If we asked our friends, and parents of Claire's friends, they would say Claire seemed fine. We would then think, "Gosh, if it only happens at home, maybe we are the problem".'

A lot of people also commented that their own children displayed similar behaviours to Claire, particularly withdrawing from family activities, spending long periods alone in their bedroom and being away from home at mealtimes. 'This caused us to consider whether what we were witnessing in Claire was simply normal adolescent behaviour', Jennifer said. It was a big step to accept that Claire's behaviour was symptomatic of anorexia nervosa. This was a stressful, uncertain time and Jennifer did not need any more worries. Before the onset of Claire's illness, she had a scare with breast cancer and a lump was removed. A year later, when Claire's anorexia was raging, she would have a second scare, this time requiring a mastectomy.

The support group assured Michael and Jennifer that Claire was not being deliberately difficult or choosing to starve herself. Also, the family doctor had it wrong – the illness, not Claire, was exerting a will to control her life. To explain, one parent likened Claire's illness to that of a bully in her head twenty-four hours a day, seven days a week. With a jolt, Michael and Jennifer began to understand what their daughter was up against.

Claire's illness had been developing for eight months when they first heard of family-based treatment during a support meeting. Jennifer and Michael knew they wanted this for their daughter, even if the clinic, The Oak House, was a four-hour drive away. Claire, although scarcely eating, had been insisting she was fine, and her parents wondered if they should wait for her to acknowledge her problem before seeking assistance. On hearing their account, however, the family therapist at The Oak House said not to wait and arranged an appointment for an assessment the following week. As soon as they entered the family-based treatment clinic, Michael and Jennifer felt they were on the right path and were cheered by thoughts of a positive outcome. For a start, the therapists were interested in more than food and weight. They were interested in supporting every member of the family and were not suggesting Michael and Jennifer were overreactive parents.

Until that first meeting, Michael had continued to believe that Claire's 'morselisation' of food was a frustrating habit rather than a symptom of a deeper illness. Now he began to see that her illness was more than physical. It was more than skipping meals and eating dry rice cakes for school lunch. Besides talking to the therapy team, sharing with other parents at the clinic and in the local support group helped enormously in understanding Claire's struggle. For the family's first few therapy sessions, for instance, she did not speak.[2]

Another challenge rose when Michael went overseas for work for three weeks. He returned to find Claire's illness had thrived in his absence, with a lot of shouting, bad language, an incredible determination not to eat, and many plates of food thrown on the floor. Sometimes Claire would hit out at Jennifer, or Michael now that he was home, and everyone would become distressed.

But just as attempts to fight the illness seemed to be degenerating, the family-based treatment empowered Michael and Jennifer to stand their ground and insist Claire eat. They felt a definite need for this permission, their family doctor having specifically removed it months earlier. At last their confidence as parents was being restored. Just the same, if the therapist had not forewarned that Claire's illness would worsen before improving, they would have thought their doctor's advice was correct. Assured that they were on the right track, they agreed to support each other, and to learn to recognise when the other was struggling. The manipulative and hurtful illness was pushing the buttons of each family member, especially Jennifer's, whose blindness was a point of vulnerability.

Claire strongly objected to her food or plate being touched, which Jennifer needed to do to check that everything had been eaten. To overcome this hurdle, another family member sat at the table to be Jennifer's eyes at mealtimes. This was usually Michael, Rhys or a close relative of the family. A roster of friends and extended family also provided transport for Jennifer to take Claire's lunch to school. Having to depend on others in battling anorexia made Jennifer want to scream and shout in frustration.

'While I greatly valued the dedication of friends and family in helping out, this dependency brought its own complications', Jennifer said. 'Claire struggled to eat in front of others, and coordinating times and accommodating last-minute changes in school timetabling or someone's availability was aggravating for me.'

Even when both parents were present, the anorexia involved horrendous times. Jennifer described the daily struggle:

> At 5 p.m. we could be waiting for Claire to eat breakfast – two whole mouthfuls of cereal. We actually would have intended for her to eat a full bowl but would have negotiated down to two mouthfuls. One day during the first week of Phase One we got to 5 p.m. and she had not eaten ALL day. She was due to start her part-time job at 5 p.m., and we said that unless she ate those two mouthfuls we would have to call her employer and say she couldn't go to work. In the past she had eaten in response to this strategy but this particular day she refused. We felt awful but had to keep our word and cancel her shift. Eventually she ate one mouthful of cereal, but too late to go to work. That was a stand-up, drag-out day.
>
> We had phoned our therapist around noon to say, 'We are sitting here, encouraging Claire to eat breakfast and it is not happening. We want to know, how long do we need to sit?' And the therapist patiently replied, 'You have to sit just a little longer than the illness'. One part of me wanted to reach through the phone and hit the therapist, 300 kilometres away, and the other part said, 'Okay, we have to be more determined, and however long the illness hangs out we will hang out longer'.[3]

Michael and Jennifer were fast appreciating the strength of commitment and persistence required to beat the powerful illness. Michael needed time out from his job. First, he used part of his holiday entitlement and then his supportive employer rearranged his work hours into four days instead of five so he could attend the weekly therapy sessions. Even with the therapy sessions and help just a phone call away when at home, Michael and Jennifer often felt uncertain in the choice of strategy. They couldn't think further ahead than coping, hour-to-hour, with the next meal. Most challenges revolved around food, but anorexia's variations of confrontation were unlimited.

Responses to Claire's anorexia, compared with Jennifer's cancer, had differed markedly. Concern and compassion flowed into the home following Jennifer's diagnosis with breast cancer. People could grasp and be sympathetic to her situation. After all, she had not chosen to have this real and potentially deadly illness. She received flowers, phone calls and get-well cards, and casseroles of food landed on her front doorstep. But as Jennifer explained, it was a completely different story with Claire's illness:

> As for Claire's anorexia, we might as well have said we were washing our dog. People didn't want to know about it. They seemed to believe Claire chose to have her illness. But she did not choose anorexia, any more than I chose breast cancer. Some people implied Claire was 'a wilful brat' and should 'snap out of it'. They didn't grasp that the anorexia, not Claire, was trying to manipulate and gain control; and they didn't understand that this torment went on all day, every day.

Such reactions were due to an inability rather than an unwillingness to understand: 'In contrast, people could relate to my cancer because it was a physical illness'.

Family life contracted to revolve around a few friends and the therapy team. Michael learnt to say nothing to most people, because unless they had experienced anorexia they didn't understand. As for Claire, her teenage peer group lacked awareness about her illness but remained supportive. The illness was difficult for Rhys to understand, too. An insulin-dependent diabetic since the age of seven, he had to eat regular meals to keep well. Not eating didn't make sense! He had begun attending the weekly family therapy sessions with his family, but had to cease due to missing important classes at school. 'If we hadn't had to travel such a long distance, Rhys would probably have continued to attend all family sessions', Jennifer said. 'He did all that he could to support Claire and was very tolerant of the time and energy that needed to be poured into her care.'

Claire reached a healthy weight within eight months and yet, although maintaining it, was having difficulty officially moving on to Phase Two of family-based treatment, which involved resuming control over her eating. After twelve months of treatment, Michael and Jennifer did not quite have their daughter back but were feeling positive. Jennifer explained:

> Twelve months is an average, but you can't help taking it on as a goal because you want it to be over. You want this illness to be gone. You also have a perception that it is a gradual steady climb up and, when you slip a step back, you think the whole thing hasn't worked and you panic. If we had a really bad day, I reminded myself we were further ahead than a year earlier. A slip didn't mean we were spiralling down; we were simply having a bad day. Personally, I prayed a lot. When it got really bad, I screamed 'I can't hold on, I can't do this right now', and asked God to hold on for me. You think you must cope at all times and sometimes you don't. You say and do wrong things.

On one particularly frustrating day, Jennifer spilt a bowl of custard over Claire's head. The situation went from bad to worse with Claire refusing to stay at home and moving in with friends for two days. Jennifer phoned the therapist in tears, thinking, 'We have been told to be totally hands-off and now we will be chucked out of the program'. To hear the therapist say 'You are not the first parent to experience this' lifted Jennifer's spirits enormously. The therapist told Jennifer to accept she was fallible and think about what she could learn from the experience; to accept that sometimes, despite best efforts, everything would go pear-shaped and things like this would happen. After emotionally beating herself up, Jennifer thought, 'Damn, the illness won that round. It made me do this. It pushed me'. She resolved to be stronger and more determined.

'When you start this treatment you have ground rules – you are to be hands-off, calm, and firm but loving', Jennifer said. The phrase 'firm but loving' was one Michael and Jennifer came to hate. They said it over and over: 'We will be very firm and loving'. But they could not just flick a switch, and at times they would think, 'Oh, my goodness, I don't suit the program', so reassurance was very important.[4]

Michael, like most fathers, thought he knew how to manage his children, but anorexia put Claire on a collision course with him. He'd had few confrontations with Claire until they began family-based treatment. Then she changed dramatically – from someone loving, trustworthy, thoughtful and mild-mannered to someone uncooperative, untrustworthy and manipulative who used words he never knew she knew. Going toe to toe with his child, asking her to eat her dinner, became a frightening battle of wills. Did he do everything right? No. He found his role hard to follow. Sometimes dinner would be thrown across the room and plates smashed on the wall. So Jennifer would cook another batch and he would stand in the doorway until Claire ate the food on her plate. He tried hard to remember that the illness was making his child repeatedly yell 'I hate you', but he would be shaking inside and sometimes he'd lose it. He would yell back, 'Eat your dinner!' At times, he would thump the table in frustration and send glasses rolling.

The hardest times for Michael were when the hate was targeted at Jennifer. Early on there was a brief period when Claire would hit out at both parents, and both had bruises. Michael was well built but Jennifer was small. He could take a lot of insults, but if his wife was attacked or given a hard time, all bets were off and he could become infuriated.

The family therapist persisted in helping Michael see that the illness, not Claire, was giving Jennifer a hard time. The biggest tool family-based treatment gave him was permission to fight back and browbeat anorexia. 'Put the potato on your fork, put it your mouth', he would say to Claire over and over, for hours on end. He had to take many deep breaths and remind himself not to take it personally. No matter how much he wanted to retaliate with words, he knew that would be a mistake. Shouting would not help – worse, it would strengthen the anorexia. 'We would not have persevered without encouragement from our therapist', Michael said.[5]

Challenges were never-ending because anorexia allowed no time out. To see Claire wasting away before his eyes, having been told she may die or suffer for the rest of her life, motivated Michael to keep fighting the illness. There were times when he and Jennifer feared Claire would run away, so he locked their doors. They had her sleep in their room when she went through a stage of self-harm. One day Claire came and said, 'I have done a silly thing, I have attempted an overdose of paracetamol'. She was feeling angry enough to swallow the pills but not angry enough to want to die. She had felt scared and found the courage to tell her parents, who took her to the hospital immediately. The charcoal, 'flush the system' type of solution was unpleasant for Claire, and Michael and Jennifer felt upset, too.

Encouragement to persevere came not only from the therapist but also from Claire, when she began to provide glimpses of 'coming back'. Michael and Jennifer were delighted when, without prompting, she began to tell them of something that happened at school. At first, Claire's illness would interrupt after she had said a few words and she would withdraw, but more of her personality began shining through. It was a big moment when she came home from school and shared an entire joke she had heard that day. Gradually, Claire was able to open up and let her parents into her life a little more.

However, sometimes, just when Michael and Jennifer began to think the bad days were behind them, the illness would strike back with a sudden mood change or total refusal of a meal with no indication why. A couple of those bad days in a row could make them wonder, 'Goodness, are we going backwards?' It felt like going back to nappies after years without them. This was demoralising, but giving up was not an option. Along the way Michael and Jennifer learnt a lot about themselves, with anorexia helping them discover weaknesses such as impatience or laziness.

A joke sent by SMS gave another glimpse of Claire 'coming back'. She thought the joke funny and wanted to share it with them. This small, simple gesture was incredibly special to her parents. Michael and Jennifer had a hearty laugh over it and, for a precious moment, anorexia was absent. Sometimes, when away from home, Claire would text a message 'I hate you' to her parents, and they learnt to laugh at that, too. They figured it had become Claire's way of saying, 'I'm thinking of you'. As Jennifer said:

> It wasn't so much that we laughed over these messages, rather that they were predictable. Michael and I made a conscious choice to interpret them as Claire's acknowledgment that she was thinking of us – if we had taken her messages at face value, we would have felt hurt and depressed. Because anorexia had manifested itself in Claire through silencing much of her communication, her phone texts were an important link. This was one way Claire felt able to reach out.

Michael and Jennifer began to find that when handing things to their daughter, she was not flinching or shying away from near physical contact and, when a close family friend died, a distraught Claire went to her mother for a cuddle and a cry. No touching had been allowed for months and, although her parents felt sad a tragic event had been the catalyst, Claire's reaching out for comfort again marked a little progress.

Claire, now eighteen, is in her final year at high school. Throughout her illness and recovery phases, her school-teachers have helped her to catch up on missed classes and keep study stresses to a minimum. While she has reclaimed much of her sense of self, Claire acknowledges this process is continuing. For now, she likes her parents to give her break-fast in bed and they are happy to do this. At school she eats her midday meal in the company of an understanding welfare coordinator, as she is not ready to eat with friends, and arranges her own morning and afternoon snacks.

'I now have more contact with people outside my home', Claire said. Her increased social interaction has been accompanied by a renewed interest in clothes and fashion. While pleased with this normal teenage behaviour, Jennifer expressed concern when she noticed Claire was spending most of her social time with girls who had eating disorders. Jennifer did not wish to discourage this but wanted Claire to extend her circle of friends. Claire has since be-gun to renew the friendships she enjoyed before anorexia intervened, but said it was helpful to have friends 'who have been there':

I can say to them that I have had a bad night and they understand and are consoling. It is also good when you make a small accomplishment. Others look at you as if to say, 'What's the big deal about?' But my friends who have had anorexia can appreciate it. I go out to dinner with one of these girls and we support each other. We talk about stuff other than food, too.

I can hug girlfriends but hugging my parents remains a challenge. With them I remain quite angry and feel like 'this is my space and you have done this, and I still hold you responsible for me putting weight on'. I don't want them to touch me and feel how much weight I have put on – even the thought makes me feel anxious.

I'm talking with my parents more – I still don't have great communication with them, but I'm getting there. I suppose I feel this way because they took control of my eating and made rules and I got angry. I would wake up in the morning and would not want to get out of bed. Then I would think, 'I suppose I have to deal with them', so I would put on my happy face and face the day, with this churning going on inside me.

Overcoming the physical effects of anorexia nervosa by restoring weight to a healthy level is a major step towards recovery, but emotional and mental scars also require healing. As Michael and Jennifer have discovered, parents tend to remain a verbal punching bag for the sufferer until an emotional sense of self is restored. Because they have fought the illness so their child can eat, there are confusing moments when a healthy weight is reached and they start to pass control back to the child. A gap remains within and it needs to be filled, not with food but with self-love.

Without it, constant sabotaging occurs. It's not about the food so much. Claire can eat food now, but sometimes she feels a 'payback'. Her guilt has generally manifested in feelings of anger but she said that this depends on who is present. Eating away from home, in front of others who haven't suffered from the illness, remains a challenge; the thought alone may trigger anxiety. Claire thinks others are watching her, analysing what she is eating. Her fragile self-esteem magnifies the imagined scrutiny into messages of strong disapproval and she wants to hide. She feels more comfortable and secure eating at home with her family, preferably sitting in front of the television because it is a distraction and she can relax more easily.[6]

'I'm gradually finding I can eat in unfamiliar circumstances, like going on a year 12 retreat for a week, without feeling guilty afterwards, and I am glad', Claire said. This confirms another big step in her recovery. Besides her studies, Claire enjoys working six hours a week in a pharmacy and participates in a leadership service program. 'I hope to study nursing', Claire said. 'I am interested in paediatrics and finding a way to help people with eating disorders because I don't want others to suffer as much as I have with my illness.'

Claire is embracing the freedom of dreaming, having ambition, making goals and filling her calendar with dates and events to work towards and look forward to. Some things may not be perfect right now but they will improve as her recovery continues. Summing up her journey, she said, 'Getting your life back and being able to live free from anorexia is worth the fight'.

8

Kylie

Sean's fears manifest in a recurring nightmare. His dream starts when he takes his 12-year-old daughter Kylie to the beach. As soon as they hit the sand Kylie drops her towel and races off, as she always does, jumping over and ducking under waves as she heads out for a swim. Sean, basking in the sun as he watches her, suddenly leaps to his feet and races to the water's edge. His daughter is in trouble.

Sean calls out, 'Tread water, help is coming'. Striving to keep her afloat until he can get her safely to shore, he throws a lifeline but it falls short. Kylie cannot reach it and, in disbelief, Sean realises she is making no effort to grab it. He yells at her to take hold, but a powerful force is holding her back, pulling her down. Realising he is watching his child drown, Sean turns to the crowded beach and screams for help. Families and friends sunbaking on the sand lift their sunglasses and dismissively say, 'You have taken her swimming before and she has never drowned, so why worry now?' No one takes Sean's plea seriously and no matter how close he throws the lifeline, Kylie will not reach out and take it. The hidden force is draining her will.

With relief Sean notices a string of clinicians strolling along the beach. First in line is a white-coated family doctor who pauses to say, 'Stop worrying, she will float and make her own way back to shore'. Next is a paediatrician who looks out to sea, frowns and says, 'She is naughty and needs stronger discipline; she knows she shouldn't be swimming there'. A dietician smiles warmly and says, 'All that exercise will be good for her'. A psychologist and a psychiatrist come at the tail of the beach procession. They glance at the tiny child barely visible in the bucketing waves and say, 'She's fine.

She is exerting her independence. You're overreacting as usual'. Weak and gulping for air, Kylie is losing her struggle against the pull of the sea. She is definitely DROWNING. WHY WON'T SOME-BODY HELP?

Awakening with a jolt, Sean sits up in bed and breaks into a sweat as he fights to think rationally, 'Is this the day my child dies?' or 'Is this the day she is saved?'

Sean's dream, which recurred during a fourteen-month struggle to find help for Kylie, presents a frightening analogy of public perception. Sean said:

> When watching your child develop and suffer anorexia nervosa, these are the unhelpful comments you get. If your child was literally drowning or had developed cancer and people responded with those comments you, rightfully, would want to punch their nose. You would expect your call for help to be taken seriously, for alarm bells to ring, and rescue and medical emergency teams to respond swiftly. You would not expect to be told you are worrying over nothing, but that's how it was for us with anorexia nervosa.

Unhelpful comments, Sean said, came from not only health professionals but also family and friends:

> This added to the destructiveness of the illness because as parents we felt isolated and misunderstood, and began questioning our parenting skills. We began to ignore comments like 'give her a smack' and 'she is only being naughty' by remembering that people who have never lived with a child who has anorexia would find the illness extremely difficult to understand.

Sean and his wife Naomi live with their two daughters, Kylie and Sara, who is two years younger than Kylie, near a capital city. Sean works outdoors and is self-employed, and Naomi works part-time. When Kylie developed anorexia nervosa, her parents began battling a sea of medical indifference. Many tears have been privately shed in their quest to free Kylie from her illness so she can enjoy her teenage years.

Of small build, Kylie always had a light appetite and was underweight. So her parents were a little bewildered when they looked out their kitchen window one evening and saw her running laps in their backyard. Their bewilderment turned to concern when they observed she was developing a strict and ever-increasing routine, determinedly running every night after the evening meal.

Mealtimes also were becoming regimented, with Kylie insisting she would eat only low-fat food. She flatly refused treats like ice-cream and chocolate. Next she eliminated meat from her diet, telling her parents she had decided to be a vegetarian. One day, after catching her daughter determinedly counting star jumps in the lounge room, Naomi decided, 'Enough is enough'. She called the family doctor for an appointment. She had heard media reports that childhood obesity was a problem and exercise was to be encouraged, but Kylie was taking it too far.[1] The doctor advised Naomi and Sean not to confront their daughter but instead let her make her own decisions. 'She won't starve. She will eat when she is hungry', the doctor said. While respecting Kylie's choice to be a vegetarian, however, he suspected something 'wasn't right'. The doctor suggested Sean and Naomi keep an eye on Kylie, but not until several consultations later did he concede there may be a serious problem. He then referred her to a psychiatrist.

All the while Kylie, who had never had a spare gram of fat on her body, was fast going from thin to skeletal. Despite her emaciation, she remained steadfastly committed to completing her daily exercises and to eating less every day. Doctors, of any sort, were at the top of her unwanted list. Her parents had to force her to attend her first psychiatric session and, unfortunately, the experience strengthened Kylie's illness more than herself. Accompanied by Naomi, she waited more than an hour for her appointment, and then the psychiatrist called her by the wrong name, spoke mostly to her mother and explained he was running late because new office furniture had been delivered to his consulting suite.

Quite likely the psychiatrist made an innocent mistake in addressing Kylie, but sufferers of anorexia nervosa are extremely sensitive. As such, Kylie could easily conclude the psychiatrist had not checked her name because she was unworthy of his attention. Her distrust of him was immediate. Not only did he forget her name, and ignore her, but he rated his furniture more highly than her. She refused to see him again, and this time her parents didn't pressure her.

By now, Naomi and Sean were drawing their own conclusions, suspecting that Kylie was developing an eating disorder. They were confused because they thought anorexia nervosa happened to girls who thought they were overweight, and Kylie definitely didn't fit that description. But something was wrong. Something was stopping her from eating, and making her withdraw into herself. Initially, Naomi and Sean thought help would be easy to find, but soon they were wondering where to turn next. A phone call to the state's eating disorder association led them to attend a seminar at which the main speaker drummed out frightening statistics, including that up to 20 per cent of sufferers died from the illness and that there had been 'no breakthroughs' in treatment for more than sixty years. The speaker, introduced as a leading psychiatrist highly experienced in treating anorexia, sent chills through Naomi and Sean. They had gone to the seminar hoping for encouragement and guidance in helping Kylie. Instead they listened to a portrayal of doom and gloom. The couple were tearful as they left the auditorium, and on reaching their vehicle they sat in it for a long time, too distressed to start the drive home. Other parents, they noticed, were equally upset.

They had been painted a dark picture of their daughter's future. They were wasting time looking for an answer because Kylie would either kill herself or die from malnutrition, and there was nothing they could do about it. The conveyor of the grim outlook was head of their state's prominent eating disorder clinic, and they felt unable to question such a high authority.

By the time they arrived home that night, however, Sean and Naomi had rallied. Determined to keep Kylie from the psychiatrist's pessimistic basket of statistics, they vowed to seek help elsewhere. They tried several health professionals during the next few months, but Kylie's weight continued to plummet and she was on the verge of requiring hospitalisation. Her exercise routine had intensified, her mood swings had increased and she was more tearful. At the same time, this deeply conscientious little girl strove to keep up her school attendance and excelled at her studies.

Through a family friend, Sean and Naomi heard of a counsellor who ran a private 'food without fear' program for adolescents. Kylie was persuaded to attend for six months. The counsellor's method was to gain Kylie's confidence by showing her how much she could eat without gaining weight. Naomi and Sean knew little more than this because they were not included in the consultations or told about what went on behind closed doors.

At the same time, Naomi took Kylie to see a paediatrician at a public hospital who agreed she was seriously underweight. He asked Kylie point blank, 'Do you feel you have to do ten sit-ups?', 'Do you know what anorexia is?' and 'Have you looked up eating disorder websites on the internet? You might find something helpful there'.

Within the mind of a child with anorexia, questions about exercise could spark anxiety. If not already doing ten sit-ups, the child could feel compelled to add them to the daily routine – probably double that amount, to ease the guilt of not doing them before. Naomi felt this paediatrician was encouraging Kylie to get worse instead of better: 'He was putting negative ideas in her mind. He basically told Kylie to go home, do more sit-ups and learn more about anorexia by searching the internet. He couldn't be bothered taking the time to connect with her and explain her illness to her'. By now, Sean was concluding that local clinicians were reluctant to apply their skills, knowledge, time or effort in finding a solution. He had searched the web himself and was horrified to find that some websites, by encouraging competitiveness among sufferers, fed the illness with manipulative strategies and health-threatening goals. Kylie didn't need such encouragement.

After several visits, the paediatrician suggested Kylie see a psychologist and another dietician. Sean and Naomi immediately said 'Yes!' for they were getting nowhere fast. However, there was a two-month wait for each appointment. This was two months too long because Kylie needed help immediately.

She was thirteen by now and more than a year had passed since she began running around the backyard. Sean intensified his own research on the internet and felt a glimmer of hope when he clicked on a site describing the Maudsley Approach. He called his capital city's eating disorder association to ask if this family-based treatment was available locally, but staff assured him no such therapy was available in their state. Refusing to give up, Sean went back to the internet, like a terrier scenting a trail, and discovered the therapy was available interstate at a private outpatient eating disorder clinic, The Oak House. He clicked on to this clinic's website, and his hopes rose. The only catch was the clinic was more than 800 kilometres from home. It was a long way to go for a lifeline.

Sean provided the clinic's details to his state's eating disorder association. If he could sense the potential of the Maudsley Approach, surely the local experts could, too – hopefully they would be inspired to train and offer the treatment. But the local experts repeated they hadn't heard of the Maudsley Approach, and therefore could not recommend it.

By now Sean and Naomi had concluded that the health system in their home state did not cater for children with anorexia nervosa. They could not find a health professional with experience in treating eating disorders in their daughter's age group, or anyone willing to try anything other than the 'old methods of medication and hospitalisation'. Feeling abandoned locally, they contacted The Oak House and two months later the family, including Kylie and her sister Sara, now eleven, made the eight-hour car journey for an assessment.

'Our experience to this point had been negative', Naomi said, 'but now we were given hope'. The family was accepted into the program and began family-based treatment immediately. Sean and Naomi had accessed books on the internet already, and understood that they would need to work through the three phases of recovery.

Initially, Kylie had been excited when her parents told her about the family-based treatment and looked forward to her first session. She was optimistic, but her expectations were unreal. She thought she would be 'talked to' and suddenly be set free of her illness. However, when she learnt that the road to recovery would be long and hard, she fell silent. Her illness had a big win.

'It was like she was in a trance', Naomi said. 'Her illness tried to block out everything that was said in our family-based treatment session.' For Kylie, the therapy session was like a punishment. She didn't want to increase her food intake or gain weight – her silence was a powerful weapon. The first time she said one word to the therapist was a major breakthrough.

'It is not just the struggles over food that sap your energy and coping skills', Naomi said. 'It is the hate. Kylie can't see that she is underweight. Her illness convinces her she is fat and ugly. She says horrible things to us and she tells lies. We try to help her feel loved but sometimes she absolutely detests us.'

A month after starting therapy, Sean and Naomi were feeling tired at the end of their long drive home from a session, and pulled in to a fast-food outlet for their evening meal. They had been advised it was time to introduce Kylie to foods that were higher in fat, and bought a fish burger for her. Her reaction was swift. Sean and Naomi tried to appease her anxiety, but she hated them and refused to speak for three days. 'It was like a demon possessed her', Naomi said. Over the coming weeks, they returned to that fast-food outlet several times and ordered another fish burger for Kylie. They met with the same resistance each time. When Sean and Naomi tried to reason with their daughter, she switched from silence to a 'raging outburst'. The anorexia counted on the parents accepting the silence as the easiest option.[2]

At home, Kylie at first struggled and resisted, and the completion of one meal would coincide with the start of another. Food would be thrown off the table and there would be tears of anguish as her illness made her cry, 'I can't eat it', 'You are making me fat' and 'I can't fit it in'.

For months they had no friends or family around for a meal and did not accept invitations elsewhere. Family life revolved around Kylie's next meal or snack. Her grandparents, aged in their eighties, lived nearby and wanted to help. They looked after her for a few hours one day and Kylie was to drink a strawberry milkshake as a snack. When Sean and Naomi returned home the grandparents said proudly that Kylie was excellent and had drunk all her shake. But Naomi found traces of strawberry in the bathroom handbasin. The manipulative anorexia had outsmarted the loving grandparents.

Four months after starting therapy, Sean and Naomi were encouraged to introduce others to their meal table as a strategy in continually challenging the illness.[3] Kylie's grandparents were the first to come. They had been on hold for a long time and were excited when told mealtime visits were to resume. They were cautioned to say nothing about food or Kylie's appearance. She accepted their presence under sufferance and their visits gradually became more regular. Also encouraged to eat out socially, the family visited a local bakery for a Saturday lunch. Sean and Naomi ordered a bowl of vegetable soup and a buttered bread roll for Kylie, but the sight of all those calories and the feeling that everyone was looking at her made Kylie uptight. In an effort to suppress her rising anxiety she tightened her control, eating the soup because it contained fewer calories than her normal meal at home and refusing to touch the roll. Anorexia won that round.

The parents have come a long way in bringing their daughter back, but there is still much to deal with. Besides the ongoing daily battle with food, Sean and Naomi have had to budget carefully to meet expenses associated with Kylie's family-based treatment. Ideally they would attend weekly therapy sessions, but the cost regarding time and money is prohibitive. To cope with the long distance, the family makes the eight-hour drive to the interstate city on alternate Sundays, stays overnight, and attends the therapy session on Monday morning before starting the long drive home. This way Sean loses only one weekday's work every two weeks. He explained:

If Kylie had cancer, we would qualify for accommodation and fuel cost assistance, but because she has anorexia nervosa, we miss out. We have been told we would qualify for a carer's allowance from our national health benefit scheme, but there is no appropriate box to tick on the forms they provide, so we miss out there, too. Families must show they provide twenty hours of care to get the carer allowance – we do far more than this but get nothing. We are worn out from trying to prove we qualify for this allowance. Assistance is also available for ongoing psychiatric visits to a maximum of eighteen per year – but we must show that Kylie is progressing and improving; if we can't prove this we don't qualify there either. There needs to be defined criteria for anorexia because this illness convinces the sufferer that they do not want to get well.

Sean and Naomi, who meet their expenses from retirement savings, want family-based treatment to be available 'everywhere' – in capital cities and large regional centres – and supported by national health benefit schemes. Their dream is for families to avoid the struggle they have had in seeking and acquiring help for Kylie.

Sean is convinced that a major part of the problem is that many people, including those in government and in medical circles, do not consider childhood anorexia a serious illness. He believes the illness is not attractive to the marketplace generally, and affected families are so caught up in battling the illness 24/7 that they don't have the time or energy to lobby for assistance. 'Our government won't acknowledge Kylie's anorexia, but if she had a heart attack or cancer, or if she was overweight, it would support us in caring for her', Sean argued.

The marketing of weight loss is a lucrative business, but anorexia has no advertising appeal. It isn't sexy or attractive and is not a money-spinner. Paradoxically, the promotion of weight loss, eating 'healthy' food and exercising, while helpful for some people, can disguise early symptoms and aid the spread of anorexic behaviour in others.

When a child refuses a favourite sweet, like a chocolate bar, they may be trying to be more health-conscious or simply not be hungry, but if refusal of sugar- or fat-rich foods intensifies, and is accompanied by mood swings, the child might be responding to the torment of a budding eating disorder. Continued denial of favourite treats should be treated with suspicion.

A group of teenage girls at a school in Kylie's neighbourhood formed a pact not to be seen eating in public. One girl developed an eating disorder; others were borderline. Greater awareness of the serious impact of eating disorders was vital to discourage such worrying behaviour.

Sean and Naomi's younger daughter, Tara, had a sports day recently and, noticing one little girl had lost a lot of weight, Naomi spoke to her mother. When told the girl had developed a habit of checking the caloric values of packaged foods from the supermarket, Naomi explained signs that might indicate an eating disorder was developing. The mother was grateful and vowed to be vigilant.

Naomi encouraged parents and carers to be aware:

We took a long time to accept the fact that Kylie had a problem. We told ourselves there was nothing wrong, that she just had a fad. If we had taken action when we had first noticed her changes in eating behaviour and her obsession with exercise, her illness would be over by now.

Checking the small print on food packets, insisting she wanted to be vegetarian, cutting out items in her diet that she would normally like – Sean and Naomi didn't know these were warning signs. If she had known these were symptoms, Naomi said she would have acted on Kylie's behaviour earlier, even on her sudden passion for vegetarianism. 'I would have been stricter and told Kylie "You will eat the same food as us and you will sit there until you eat it". When I was small, my mother made sure I sat at the dinner table until I cleaned my plate.'

Naomi warned parents against being 'too soft'. In her experience, giving into a child's plea not to eat could give the illness time to grow:

> Parents must be aware of anorexic symptoms so they can stem its spread. If worried, your first step should be to see your family doctor. Many dads are at work so mothers are often the first to notice the little changes that might indicate the illness is creeping up. Siblings, friends, teachers, dance or gym instructors, or sports coaches can also notice symptoms, and it is important to share concerns with the parents as soon as possible.

Sean and Naomi strongly believe that their marriage has grown stronger and is more united as a result of fighting Kylie's illness. They have been tested by many tense moments that tried to pull them apart, with the illness often playing one parent against the other. 'You say something that feeds the illness and your partner picks you up on it', Sean said. Together the parents have learnt much about communicating and resolving conflict.[4]

Eating meals together, sitting around a table with the children, is vital, Sean said.

> We didn't do that, and I wish we had. Knowing what we know now, we would have seen early changes and talked it out. Before Kylie became ill, one daughter would be in the study on the computer, and one would be watching television in the family room. And often neither would move for a meal.

By eating as a family with both the computer and television switched off, Sean said meals become a social event with parents talking with their children and each other.

Sometimes Sean and Naomi look at each other and ask if Kylie is behaving like a normal teenager or if her anorexia is playing up. Sean described the difficulty of separating the illness from his child:

> When Kylie talks back, we wonder whether to ignore her

because it is her eating disorder, or discipline her because she is exhibiting normal teenage behaviour. If she refuses to help with the dishes, we wonder if her illness is angry because she ate a new food, or if she is rebelling as a teenager.

Sometimes trying a new activity, like a family fishing outing, is more hassle than it's worth. Besides the fishing gear, Sean and Naomi must pack Kylie's special snacks and lunch and ensure she eats them. It's easier to focus on the ultimate goal of recovery.

The not knowing – of when meals will be eaten without supervision, of when the child will be free to live without torment – takes a heavy toll on parents. Many tears are shed in anguish and helplessness. Sharing the load with others who understand is vital to maintain a sense of well-being.

When pressures mount, the family-based treatment provides a supportive setting in which Sean and Naomi can release and discuss any pent-up feelings. 'With the therapist, you feel free to say things you haven't told your partner', Sean said. 'You try not to cry at home because you have to be strong, but in the presence of our therapist, we can cry and it helps.'

Sean and Naomi also find comfort in their strong Christian faith. 'Our faith will get us through', Sean said. Kylie attends Bible study meetings and church with her parents and sister, but the anorexia seems to isolate her, sabotaging her ability to belong and connect with others. At home, the family continues its tradition of saying prayers before bedtime; Kylie participates but recites a prayer rather than create her own as she did before her illness set in.[5]

Today Kylie is almost fifteen, and while her illness continues to impact on both family and faith it is gradually losing control. Mealtimes have become almost normal. Although sometimes displaying anxiety and requiring prompting, Kylie often eats her meal in the same time as her parents and sister. To take fifteen minutes instead of two hours for breakfast is a huge step forward. There is even some joking and laughing between meals. Kylie has almost reached her target weight, and Naomi and Sean are hopeful of more progress when her weight restoration is complete. Sean is confident that a few extra kilograms 'as a buffer' will make 'all the difference'. Kylie's anxiety levels have dropped and she is also more socially active, although she rarely goes out for a meal with friends because, without a parent by her side, her illness does not allow her any food or water. Her eating remains heavily dependent on her parents' supervision.

Now in year 9 and an 'A and B' student, she plays in a netball team and enjoys other sports, too. Sometimes she goes to discos for a few hours with her friends. All this seems pretty normal for a teenager, but anorexia lurks in her mind. Sean is hopeful that when no longer pressured to gain weight, Kylie will feel free to share her feelings. 'If someone says "I am depressed", you have a clue on how to help them', Sean said, 'but Kylie won't give a clue so we can't say anything'.

Sometimes Kylie seems happy for a few weeks, but every time her weight goes up a full kilogram, her illness strikes back, giving her and her parents a hard time. Usually this means a few days of 'no talking'. At times like this, the therapist helps Sean and Naomi keep on track. Knowing they must increase Kylie's weight before their next appointment spurs them to keep challenging the illness. Without the therapist, it would be easy to let the momentum slip and not push Kylie to eat her next meal. It would be easy to say, 'Let's forgo our 1600 kilometre round trip this week', but that would give the illness the upper hand. The next therapy appointment shines ahead like a beacon. For now, every gram of extra weight means a little less illness and a little more Kylie.[6]

9

Billie

Billie was a frightened 11-year-old girl when admitted to a big city hospital far from her home in the country. The doctors placed her in an adult psychiatric ward. They confiscated all her keepsakes, including jewellery-making beads, saying she could use them to commit suicide. Billie's illness grabbed hold of this idea; until now, she had never contemplated killing herself . . .

Fun loving, 10-year-old Billie was in fifth grade when her mother, Carolin, noticed a growing obsession with early morning runs and cookery books. Both were out of character. Billie was not into exercise and, while happily baking gourmet cakes for others to enjoy, she was refusing to eat any herself. Billie was tubby, unlike her tall, slim mother and string-bean siblings – Rebecca (eighteen) and Juno (fourteen). She had told her mother she was being teased at school about her big size. She also looked a little different from the other children as her dad, Eddie, was born in Japan to a Japanese mother and Australian father, and she had inherited some Japanese characteristics. Most of her classmates were Caucasian.

When Billie eliminated not only cakes but everything except salads from her diet, Carolin was pleased, thinking some weight loss would help her youngest child feel happier and, hopefully, the teasing by her peers would stop. Eddie also was pleased, silently praising Billie's efforts in losing weight because the media catchwords were 'childhood obesity' and it was not easy to 'keep kids off junk food'.

Lettuce and salads were all very amusing, for a little while. Billie is a good girl – she was always one to toe the line – but suddenly she began having mood swings, becoming openly rude and vitriolic. And sneaky! She came up with brilliant ways of hiding her food. Within a week or so, we started to wonder what was going on. By then, perhaps, it was already too late? At that point, we had no idea what was going on. Easy access to the latest information right then would have been helpful, because her illness snowballed.

One day Billie came home from school looking decidedly downcast and, when Carolin asked what was bothering her, pulled out a girls' magazine from her bag. Turning the pages, Billie pointed to an article containing a checklist of anorexia nervosa symptoms and said she met the criteria. She asked her mother to read the article and call the listed helpline number. Concerned at her daughter's disclosure, Carolin did so and information about eating disorders was sent in the mail.

Carolin had heard the word 'anorexia' before Billie developed her illness but knew little about it. A few years earlier, people had asked if her older daughter Rebecca had developed anorexia, but Carolin had laughed that off, saying she ate everything and was naturally thin. However, Billie was not naturally thin, and the realisation that she had symptoms of anorexia nervosa was a shock. Carolin was certain Billie didn't choose the illness, so how and why did she get it? The literature received in the mail had provided few clues and, without a computer at home to help in her quest for answers, Carolin went to the local library. There, she read that she and Eddie were a probable cause of their little girl's illness. As Billie's parents and major caregivers, they had the most influence in moulding her feelings and attitudes since birth. Therefore, they must have slipped up in their parenting skills and should consider themselves part of the problem. In disbelief, Carolin paused to reflect on Billie's short life:

I knew we weren't guilty, and I could pinpoint only one

possible trigger. When Billie was three years old, Eddie and I went overseas to trek for several weeks. We left our children with Eddie's parents and this has played on my mind a little, wondering if our absence caused some anxiety in Billie. As well, some members on my side of the family suffer mental illness.

Whatever the cause, Carolin knew her focus must be to help Billie get better. First, she took her to the family doctor, who recommended they keep a food diary for a week and return for another visit. One look at the diary confirmed the doctor's suspicion that Billie was undernourished, and he referred her to a paediatrician. By now she was eleven years old and had lost more than 20 kilograms. The paediatrician admitted Billie to the local rural hospital, which had no specialty unit for children or adolescents suffering anorexia nervosa. When she refused to eat, they placed her on nasogastric feeding.

Gradually Billie's weight was stabilised and she was slowly reintroduced to solid food. She returned home but her illness continued to rage. The next three years became a journey of 'protracted horror and misinformation' as Carolin sought help to save her daughter.

The local paediatrician had wanted to send Billie to the state hospital for what he considered would be more appropriate treatment, but Carolin shuddered at the thought, having heard of unhappy experiences by other families, and instead chose to take her daughter 2000 kilometres interstate to a private, outpatient, eating disorder clinic. By now, Billie was in a critical state, requiring another nasogastric tube. She was medically monitored while attending this clinic and was offered a bed in that state's main children's hospital; however, on learning that parental visiting rights would be restricted there, Carolin declined the offer and took her daughter home. With Billie too ill to travel so far by car, the trip home was made by plane. The homecoming was not happy, with Billie complaining that she could not see and that her ears were ringing. She was also having difficulty breathing and her body was racked with pain. All but swamped by her eating disorder, she managed to exert a thread of will to live, whispering to her parents, 'You have to get me to hospital'.

On dialling their local hospital, Carolin and Eddie were told not to wait for an ambulance to make the hour-long trip out to their rural property but to rush Billie to the hospital's emergency section in their family car. When Eddie picked his little girl up to place her in the vehicle, she cried, 'Don't touch me, everything hurts'.

A staff nurse, a family friend, was on duty when the car pulled up at the hospital's emergency entrance. She masked her feelings in taking charge of Billie's care, but later said to Carolin and Eddie, 'You don't know how close she was to death'. The medical staff monitored Billie overnight and the next day an ambulance transported her to the state hospital – the very one Carolin had wished to avoid – where she spent several days in intensive care. The staff worked on rehydrating her and stabilising her condition while discussing what to do next. The dietician and gastroenterologist shook their heads and said to Carolin, 'What have you done to your daughter?'

'I had no idea how to help her', Carolin said. Instead of being told about the option of family-based treatment early in Billie's illness, Carolin received mixed messages. The state's eating disorder association said she wasn't to blame, but a clinician in the state hospital suggested she was an overcontrolling mother.

Billie was moved from the hospital's intensive care ward to an adult psychiatric ward containing sufferers of schizophrenia and depression, some contemplating suicide. One patient asked her if she would like some drugs. 'She didn't get drugs but she did get chronic diarrhoea', Carolin said. Two weeks passed before Billie was transferred to a more suitable ward, where she remained for four months.

For the first month, Carolin obtained accommodation in a nearby Ronald McDonald House so she could visit Billie in the short breaks when parents were allowed. On one such visit, she discovered that Billie, suffering extreme anxiety, had self-harmed with cuts on her arms, and covered her body in graffiti with the messages 'I am fat, I want to die'.

Horrified, Carolin asked the nurses to keep a close watch

on her daughter. 'Some days when I visited she would be going through nightmares and hell', Carolin said. 'I obtained permission to take her on a little outing and this distraction helped to bring her back into her self.' As she gained weight via the nasogastric tube, Billie was able go out with her mother for several hours, usually taking the bus to the nearest shopping centre. Eventually, with both weight and heart stabilised, Billie was told she could go home on a nasogastric tube.

However, no assistance was offered with medical supplies and Carolin wondered if she could afford them: she had no time to go to work, and Eddie was trying to build a house for the family. Fortunately, the local hospital was helpful, arranging a pump and fresh supplies for the tube. For the next eighteen months, Billie ate no solid food. Apart from a nutritious chocolate and malt milk beverage, that she tried to avoid swallowing, the tube was her lifeline. Medical staff eventually conferred and asked, 'Billie has been on the tube for a long time, what will we do?' A visiting consulting psychiatrist came and said, 'Let's see what we can do to get her eating solids'.

By now some hospitals didn't want Billie as a patient due to her long illness, and Carolin had a tedious time looking after her at home. 'Billie would be fed during the night and I had to tape the tube to her and sleep in her room or she would pull the tube out', Carolin said. 'Overall, Billie didn't mind the tube but she was becoming dependent on it and was not making any progress towards recovery. Somehow, we had to get her off it.' The medical team at the state hospital would not take Billie back, conceding they could not help her. It was at this time that the consulting psychiatrist told Carolin and Eddie, who were running out of options and hope, about a family-based treatment for anorexia nervosa in its infancy at another major hospital, the Children's Hospital at Westmead.

Billie was thirteen by now and, after years of being discouraged from participating in her daughter's recovery, Carolin believed at last she was on the right path. She wondered why doctors in some mainstream hospitals had not kept up with new methods as part of their medical practice and why she had not been told about family-based treatment earlier. Carolin could not understand why caring parents were being blamed, isolated and pushed away from their children at a time when other hospitals were achieving encouraging results through therapy that incorporated families in the treatment. Medical teams in hospitals and clinics in three capital cities had applied what they said was their best method, but Billie had kept edging closer to death. Carolin said:

> Until we began the family-based treatment, doctors had saved Billie's life but had not treated her illness. We weren't the only family experiencing this. One hospital had a room like a padded cell and a sufferer was put into this for stepping out of line. A body-lock system was used when patients were out of control. And they had a very overweight lady on staff who literally sat on patients when they didn't conform. The treatment in that hospital was archaic, and the inference was 'Leave Billie with us and we will fix her up'.

Now, on learning about family-based treatment, Carolin and Eddie did not care for a moment that the Children's Hospital at Westmead was more than 800 kilometres from home. Their local rural hospital, keen to assist, rang and arranged for Billie to be admitted for an assessment. The response was immediate. 'I was told that if I wanted to accompany Billie on the plane and thereby spare them a nurse, I had two hours in which to go home and pack my bag', Carolin said.

The medical and family-based treatment teams accepted Billie into their program. By now she had been suffering anorexia nervosa for three years. For the first time, Carolin and Eddie became hopeful of a positive outcome. Carolin had been teaching part-time again and was also studying, but had dropped both so she could focus on Billie's recovery.[1]

'The upheaval was worthwhile', Carolin said, 'because this treatment turned out to be the best thing ever. For the first time we felt accepted as a family, and for the first time the medical staff externalised the illness, separating it from

Billie's sense of self'. This was an enormous step forward, but there were fresh obstacles. A funding shortage meant nursing staff could not offer 24/7 support, and Billie was placed in a ward with other children who were not experiencing anorexia. Without constant vigilance, her illness maintained its hold but Carolin persevered. She visited her daughter every day and obtained a teaching job within the hospital to help meet the cost of living away from home. Three months slipped by. As an in-patient, Billie was being kept alive but was showing no improvement.

Convinced that more intensive confrontation with the illness might achieve the longed-for breakthrough, Carolin told the therapy team, 'I am a resource you could use to help my daughter get well'. She offered to provide the much-needed 24/7 care. The therapy team agreed to her participation as 'care by parent', but without medical training, Carolin wasn't allowed on the ward. So the team put a proposal to the hospital's ethics committee and gained approval for Carolin to supervise Billie's meals with backup medical support in the form of outpatient therapy.[2]

'This was the best thing ever', Carolin said. She asked the team, 'Why don't you establish this facility so other parents can experience what treating this illness involves? Parents of children with anorexia need the same support provided to parents of children with cancer'.

Fortunately, funds were found for Carolin and Billie to be accommodated for a month at the hospital while adjusting to this new phase in Billie's recovery program. Carolin took her role in providing 24/7 care seriously, pouncing on any sign of anorexic behaviour that was keeping her daughter a prisoner. When Billie confided to her sister Rebecca that she had developed the habit of draining her nasogastric tube while taking a shower, Carolin spoke to the therapy team and a decision was made to pull the tube out – and leave it out. Billie would have to eat. And she did! Because she had not eaten for almost two years the reintroduction of solid food was gradual, starting with six small snacks a day.

Nutritional beverages were suggested as a way of increasing calorie intake, and Carolin agreed this seemed a good idea. A couple of these healthy drinks a day topped up

Billie. However, apart from the physical impact of eating, emotional issues had to be resolved because the tube had become part of Billie's persona. She felt afraid: 'If I get rid of my tube, no one will know I have anorexia'. At home she had taken it out during the day while she went to school, but in hospital the tube had been left in day and night. Billie had gone shopping and to the library with her tube and she didn't mind. It was her identity, and it showed the world that she had anorexia nervosa: 'This is me'. It was scary to let go. When the month's stay at the hospital was up, a further two months' accommodation was arranged for Carolin and Billie at the nearby Ronald McDonald House.

By now Carolin had been away from home almost continuously for more than two years in her bid to save Billie. Eddie had stayed home to complete the house, work and look after Juno, who was completing his secondary school studies. Their other daughter Rebecca had moved to the city to gain work as a model, which, Carolin said, 'probably didn't help' Billie's self-image. At the same time, though, Rebecca had been Billie's main 'support person' during the family-based treatment and, Carolin said, 'This important role of sibling support cannot be underestimated'. Besides the 'draining the nasogastric tube' revelation, Billie gave Rebecca many insights into her illness that became the catalyst for change and progression in her recovery.

Carolin and Billie were at the Children's Hospital at Westmead for almost eight months. 'I coped with being away from home so long by learning to live in the here and now', Carolin said. 'I would listen to other parents and think I didn't have it so bad. Oncology patients, especially, really touched my heart and Billie also gained an understanding of the suffering of others.'

It wasn't all smooth sailing, however. Billie's illness fought back and her dislike of her mother intensified. The nasogastric tube had enabled her to avoid dealing with the problem of eating, but with her mother insisting she eat solids, the more weight Billie put on the angrier she became:

> My mother studied me, like she was making a career out of it. Sometimes she became paranoid, suggesting that if

I didn't eat I would end up in intensive care again. She was overprotective, pushing until I got angry and she could feel justified in saying, 'See, your anorexia is coming back'.

Fortunately, by the time mother and daughter were residing at Ronald McDonald House, Juno had moved to the same city to study at university. This meant that he, along with Rebecca, could visit them at the 'House', and this strengthened the family support base.

When Carolin and Billie finally returned home to the country, resettling into family life and adjusting to both the illness and relationships took time. The therapy team eased the way, communicating with the family via video conferencing. They linked up once a week to talk through tactics and strategies, gradually reducing to one link-up a month. The local doctor provided Billie with weekly physical checks. Carolin slept in the same room as her until convinced that the long-time urge to over-exercise had subsided. Billie, who had missed a lot of school, slowly resumed her studies. Carolin took her lunch to school and insisted her daughter eat everything on the plate before returning to the classroom. Her vigilance was unrelenting. 'At last we were on the right track', Carolin said. 'Often I had been called an "over-controlling parent", but if I had not cared and persisted, we would not have gotten our kid back.'

At fifteen, a third of Billie's life had been dominated by anorexia nervosa. She continued her schooling, completing year 12 at eighteen years of age and, at the time of writing, is taking a year to work and explore life a little before undertaking tertiary studies. Billie has required no hospital admissions and has taken big steps towards living independently. This has involved moving away from the family home and returning to the city, 800 kilometres away, where she lives with her now-married sister, Rebecca.

Billie has her own version of how her illness started:

I was a tubby 10-year-old and my mother said, 'If you want to lose weight, exercise more and eat right'. When I started to lose weight I was getting compliments like, 'Hey, you have lost a lot of weight' and 'You look great'. So I thought, 'If I lose more weight I will look even better'. My best friend was called 'anorexic' in primary school, but she was naturally skinny and ate like a horse: thinking back, I was probably jealous and thought, 'I want to be like you'.

At first, Billie knew only that lettuce leaves were less fattening than potato chips. It wasn't much to go on, and it meant she ate a lot of salad. 'Only when I went to hospital did I learn about calories. The doctors would push kilojoules and calories; they counted them. So I started to learn the values of food and counted calories, too.'

When Billie refused to eat, the medical staff confined her to bed. 'In one hospital I was kept in solitary confinement', she said. 'Eventually they transferred me to a children's ward, saying, "This is for SICK children, not children like you".'

The experience was traumatic and at first, when introduced to family-based treatment, Billie was sceptical and hated that, too. For three months on the ward-based program, she took no steps towards recovery.

I didn't like the other girls with anorexia, as they were really competitive. They would copy my menu if I knew more about calories than them. They reminded me of what I was like when I was eleven, but I was fourteen by now and was past all that.

With my mother nagging, the medical team developed a program to let me out of the ward. This was when mum took over my care as part of the family therapy and very soon I started to hate her. Having my mother supervise my meals was much better than sitting in hospital and being told I had half an hour to eat, but she watched me all the time and this annoyed me.

The weight restoration process was particularly hard for Billie to accept. She would feel irritated when her mother insisted she eat, saying, 'It is only this much; it is only this much'. For Billie, the issue was black and white: she was being asked to eat calories and they would make her heavier. For Carolin, the issue was equally black and white: Billie needed to consume calories to beat her illness. Gradually, Carolin's unrelenting stand against the anorexia produced encouraging signs. The mother's love for her child won out.

Today, Carolin has resumed her teaching career, volunteers as a Lifeline counsellor and promotes eating disorder awareness at every opportunity. Her life is full but she remains a concerned mother. She believes Billie was 'probably more socially engaged' in her local, home environment and, six months after her move to the 'big city', continues to fear the triggering of old eating patterns. When Billie calls for a chat Carolin cannot stop herself from asking, 'Are you eating properly?' Billie's reply to her mother is always a prolonged sigh and 'Yes'. There have been slips and slides, but progress, too.

'Billie is still finding and rebuilding her sense of self', Carolin said. 'She missed out on a lot of teenage years but her friends have helped her to come out of her shell and be Billie.' Outside the family, Billie presents as a beautiful young woman – delightful, caring and sharing. At home, Carolin occasionally sees signs of anorexic behaviour. However, aware that Billie needs to develop her own managing skills to be independent, Carolin has the new challenge of deciding when to step back and when to speak up:

> I tell Billie that I love her for who she is, but I don't like her eating disorder. I liken it to having a child with diabetes. At some stage you have to say 'you have to deal with it', but right now I don't expect Billie to have all the skills to deal with her illness, plus a new job and living away from home for the first time. When she adopts more strategies to maintain good health, I will feel more comfortable. I have offered to pay for a therapist for ongoing support, but she has declined this.

While acknowledging family-based treatment has been the key to her recovery, Billie believes her will played a part, too: 'I wanted my life back. I wanted to be normal, so I began to eat'. Importantly, Billie agrees with her parents that the treatment reunited their family:

There are many pluses, I know. I have a life now. I am not as driven. Sometimes I admit to myself, 'Oh shit, I have eaten way too much today and will have to go for a run', but this is a big improvement on a few years ago when I would do 500 sit-ups, and not allow myself to wear a sweater when feeling cold so I would use more body heat.

Billie has worked hard to catch up on lost time and rebuild her life. She had been the best of friends with her brother, Juno, before developing anorexia but, due to her long periods of hospitalisation, hardly saw him during the four years before starting family-based treatment. 'I think he thought I had stolen our mother because she was away with me so much', Billie said.

However, Juno, fourteen when Billie developed anorexia, did not begrudge the time his mother was away from home; rather, he felt sad about losing his little sister. The personality of the Billie he knew 'disappeared' and when Billie came home after starting the family-based treatment, Juno was studying at university, leaving little opportunity to rebuild a relationship. Despite accounting for the passage of time, Juno said, 'Occasionally it was and still is hard to see Billie, and I know this is largely due to the anorexia. The illness seems to have suppressed parts of her. It robbed her of her teenage years, and robbed me of a sibling, pretty much'.

Today, brother and sister catch up socially in the city, and Juno is impressed with Billie's efforts in developing her emotional and financial independence.

At work, Billie keeps her eating disorder struggle under wraps, but food remains a bugbear. 'Even when I'm my dream size 6, I feel uncomfortable with my body', Billie said. 'I can't take compliments; if someone says I look pretty, I think they are lying.'

Billie can look forward to food issues dissipating when she's able to acknowledge that feeling comfortable with her body has nothing to do with dress size or weight, and everything to do with self-love and acceptance. Until then, an evening out with friends looms as a challenge for this young, attractive and bright young woman. While others are happily chatting around the dining table, Billie sometimes becomes aware she has been lost in thought, looking at the food on her plate and subconsciously counting the calories.

This nudge of anorexic behaviour annoys her because she knows she must maintain her recovery to realise her life dreams, a prominent one of which is to study fashion design and become a styling assistant, 'dressing up celebrities for photo shoots'. Being aware that food-obsessed thoughts belong to her illness is testimony to the long way Billie has come in regaining her identity. If one diversionary strategy fails, she tries another.

Throwing the bathroom scales away was easy, but Billie says her weight continues to yo-yo around. She has her 'skinny' jeans and her 'fat' jeans. To avoid the temptation to be skinny again, Billie reminds herself of the bad times:

> I remember how bad it was. With each relapse my illness would draw me back and think of new tricks. When I need extra incentive to look after myself, I think of those horrible times and the repercussions – I've a long list of them. Things like having family visits restricted and phone calls limited to one a day.

Despite Billie's determined optimism and strategies, her father, Eddie, continues to have difficulty divorcing the illness from his child:

> Everything seems to centre on Billie in her mind. This makes her seem incredibly selfish and unable to see other points of view, and she seems unable to acknowledge efforts others are putting in. Now she is nineteen, I believe she must take responsibility for managing her illness in her own way. I love her and will support her, but now, how far she goes depends on how far she can dig deep in her own psyche.

Older sister Rebecca continued a supportive role when Billie moved in with her in the city:

> Her illness is still there, but for me the bottom line is that Billie is much better than she was because she has not

been readmitted to hospital since starting family-based therapy, and she enjoys some normal life. I remember thinking wistfully, hopefully, when we started family-based treatment, that if Billie had to have this illness, she was better to develop it while young rather than in late adolescence, when living away from home. I hoped that by having it younger, she would be shown skills to recover and live as normal a life as possible. I'm glad it is working out this way.

Billie's story is an amazing journey of survival. Her tenacious and determined mother, Carolin, travelled thousands of kilometres over several years searching for help. Carolin's love for Billie gave her strength to believe in her gut instinct and challenge traditional medical practice. When the help was found in the form of family-based treatment, the challenge was far from over. Carolin was happy but Billie was not. For a long time Billie maintained a comfortable relationship with her illness, until one day she decided she was fed up and wanted to get her life back. Billie has yet to admit it, but her mother's perseverance had won through! As Billie's sense of self strengthens, she will be more able to appreciate and acknowledge the efforts of her mother and other members of her loving family. For now, Billie continues to see her mother as more of a bother than someone who saved her life. Her mother does not mind at all because she can see Billie is well on the way to recovery.[3]

10

Annabelle

Maree's frustration with Annabelle's illness was suddenly over-taken by the humiliation of having several police cars parked outside her home. 'Can't you just go? People will be wondering what we're doing', Maree beseeched the six police officers as they entered her front door. She did not want the embarrassment of facing the neighbours on top of all else she had to deal with. This was one of Maree's lowest points.

Maree was putting clothes away in 16-year-old Annabelle's bedroom when a discovery sent her into a whirl. All had seemed calm in this family comprising Maree, husband William, and their daughters Annabelle and Isabella. But a storm broke that afternoon when Maree pulled open a drawer and found a cache of diet pills.

Two years later, as she turns the pages of the family's photo albums, Maree asks how she and William did not realise something was wrong earlier. Anorexia, however, is a silent intruder, and can be difficult to notice even when living with someone suffering the illness. There had been no inkling that Annabelle was anything but carefree. A new school year in her rural town had begun and she was blossoming into a young woman; she seemed fine.

Maree and William did not know their daughter had a storm brewing within her until the diet pill discovery. Putting away the clothes while her daughters were at school, Maree noticed one drawer in Annabelle's bedroom was so cluttered it would not budge. She began emptying the drawer, placing the contents – which included a basket – on the bed so she could repack it neatly. The basket slipped from her hand and the lid fell off, exposing the pills. 'Oh my God', Maree thought, as she saw them, her mind in a spin. 'Why does Annabelle have diet pills? She is already slim!'

Maree waited until William came home from work and drew him aside, saying they needed to talk. They decided not to approach Annabelle about the pills until the next day, as friends were about to arrive to share the evening meal. Maree called the friends in advance to explain she would not be her normal cheery self. The friends were a good distraction, and Maree and William did not want to jump in too hastily in approaching Annabelle. 'I don't think it filtered into my mind that she had an eating disorder', Maree said. 'I felt alarmed more because those pills seemed out of character for her.'

William and Maree stayed awake a long time in bed that night, discussing how to confront their daughter. Next morning they sent their younger daughter Isabella to her room, which was not wise in hindsight, but at the time they wanted to talk solely with Annabelle. Isabella knew only that a discussion was going on and that she had to stay in her room until her parents said she could come out. She sat on her bed for most of the day, wondering why she was excluded and if she would be allowed out, even to go to the toilet. Not until the following day did her parents offer her an explanation. When asked to explain the pills, Annabelle had readily admitted she had hidden them and announced to her stunned parents that she thought she may have 'a small eating problem' but was 'not developing' anorexia nervosa.

Now that she was alerted, Maree swung into information overload, leaving no avenue of help unturned. She rang a close colleague at work for solace and advice. She then contacted a city-based clinic about a two-day program aimed at educating families on how to treat eating disorders. The earliest appointment was a month hence and, not prepared to wait, Maree and William consulted a family doctor, a dietician, a psychologist and eating disorder clinics and associations in the state capital 300 kilometres away. Late into the night Maree downloaded information from the internet and during the day she looked for answers among the medical services in her home town. She searched the health and nutrition shelves in the local library and bookshops, picking up anything related to eating disorders, but nothing was helping.

'I went into total madness', said Maree. She became obsessed with finding an answer for her daughter. The family doctor was upfront, saying he had little experience with eating disorders. He offered to do a physical check, however, and mortified Annabelle by lifting up the back of her shirt to test her with the stethoscope. Maree was mortified, too, when she saw how thin her daughter had become, and her fears mounted as she listened to Annabelle telling the doctor that she thought she had fat thighs. The doctor asked Maree to leave the room so he could speak to Annabelle alone. Bringing her back in, he confirmed that Annabelle was possibly developing anorexia nervosa – and would need to see a psychiatrist and then a paediatrician.

There was a four-week wait to see the psychiatrist and Annabelle said after her first visit, 'Don't take me back there again'. Maree did not insist, as the psychiatrist had not seemed genuinely interested in helping – throughout the sixty-minute appointment she had kept looking at her clock, and her keys and handbag were perched on the edge of her desk as if ready for a quick getaway.

While Maree and William were busy seeking information on eating disorders and treatment options, Isabella was again feeling left in the dark. Her parents, she said, did not share the information they found, would not answer her questions and held discussions in her absence.

As for Annabelle, she was forming a relationship with a counsellor who she saw as the only person who could understand her pain. 'I attended the sessions merely to have somebody to talk to', she said. The paediatrician said Annabelle's weight was 'rather low' and arranged blood tests, the results of which were normal. A dietician suggested a snack plan of seven meals a day, but Annabelle refused to try it. By this time, Maree and William were serial appointment keepers. Unable to find the right help, Maree was haunted by thoughts of her daughter's very thin features and feared she would be hospitalised. 'On reflection, I was numb. I was running about like a hen with its head cut off', Maree said. 'I was on autopilot, in a daze, looking for an answer.'

The answer came unexpectedly. Several weeks had gone by when Maree, while resting with her feet up and browsing the newspaper, noticed an article about a local girl who had undertaken family-based treatment for childhood anorexia. The article included the telephone number of a local support group for parents with children with an eating disorder, and Maree attended the group's next meeting. On learning more about the family-based treatment Maree instinctively knew that this was what she and William were looking for. The relief of meeting other parents that were experiencing the same feelings had eased Maree's anxiety, and she went home feeling consoled and purposeful. After conferring with William she rang the private eating disorder clinic offering the family-based treatment, and was told her family could attend an assessment in four weeks time. The clinic, The Oak House, was a four-and-a-half hour drive from home, but the distance would not matter if the treatment would help their daughter recover.

By now, two months had passed since the diet pill discovery and Annabelle was losing a lot of weight. There was little recognition of the easy-going, happy girl with a warm and caring nature that her parents knew and loved. Annabelle had been cuddly and affectionate, but now her illness would not let her mother touch her, and she no longer tried to hide her secret. At breakfast time, in front of her mother, she would place a measuring cup on the kitchen bench to painstakingly measure half a cup of cereal and 'two drops' of milk.

Wanting to repel the monstrous illness that was causing her daughter to starve and behave in strange and hurtful ways, Maree tried some manoeuvres of her own. 'I tried to be sneaky', Maree said. She had a win when she bought a bottle of skim milk and replaced it with whole milk. 'Annabelle did not notice!' Pleased, Maree added a few extra calories to recipes at every opportunity. When she cooked a favourite stroganoff casserole, the family said it tasted a little different but loved it anyway. They did not know that Maree had added some brown sugar. She added extra butter where she could, in mashed potato or sandwiches, but her efforts were soon to no avail as Annabelle, nudged by her illness, refused to eat meals prepared by her mother.

The dietician suggested to Maree that hiding the measuring cup might help, but this had a negative effect in that Annabelle then judged her amount of cereal by sight and allowed herself much less than a perfect half cup.

When the family-based treatment began Maree learnt that trying to outwit Annabelle was wrong, because she needed her trust: 'I had to cease being sneaky, and this was hard because I just wanted her to eat more. I would look at her and think "if only you could see what you're doing to your body and consider the health ramifications later on" '.

Annabelle's illness flared up again when introduced to Phase One of family-based treatment. Annabelle kept screaming at her parents, 'Leave me alone'. When they refused, she became reclusive and did not speak to them for months. Annabelle was keeping a secret pact with her anorexia. She was eating just enough to live so she could perform in a school drama that would take place within eight weeks. She had negotiated with her illness because the play was important to her, and vowed that after it she would quit eating. She bargained, 'You can have everything else but I love my music and drama, so let me have this one performance and then you can have all of me'.[1]

The crunch came the day after the drama performance, when Maree met with Annabelle to supervise her lunch at school. Annabelle got in the car beside her mother and refused to take her sandwich, saying, 'I'm not eating any more'.

From there, the day deteriorated into a real-life drama between mother and daughter, with anorexia the choreographer. When Annabelle refused to eat Maree did not allow her to return to her classes, as the deal was if Annabelle did not eat she could not attend school. She had no choice but to take her home. Feeling frustrated and helpless, and unable to call William as he was working away from home for the day, Maree snapped, 'I've had enough. I can't take any more!' On the way home, she pulled in at the local pharmacy with a prescription for some antibiotics and told Annabelle to sit in the car. Annabelle began to feel anxious, more so when her mother returned to the car. With verbal exchanges intensifying, mother and daughter became increasingly uptight and upset, and by the time they reached home, tensions were soaring. Maree pleaded with Annabelle to eat her lunch but she was adamant she would not. Distraught, Maree said, 'That's it! I am leaving. I'm taking your medication and I am not sure when I am coming back!' Annabelle's illness would not allow her to communicate her fears and, when her distraught mother ran through the house, intending to jump in the car and go for a drive to help regain her composure, Annabelle felt sure she was going off to kill herself.

Annabelle's version of this incident varies to that of her mother, who insists she was intending to go for a drive while she calmed down and that there was no emergency. She was taking Annabelle's medication with her because she felt worried Annabelle might take an overdose while alone in the house.

Anorexia was having a big win in fuelling the drama between mother and daughter, but then its plot began to falter.

Fearing her mother might harm herself, Annabelle's concern for her mother suddenly overrode her illness, and she sprang into action. Her mind racing, she blocked the door and would not let her mother out, and thought, 'I don't know what to do next in this situation'. She tried calling her dad on the telephone, but Maree continually cut the connection. Panicking, Annabelle dialled 000. When the helpline operator sought details of the emergency, Annabelle said, 'My mother is going to take pills and kill herself. Please, you've got to help me!' She managed to provide only her name and the town before her mother cut the phone connection again.

The call was out, however, and within minutes six uniformed police were knocking on the front door. Maree's frustration with Annabelle's illness was abruptly overtaken by humiliation at the sight of several police cars pulled up outside her home. 'Can't you just go? We are fine. People will be wondering what we're doing', Maree beseeched the police officers as they entered her lounge room. She did not want the embarrassment of facing the neighbours on top of all else she had to deal with. 'This was one of my lowest points', Maree said. 'Annabelle had to be reassured that I would not take my life. This did not happen overnight. Three months were to pass before she would trust me again.'

Annabelle's illness made the most of this family disharmony. However, assisted by the Maudsley Approach therapist, she managed to restart the first phase of her recovery program, and this time her improvement was quite swift. Ultimately, Annabelle's concern for her mother had enabled her to reconnect with part of her real self. 'I thought "I can't put everyone through any more pain".' She made a new deal with herself: she would pretend to go along with what her parents and therapists wanted her to do for twelve months. This would be acceptable, she thought, because she would be eating only because they were making her do so. She would eat to make them happy, no matter how much it hurt her and then, when they were fooled, would revert to her anorexic way of living.

However, halfway through the three-phase family-based treatment, Annabelle began to think, 'I don't want to go back there'. Without intending to, Annabelle had regained enough of her sense of self to see that starvation was not making her happy. She began to withstand the pull of her anorexia. She became less reclusive, finding her recovery program was helping her parents, sister and herself communicate more effectively with each other. The journey was far from over, but she was getting there.

Getting back to those diet pills, when Maree discovered them in Annabelle's bedside drawer, she seized only half the stash. She did not know Annabelle had hidden them in two places. Annabelle explained:

I did not have any money, so I stole the pills from a local supermarket. I realise now that my illness told me to do this. I did not actually swallow any of the pills for a long time because I was losing weight without them. I just felt a need to have them. Then I wanted to go on a drama group trip, and I started taking the pills because they contained an energy stimulant, but they smelt like pee and had no effect! They were pointless!

Annabelle's development of anorexia was slow. In year 7, when she was twelve, she was feeling overweight. 'I thought I was fat even though part of me knew that I was not', Annabelle said. By year 9 she was cutting food out of her diet and counting calories. By year 10 Annabelle was aware that some of her thoughts and behaviour were abnormal. She observed that her friends could eat anything and not worry about it, while she worried about every crumb. Sometimes, unable to restrain her concern, she would blurt, 'But that contains 200 calories!', and her friends would look at her and say, 'So what?'

Annabelle felt scared. She did not want to tell her mother about the powerful, nagging thoughts that were increasingly occupying and casting doubts in her mind. She wanted to be carefree like her friends but she still felt fat. Baggy clothes hid her weight loss and efforts to disguise her inner torment were making her withdrawn and moody.

Maree and William felt shocked when they learnt that Annabelle's illness had been tormenting her for three years before they knew about it. 'Family members and friends later said they had noticed changes in her, but did not like to say anything', William said. 'They did not want to intrude, but the longer this illness goes unheeded, the harder it is.' Although they saw Annabelle every day, William and Maree were unaware of any signs that indicated development of anorexia nervosa.

This was despite being reasonably informed about the illness. Both parents had read about it in magazine articles and watched television documentaries and current affairs programs. William was aware anorexia nervosa was more than a physical illness and would take more than saying 'eat this' to fix, but like Maree he had no idea how tough the illness would be to beat.

Maree had dealt with some extremely challenging situations in her work as a drug and alcohol counsellor, but none of her training or experience prepared her for fighting anorexia:

I became very angry at first. We had little conflict in our home until anorexia came along. It made Annabelle say and do ugly things and I reacted. If you had told me at the start what fighting this illness and helping our daughter recover would be like, I would have said, 'I can't do it'. I still feel astounded at how I managed![2]

William felt the same way. 'We had no idea this illness could be so voracious', he said. 'Local doctors initially thought they could help, but soon found they could not. Seeing a doctor for an hour every few days was nowhere near enough to combat this illness that was putting thoughts in our daughter's mind 24/7.' William liked the team approach that family-based treatment emphasised. He understood why the founders of the treatment decided the key was to empower the parents. 'Who else would take all the crap?' he said. Sometimes, although he loved his daughter, he found the going tough and wondered how he could persevere.

'I am fairly relaxed most of the time', William said, 'and I thought that if I could not maintain my perspective I would not be much help to my family'. So, on the rare moments he had some free time, William went camping. Those little escapes did wonders in helping him balance his outlook and maintain the fight to get his daughter back. The moments available for relaxing were indeed rare, because William lost one day of his working week attending family-based treatment sessions and made up the lost work time by doing extra hours at night. A partner in a business, he was grateful for the understanding shown by his colleagues.

'Anorexia wears you down', William said. 'You take over your child's life and run it for them. In the re-feeding stage especially, Annabelle did not have any concept of what was best for her.'

William was 100 kilometres away on the day of the high drama with the police, and when a phone call alerted him to what had happened, there was no one he could call on to comfort his wife and daughter. He explained:

The grandparents would have been upset and added to the emotional upheaval, and it was too involved for my friends. I was out of phone range most of the way home, and wondered what I would find when I arrived. At tough moments like this you have to diffuse your emotions, get them down a bit. I was sad I was not there to support Maree, but this big bust-up seemed to move a big boulder in Annabelle. She began to eat! As the months went by she would suddenly burst into song, as singing had been her passion. She became increasingly happy and I could see the light coming back in her eyes.

Annabelle's sense of self began returning 'like a switch going on' shortly after reaching a weight that was enough to ensure a healthy body and some in reserve if she became sick with a flu or bad cold. This was eight months into therapy.

A test came in the second phase of family-based treatment when Maree and William decided to maintain their annual Easter tradition of camping with friends. They briefed their friends beforehand, asking them to avoid any reference to food in front of Annabelle. The friends found this abnormal request difficult and were very 'tippee-toe', trying to do the right thing. Chocolate eggs aside, roasted marshmallows and barbecues were synonymous with camping and socialising around the campfires. Although Annabelle looked 'well' by then and was able to cope with eating in restaurants with her family, she was not ready to eat in front of other people she knew. She felt they were watching her like a hawk. 'What do you know? You don't understand', Annabelle would rage, and eventually her father would respond, 'I don't understand, but I'm trying to; we're learning along the way'.

The family moved through the therapy program and completed the three phases of treatment in about twelve months. 'We were told not to start the program unless we could commit to it 100 per cent, because anything less than that and it would not work', Maree said. 'I decided I would rather do this 100 per cent and have our lives turned upside down for one year rather than have the illness drag on year after year. In hindsight it was hell on wheels.'

The nine-hour round trip for the weekly therapy session was often a trial in itself. After each session Annabelle would huddle in the corner of the car's rear seat, her lower lip quivering, silently crying for most of the four-and-a-half hour trip home. Maree would reach over from the front passenger seat to comfort her and be rebuffed. Even when Maree swapped places with Isabella and sat in the back, Annabelle would pull away. At such moments Maree fought feelings of rejection – her heart was breaking. The trip home from therapy was usually worse because Annabelle would be upset at her weight gain and issues brought up in therapy. Her illness fought against this confrontation and there was no escaping it in the car. At home Maree could go into another room and try to detach herself from the situation, but in the car she was stuck.

Annabelle did not become physically aggressive at her parents but, on another occasion in a fast-food restaurant, she could not stand the smell of the food as she believed the smell would create calories. She swiped her arm at her mother and stormed out. She was curled up in the car, sobbing, when Maree climbed in and told her she had caused a scene with her bad manners. Annabelle was already distraught but now felt more so at her mother's misunderstanding of the situation: she hadn't meant to be rude – her illness had made her leave the restaurant.

Sometimes when traffic flow was smooth, the family arrived thirty minutes early for their weekly therapy appointment and would walk along the city street, window-shopping, and Annabelle would brighten and be totally different. Maree initially thought, 'You little brat, you're playing games; you have control over this'. Annabelle seemed to be able to switch her illness off and on, but in fact she had no control. The therapist explained that the shopping was a distraction from the illness, allowing Annabelle to be herself for a moment.

The most successful distraction at home during mealtimes was card playing, with Uno the most successful ploy. Sometimes Annabelle tossed the cards off the table, but gradually her focus on the game increased, and meals passed more peacefully. A distraction from exercising or purging did not seem necessary, with Annabelle convincing her mother she preferred not to eat in the first place, rather than run it off or bring it up later.

The intensive family therapy produced unexpected revelations, with Maree discovering a new depth of emotional strength and resilience within herself. 'I'm glad', Maree said, 'but it was a hard way to find out'. She also learnt she was more capable:

> We as a family are still scarred by the illness but have become more connected and appreciate life more. We had always communicated well, and this has improved. I don't sweat the small stuff now. Things I would have stressed over before Annabelle's illness don't bother me. I was pedantic about the housework – I could be half dead with pneumonia but if it was a Monday, my cleaning day, I would still do it. Or if anyone were coming to visit I would race around getting things in order. Now I can go three weeks before mopping the floor and my friends have commented I am less highly strung and more relaxed, transformed!

As with many families, extended family and friends had difficulty understanding the seriousness of Annabelle's illness. One day Maree was making a sandwich for Annabelle when her mother called in unexpectedly and insisted she could persuade Annabelle to eat. Sitting beside her granddaughter she said, 'Come on, Annabelle, you will eat this for me, won't you?' Later, the despondent grandmother said, 'Nothing I could say would convince Annabelle to take a bite'. Annabelle had growled accusingly and scattered food and plates everywhere in the kitchen. She thought she had been tricked, that her mother had asked her grandmother to come and implore her to eat. Her grandmother went home with a heavy heart that day. She had believed Annabelle would do anything for her, which she normally would, but not while in the clutches of anorexia.

Guided by the therapy team and reinforced by parents of other sufferers, Maree and William had felt relieved, when weight restoration began, to see glimpses of Annabelle's personality coming back in the form of little snippets of conversation. A monumental moment came during a session in month six of family-based treatment when she said, 'I want to fight this illness'. She was crying and, fighting a battle inside her head, added in a whisper to her parents, 'I want to

help you fight this illness. I am on your side'. It was Maree
and William's wedding anniversary that day and Annabelle's
courageous words were the best gift they could wish for.
They knew she had fought hard to say it.

With Annabelle consuming much of her parents' attention, younger sister Isabella continued to feel isolated. 'The
worst part was the yelling and fighting at mealtimes, with my
parents trying to persuade Annabelle to eat', Isabella said.
Also, she felt forgotten at home and increasingly isolated at
school. After the first phase of family-based treatment, her
friends often commented that Annabelle was 'obviously
better' because she looked a healthy weight. Isabella could
not convince her friends that 'appearances' could be deceiv-
ing. Eventually she found it easier to pretend that Annabelle
was well and that life was good rather than talk about her
troubles at home. She found she had matured faster than
many of her friends and therefore had less in common with
them. All they wanted to talk about was the 'weekend',
either the one just past or the one coming up. So Isabella
found her own way of coping. Her favourite diversions were a
boxing bag and Playstation.

Isabella was devoted to being her sister's friend and
maintaining her trust, but occasionally she felt she was bet-
raying her parents as they did not know many of Annabelle's
secrets. Sometimes Isabella herself became caught in the
illness's web, such as when Annabelle bought a box of chocolates to give a friend as a birthday gift. Annabelle had put
the box in her bedroom cupboard until the special day arrived
but then felt repulsed, knowing calorie-rich food was in her
room, and sold them to Isabella. 'I did not want the chocolates
and they did not taste great but I bought them to make
Annabelle feel a little better', Isabella said. 'She sold them to
me for the same price she bought them, so I got a bad deal but
thought I could live with that if it meant she would be
happier.'

Isabella was in her third year of high school when
Annabelle's family-based treatment sessions began. She
attended the sessions for six months but then went less regularly as she was falling behind in her studies. The time away
from school plus the effort of completing assignments, amid

the shouting at home, meant Isabella often passed her work in a week or two late. Most of her teachers understood, but several did not appreciate the impact her home life was having on her studies. 'They did not realise that handing my homework in late was enough punishment for me', Isabella said. 'I already felt bad about it but they would yell at me, or shake their heads in disappointment. So I became more anxious when another piece of homework was due, and avoided starting it.'

At home, Isabella often felt overlooked and excluded. 'People basically assumed I played no role in, or had to deal with, my family's struggles', Isabella said. Friends of her parents would say 'Look after your mother and father, and Annabelle for us', but nobody was asked to look after her. When Isabella answered the phone, people asked about Annabelle but not her. It was the same with schoolteachers. They could not see how the anorexia could possibly affect her.

Today, home life is calmer and continuing to improve. 'Everyone in our family has grown from the experience', Isabella said.

Annabelle, now eighteen and at a healthy weight, said she will never forget her assessment day with the family-based treatment team:

> We went over my life. All the horrible parts of my life.
> There were lots of tears and tantrums. I had come to
> trust a therapist in my home town, and had expected her to
> be there with me at the family-based treatment session and
> she was not. I felt let down. I spoke in the first session,
> less in the second. They did not ask me to speak much.
> I decided to stare out the family-based therapist. I thought,
> 'I won't make this easy for you. I will take the longest to
> get well of any person who has been in this program. You
> won't beat me. I won't eat'.
>
> Then it got horrible. At home my parents would not let
> me leave the table, or if I went to my room they would
> follow with the plate. There was no escape.

Weight restoration was as stressful as it was important.

There was no easy way to achieve it. Annabelle readily admits she was not capable of thinking for herself until she was re-fed, and that she needed her family to facilitate this. Reaching a healthy weight put her in a position where she could think more clearly.[3]

Two years after completing treatment, eating without supervision remains a challenge. Some of the most torment-ing times have occurred not when Annabelle was at her thinnest, but since reaching her healthy weight. Her mind would not let her rest, so unbeknown to her parents she would get up in the middle of the night and run around her bedroom and do push-ups and, during the day, walk laps around the local shopping centre.

The family-based treatment had put her in a position where she could fight on with the support of a therapist in her home town, but Annabelle believes more explanation at the outset that recovery might take more than one year would have been beneficial:

> I was told I was well but I knew I was not. I looked well, my
> weight was okay to the outside world, and people thought
> I was fine but I was not well within. The illness is with
> me all the time. I can function but it is generally there.
> I am physically healthy yet in some ways remain
> emotionally dead.

Annabelle persists in finding ways to control her tor-ment. When she goes out to dinner she avoids anxiety by allowing her friends to decide what to eat. If left to make a decision herself, she would feel compelled to select the least fattening dish on the menu or create an excuse to eat noth-ing at all. By allowing her friends to choose, she can at least manage to eat, if not enjoy, the meal.[4]

The struggle in overcoming anorexia has given Annabelle an acute appreciation of life. Every morning, she wakes up and welcomes the new day:

> When I was sick, and I had to stay home, I would think
> just to go to school would be great. I was a prisoner and
> everything was grey and when I started to eat and get well,

the light around me got brighter and I began to cherish simple things, like seeing the sun in the morning.

On the day I visited her family at home, Annabelle presented as a beautiful, bright young woman living life to the full. She had finished high school, had a boyfriend, was employed full-time and had joined her town's conservatorium to pursue her passion for music and singing. There was no sign of her silent struggle; no sign, that is, until she sat at the keyboard in her bedroom. Inviting me to sit on her bed, I became an honoured audience of one as she began to strike the keys and launched into a soulful song. 'I created these words during one of my darkest moments', she confided, 'to describe and release the pain of being a captive of anorexia'. I was deeply moved. Annabelle credits her passion for music and creativity with helping her survive the illness. Titled 'Torn', this is her song:

VERSE 1
I wanna be anywhere but here
With anybody but you
I show a pretty smile
And scream inside
You've taken everything from me
You've torn me apart

VERSE 2
You're the man I thought you were
Did you ever really care
Did you ever really love me
I gave so much to you
And I got nothing but tears
In return

CHORUS
I wanna go home now
I want things to be better
I want my heart to be whole
And I wanna dry the tears
That my soul cries

But you're still here
And I can't leave

VERSE 3
You've carved your name on my soul
I can't escape you I'll be yours forever more
And I stand here smiling and screaming
You were there when I needed you
Ironic that it was you who broke me
In the first place

(CHORUS × 1)

Today Annabelle can reflect:

Anorexia is phenomenal. It takes over your mind. Family-based treatment is the only way to beat it. No one could convince me to eat. Someone had to make me, and it had to be as quick as possible. I needed help to reach the stage where I could feed myself and be able to function at a basic level. My parents and sister have been, and continue to be, the best people to help me. As much as you hate your parents at the time, you know they love you. Your family is the biggest part of your life, your biggest resource.

11

Alice

For the first three months of family-based treatment, as they fought the anorexia head on, Neil and Cathy feared their daughter had disappeared. 'There was nothing in her eyes', Cathy said. 'Twice, in those three months, I saw them flicker. They were the only indication that somewhere in her mind, Alice was alive.' Neil felt unnerved, moving about his home. Sensing someone behind him he would turn to find a thin, skeletal body, but no 'Alice'. She would follow him, silently, a shadow of herself. 'She was more dependent than a baby', Neil said. 'We had to feed her. You have to feed a baby, but a baby has a personality. Alice had none. She was conveying one message to us and it was, "I don't want to be here". Her illness was taking her from us'.

An end-of-year concert gave Cathy the first clue that something was amiss with her 13-year-old daughter, Alice. The youngest of three children, Alice had a happy relationship with sister Pip and brother Doug. Cathy was a full-time mother who enjoyed being involved in her children's and community activities, especially sport. Neil worked long hours in his senior position as an anaesthetist at the Children's Hospital at Westmead. But life began to go awry when Alice put on her dance costume, for which she had been measured four months earlier. The costume mistress remarked 'Alice has dropped several sizes', and Cathy thought, 'Shit!' 'This had happened with Pip when she was a teenager and I felt sick!' Cathy had noticed Alice was slimming but had attributed this to a growth spurt and puberty.

'She was dancing twenty-four hours a week but was still eating well, so I thought she was okay', Cathy said.

Two months later, Alice was in year 8 at the start of the new school term and had hardly resumed her performing arts classes when the dance master called Cathy to ask, 'Do we have a problem here?' referring to Alice's weight. Cathy said, 'No, I am aware she is losing weight and changing her eating habits – I've been there before with Pip and I think I can handle it'. However, Cathy soon realised that Alice's eating disorder was different from that of Pip's. Pip's weight had fluctuated but she did not stop eating. Alice increasingly could not eat, and this was completely out of character.

Alice had always been a 'good food eater' and family barbecues, with chops and sausages, were among her favourite mealtimes. Full of vim and vigour, she was always on the go. Besides dancing, she enjoyed swimming, and sailing with her dad. When her girlfriends expressed concern at her weight loss and sudden withdrawn ways, Cathy remained optimistic. Pip's period of disordered eating had been tumultuous, and trying to find the right help had been a 'nightmare'. She had struggled to complete year 12 at school but now, at the age of eighteen, was happily settling into a job. Cathy thought Alice's love of life was too strong to let anything hold her back for long. She surely would get over her 'little self-image problem' of her own accord. But within three weeks Cathy changed her mind. Alice's weight was dropping rapidly and she was exercising at an alarming rate.

Cathy spoke with the dance instructor again, this time to acknowledge, 'Yes, Alice has a problem'. She was introduced to a counsellor at the performing arts school, who explained that Alice was showing symptoms of anorexia nervosa and asked, 'What would you like to do about it?' Unsure where to start, Cathy and Neil agreed that Alice required medical help. By now she was living on lettuce leaves, ice cubes and water.

Neil and Cathy at first were incredulous that Alice had developed anorexia. She really was a 'five chops and sausages a night girl'; she was strong as an ox mentally and physically. She had always been stubborn. When four months old, Alice had liked to stay awake at night. Becoming a mental zombie, Cathy decided to wean her but she wouldn't take the bottle. 'She starved herself for forty-eight hours before she accepted the change', Cathy said. 'I love her dearly, but right from babyhood she has been very determined. She never crawled, just ran. She has always been very agile, very sporty.'

But a strong self-will since birth counted for nothing against the insidious anorexia. Alice's weight continued to plummet. 'I kept telling myself that if I lost more weight, everything would be alright and I would be able to eat', Alice said. 'But I would lose more weight, and everything would not be alright, so I would have to lose even more.' No matter what level her weight dropped to, it was never enough.

Alice didn't tell anyone about this inner struggle:

> I think the thoughts were always there. I remember when I was nine, I could deny myself ice-cream for a week even though I loved it. My anorexic thoughts were similar. I was already very active so cutting down on junk food was my first goal. That made a lot of difference; then to slim more, I cut out other foods. Next I stepped up my exercise, and eliminated more food. When we went on holiday to the beach after the dance concert, I surfed and swam for hours every day and when we returned home, I had to maintain my extreme level of exercise.

Neil and Cathy had heard about the Maudsley Approach, a family-based treatment available at Neil's work; however, Neil couldn't get an appointment for a week. How long can a week be? In that week, Cathy could not believe how quickly the disease took hold. 'It was like it had ears', she said, for Alice went from being able to eat something to nothing. The spread of the illness was frightening. Cathy kept saying, 'I don't know if we can last this week'. The appointment day came, however, and the family-based treatment team helped the family to take stock. 'The team members helped us realise that everyone is important in the family and to each other', Cathy said.

> The family-based treatment sessions help you realise how important everyone is, interacting and supporting each

other – the paediatrician, psychiatrist and family therapist all work with you as a team. Having this support externally, as an outpatient, is preferable to being in a hospital system where the child is away from the people and surrounds they love and know. Our therapist was always there for us. She would talk to me whenever I needed support. She would say, 'You can do it'. I didn't know how much deeper I could dig and yet, with her encouragement, I would find energy in places I didn't know I had.

Alice remembers her parents taking her for the assessment with the family-based treatment team. She was confused and stressed out, but believed she was fine. 'I knew they wanted to resolve a problem and I didn't want this', Alice said, 'because I felt really content when I was hungry. I felt happy when I went to bed hungry. I wanted to keep that feeling'. By now, ice was the only 'food' Alice could eat without feeling guilty.

During her assessment, Alice felt disappointed when asked to stand on the scales. She thought she weighed too much:

I was comparing myself with everyone else, and when the doctor tried to cheer my mother by saying that my weight wasn't as low as the girls who were hospitalised, I thought, 'I will get there, I will show them'. At that point, I didn't want to be well. I hated it when people would think they were encouraging me by saying 'You look good'. I didn't want to look good. I would look at myself, and think, 'I still look dreadfully fat. I can never be skinny enough'.

Nine months of weekly family-based treatment followed by nine months of follow-up sessions became rewarding for each member of the family. Besides fighting Alice's illness, they learnt more about themselves: any strengths in the family's dynamics were identified, tested and ultimately further strengthened. Neil and Cathy were told that their job was to feed Alice. Pip and Doug were to offer support and friendship to her.[1]

Sometimes Alice would run away rather than sit down for a meal. She had been miserable for months and was prescribed antidepressants, which brightened her a little. 'I wanted my parents' help to get better, but if I ate I felt a strong need to be punished', Alice said. She was dismayed when the therapists said she must cease her dance classes until her health recovered. Believing that the classes might give Alice a reason to get well, Cathy arranged for one class to continue. This was against the therapy team's advice and Cathy soon discovered why. 'I sat in the room throughout the entire dance class', Cathy said, 'and tried to confine Alice's movements to the dance floor'. The trouble was that Alice would continue to move non-stop on the sidelines while waiting her turn. Very soon the dance instructor told Cathy, 'I can't allow Alice to continue. She won't stop moving for a second'. So the dance classes ceased, but at home Alice kept moving.

'We were challenging her illness, but when sitting at the table for her meals, she would tap her feet, shake her knees and jiggle incessantly', Cathy said. Sitting on a chair in the family room, Alice would rock back and forth, in constant motion. She liked to be cold so her body would burn more energy trying to keep warm. She exercised when taking a shower and lying in bed. By now, her personality had disappeared. 'The anorexia had swallowed Alice', Neil said. 'To discourage her from exercising throughout the night, we eventually arranged for her to sleep in our bedroom so we could keep watch on her.'

Initially, Neil was sceptical about seeing a family-based treatment therapist. He had heard a few stories about therapists and the outcomes had not been positive. He held a senior position at the hospital, and thought the therapy might be a waste of time. When the family-based treatment team's head therapist said, 'You will be required to meet here once a week as a family, all together', Neil replied, 'I can't do that – I work from 6 a.m. to 8 p.m.'. But the therapist reasoned, 'If your daughter had cancer you would take her to oncology to treat the cancer'. Accepting the severity of the consequences of the illness was difficult for Neil, and he continued to struggle to drag himself away from work until the therapist challenged him and overcame his scepticism for her profession. She had to gain his trust so she could help his family fight the illness.

Cathy understood Neil's inner conflict, but said, 'Just because you hold a senior position in your career doesn't mean your child doesn't need help. Anorexia can develop in anybody's child. The number-one thing is to be honest with yourself and with your child. You have to say, "I need help" '.

By agreeing to attend the weekly sessions, Neil had to alter his work hours and sometimes find a replacement to do his work. 'I am very lucky to have such understanding and helpful colleagues', Neil said. By this time, he knew he had no choice but to accept his colleagues' offers of assistance. Both he and Cathy knew Alice's illness had gone way beyond their capabilities. The family therapist laid it on the line for him, saying, 'This is your decision – you choose: your daughter or your work. You have a mobile phone, and you must be available at any time, so Cathy can talk to you for five minutes'. Neil had always done his shift until it was finished; he was reluctant to leave early for any reason. However, the fight against Alice's anorexia made the decision to change his work ethic easy. He agreed that if Cathy rang he could return her call within five minutes. 'There was no contest really', he said. 'I would choose my daughter every time.'

Many people asked, 'Why would you take your daughter to the hospital where you work?' I said, 'I trust these people and I'm not embarrassed that my daughter has a serious illness and is receiving treatment'. I found that by being open, very senior people would come up to me and say, 'My wife had anorexia' or 'My sister had anorexia'. They also emphasised I was doing the right thing: 'You must get this treated now', 'Don't ignore it, don't let it fester' or 'I had it as a child and still have problems'. So all these people came forward.

Initially, Alice was a shell. We had broken the disease, but we wondered if we had broken her spirit and lost our daughter as well. It was very distressing, but our therapist was supportive. She kept assuring us, 'Alice will come back', and, month by month, Alice's cheekiness did gradually come back.

With the support of the family-based treatment team, Neil and Cathy persisted and, gradually, Alice began to reclaim her sense of self. Weekly sessions with the therapist, a social worker, became times of great family sharing and occasional confrontation. 'Our therapist was truly amazing', Cathy said. 'Firm and loving, she helped us not only come to terms with the anorexic battle, but also helped us strengthen our family relationships.'[2]

School became spasmodic – for months Alice would attend a class only now and then. She was weak physically and yet teachers complained that she wouldn't sit still. The realisation that Alice's illness was affecting others outside the home was 'a slap across the face' for Cathy. She had tried to keep Alice at school, often still coaxing her to eat breakfast on the way there in the car. Breakfast would include one of twelve glasses of medical-strength Sustagen that she was to drink each day. It was the only way to get her weight back on, Cathy said. Cathy would return to the school and sit with Alice each recess and lunchbreak while she ate her snack and midday meal. All up she would clock 29 000 kilometres in car travel to Alice's school during the first year of family-based therapy.

Filling in the hours at home was sometimes a challenge. One day Alice wanted to look at old family photographs so Cathy pulled carefully catalogued boxes out of her cupboard. Alice emptied the pictures on the floor and spent hours idly mixing them up. Cathy did not mind; she hoped the pictures might help Alice connect with her self – with her life before developing anorexia.

Because Neil's job required him to be 'on call' in emergency situations, he was often away from home, leaving Cathy to shoulder much of the responsibility in caring for Alice. 'I would try to cope alone', Cathy said, 'and call Neil for support only when at my wits' end'. Pip would occasionally take Alice shopping to give Cathy a little break. Cathy said:

> I hated the anorexia! I have not had an eating disorder, and it was a shock to have two daughters with problems.
> Rather than dwell on it though, I had to look forward.
> Each night I asked myself, 'Can I dig deeper and face

another day?' Alice was not sleeping because of her compulsion to exercise, and Neil and I were not sleeping either as we had to watch over her.

Before Alice developed anorexia, Cathy had played competition netball. Now she had no time to play, but her netball friends kept her in the loop. Each Tuesday morning, a member of Cathy's family sat with Alice for an hour while the friends caught up over a cup of coffee. 'That weekly time-out helped me keep my sanity', Cathy said.

Well, most of her friends were supportive. When one woman remarked, 'How are your children?' and Cathy replied, 'Alice has developed anorexia', the woman said 'Oh, what a stupid little bitch'. The attitude of such people evolved from ignorance, Cathy decided.

Many people don't believe anorexia is a psychiatric disorder; they think it comes from external influences and is purely an image thing. They don't appreciate it is a medical condition and that sufferers don't have control over it. Having a child who develops anorexia nervosa opens up a whole new world. Perhaps for the first time, you learn the meaning of 100 per cent effort, because 1 per cent less and this illness will beat you.

One day Cathy received a call from a woman who was working on a higher academic degree. Her daughter was developing anorexia and, having heard Cathy's younger daughter was receiving treatment, sought advice on where to seek help. Cathy told her about the family-based treatment and how successful it had been for her entire family. She also suggested the woman would need to put her degree on hold, as her daughter would require her full attention for at least the first few months. The woman said she couldn't possibly defer her studies, because the academic challenge was a long-held and cherished ambition. Cathy responded rather bluntly, 'Do you want a daughter?' The woman said that of course she wanted her daughter, but that also she wanted her degree. 'There's your answer', Cathy said. She didn't hear from the woman again and felt sorry for the girl who was not as important as an academic qualification.

Cathy suggested that with more awareness of the seriousness of anorexia, the studious woman may have had a deeper appreciation of her daughter's plight and put her health first. It didn't seem fair, Cathy said, that other serious illnesses like diabetes and cancer attracted funding and yet anorexia largely missed out – despite anorexia having a significant mortality and morbidity rate. Remaining 'hidden' and unexposed suited the insidious illness. 'When parents feel ashamed and embarrassed that their child has anorexia, and feel they are to blame, they inadvertently compound the illness's destructive effect', Cathy said.

> One of the many good things about family-based treatment is its teaching that you are not to blame. It is imperative that parents feel no guilt – you don't if your child has juvenile diabetes, and it should be the same for parents of children with anorexia. Our therapist, at every session, would say, 'Don't feel guilty'.

Having a second child with an eating illness made this a little harder for Cathy to accept. She would ask herself:

> Why do I have two girls that have had to fight this disease in one form or another? It's easy to say 'do not feel blame', but getting over this was a huge mountain for me. When you have a child who has been within you, and you're the primary caregiver and have raised her, and you go through this illness, it is easy to think that it must be something you have passed on. The therapy was helpful in dealing with these thoughts.

There were two particularly worrying moments when Neil and Cathy felt they couldn't continue the fight to get Alice back. Both moments centred on a crumb. Early into treatment, Neil and Cathy had learnt to rethink the word 'big'. Tiny things, like eating a crumb, were suddenly considered a big accomplishment. A crumb of bread or cake was a reason for feeling happy. Getting their minds around this way of thinking was important. Small things were building blocks. 'We learnt to feel great about the smallest thing and to build on it', Neil said.

Each of the worrying moments occurred when a day went by without one crumb being consumed. Each time, Cathy and Neil asked Alice to pack her bags and called the hospital to arrange her admission. 'The disease is so defiant and the awful thing is, you can start taking it out on your child', Neil said. 'When Alice was so sick, we would say, "You just have to eat this. Come on Alice" '. But Alice's illness made her think her parents were the enemy and she refused to eat anything. On both occasions it so happened that no beds were available at the hospital, and Neil and Cathy had to struggle on. Amazingly, they found the strength to do so, and grew stronger for it.

The devious illness provided Alice with creative 'solutions', especially at the weekly weigh-in that was part of her therapy session. One trick was to wear two bras, and line them with small but heavy magnets collected from the refrigerator, family room drapes, the sewing basket and anywhere else Alice could find them. Her dad, who had a skilful eye for calculating body mass, solved the magnet mystery. He wondered why the scales were registering an increase in weight, yet Alice had eaten little and looked no heavier – there had to be something hidden in her clothes! Today those magnets are kept in a small tin as a reminder of how far Alice has come in her recovery.[3]

Fiery moments occurred between Alice and her mother. One afternoon they were shopping and Cathy wanted Alice to eat an ice-cream. Alice explained:

Mum said that if I ate the ice-cream, I would not have to drink the milkshake when we arrived home. Eventually I decided, 'Okay, to make her happy I will eat the ice-cream and get it over with', but when we arrived home, my mother insisted I drink the milkshake as well. I'd kept my part of the bargain but she didn't keep her part, so I didn't want to trust her any more after that.

The family discussed this situation during a therapy

session, with Neil saying, 'Yes, Cathy should have kept her word to Alice', as establishing trust was very important. Cathy conceded she had reneged, but her intention had been good in that she was seizing every opportunity to help her daughter gain weight. She learnt, however, that trying to cajole Alice to eat with false promises would not help her beat her illness. Maintaining consistency in expectation of food intake as decided by parents, and maintaining Alice's trust, were crucial in beating the anorexia.

Alice also suspected her mother was trying to take advantage of her. 'I had worked so hard to get slim', Alice said, 'and then my parents were wanting to take this achievement away without considering my feelings. This was the most confusing part of my life, the best and the worst'. For a long time Alice was incapable of understanding that the illness was dominating and manipulating her thoughts, restricting them to one thing – food.

If dining out with her family she could focus only on what was on her plate, counting calories and figuring out what she could eat and how much exercise she would need to do later to work it off. Everyone else would be chatting and laughing, and she couldn't understand why. 'Eating and drinking is natural', Alice said, 'but I couldn't do either without feeling terribly guilty. I felt isolated and withdrawn as the thoughts consumed my whole mind. There wasn't room for anything else'.

Alice's brother Doug, now in his final year of a university engineering degree, didn't take much notice at first of his younger sister's refusal to eat. He thought she was mature enough to know that she should eat when hungry. It seemed straightforward to him. However, Doug gained deeper insight during the family-based treatment sessions and around the meal table during Alice's recovery. He said:

> An outcome of this illness is that our family is really close. We have each shared everything with each other: we have had some huge blow-ups along the way, and in dealing with these we have become more aware of, and gained a respect for, each other's personality. I don't think there could be a family that's closer.

As for Alice and her battle against anorexia, I became aware that this was not a simple behavioural problem but a serious illness when I saw her at the meal table, her face scrunched up in pain and effort, as she tried to summon the strength to ignore her illness and swallow a tiny piece of bread. I thought, 'How unnatural for a person to have to fight so hard to do what the rest of us do without thinking'.

Doug admired his little sister's courage. He and Pip would try to help her by telling jokes and being with her. 'Anorexia is a horrible disease because it turns you against yourself, and it can hang on', Doug said. 'Like, sometimes even now, Alice will eat a whole piece of steak like the rest of us, and other days she will cut it into tiny pieces and check for minute pieces of fat.'

The definition of anorexia nervosa ('an eating disorder, marked by an extreme fear of becoming overweight leading to excessive dieting to the point of serious ill-health and sometimes death') didn't really explain the depth of this illness, Doug said.

Anorexia is more than being thin – that's really the smaller part. When Alice got sick that wasn't what worried me – it was how different she was, and how she was changing mentally; the way the illness overshadowed her mind was really odd. Although I worried when she was skinny, I thought that was reparable, but mentally I sometimes thought, 'Will she ever get back to herself?'

The strong family bond that has evolved from fighting Alice's anorexia has heightened Neil's love for his family. Neil said that before Alice's illness his three children were close, but now:

They have bared their soul to each other. Some people go through life without ever doing that. When our social worker asked if any good could come from this disease, Pip said, 'You learn about yourself'. Cathy and I agree! If we had not participated in the family-based treatment, we may well have divorced by now, and Alice would be still struggling to recover.

For months after completing Phase Three of family-based treatment, remnants of the illness remained and if Alice did not want something to eat, Cathy would go on high alert:

> She would come home and say she didn't want dinner because she had been eating all day or had been 'foraging' all day. I would find this hard to accept and would say, 'I want you to eat a normal meal'. Her behaviour can still send shivers down my spine. She wants to be normal so she eats cake and ice-cream, but on her bad days she can be moody, as when developing anorexia.

As Cathy explained, such days are now few and far between:

> Family-based treatment has saved Alice and our family. So many things we learnt during our therapy sessions continue to guide and support us. The therapy is not just about anorexia; it is about helping each other and recognising signs. One day our therapist asked if there was anything good about having anorexia in our family: I thought, 'What a silly question! It is horrendous. It is HIDEOUS'. But Pip said 'No, I disagree'. Through our ongoing self-disclosures, especially during family-based treatment, we became more aware of each other and ourselves. Pip found information shared in this way particularly important and valuable for her own sense of well-being. This was a big turning point for her and she became my rock when Alice was really sick. It is wonderful to have warmth and understanding in the family.

Outside the family, Cathy found honesty the best way to cope: to be able to say to others, 'I feel like shit, Alice has anorexia'. This openness had a surprising outcome, empowering others to share. Everyone seemed to know somebody who had suffered anorexia: 'I had anorexia when young', 'My sister had anorexia', 'My niece died from anorexia'. Cathy said:

It is unbelievable when you open up to find how many people close to you have been affected by this illness. Their responses sustained me; they gave me a long-term view and hope that there was light at the end of tunnel. Be honest. Don't deny someone in your family has this illness. Don't hide. It is a disease that needs to be out there.

Alice, however, did not share her mother's view. 'She hated me telling anybody', Cathy said. 'As if they couldn't see I had a skeleton beside me, that my happy bubbly child was now this shell being dragged around next to me.' Cathy knew the illness did not like to be exposed, and when Alice said, 'I don't like you talking about me', Cathy said, 'I am talking about your anorexia'.

She acknowledges that some people probably thought her crazy and were frightened by her strong words in talking about the illness, for all they could see was an emaciated Alice. Some people had difficulty separating the illness from the child. Most tried to understand, but some mistakenly believed that Alice had chosen to have anorexia. Through family-based treatment, the family members learnt how to deal with these misconceptions and along the way learnt a lot about themselves.

Neil had always been a 'glass half-full' person, trying to see the good in people rather than the bad, and he enjoyed spending time with his family in the hours left outside the demands of his career. For him, an outcome of family-based treatment was that he realised that his family was more important than his career:

Real wealth is in relationships, not materialism. You need a job so you have somewhere to live, and a means to get around. I'm lucky I enjoy my work and my colleagues, but apart from that it is not really relevant – your family and relationships are the most important things in life.

Cathy's nature included a tendency to be authoritarian, and this aspect of her personality was raised during the family-based treatment. Neil said of the weekly discussion:

It cleared the air a lot. After about two months, the family therapy became almost fun. We went from saying 'not this again', to discussing what we would talk about at our next session. We all enjoyed it, talking about things we had never been able to talk about before. My relationship with Cathy improved tremendously. Today we can talk about anything, whereas before the therapy we'd have gone off our heads about an issue and walked away from each other.

At first Alice thought the family-based therapy was patronising: 'I can see now that my parents had to make me eat, but at the time it was hard to let anyone else have control over me'. After the initial stage of not wanting to eat anything, she had adopted the attitude that if her parents made her eat it was 'kind of okay', but if left to eat on her own accord, she would go hungry. 'Giving myself permission to eat was really hard', Alice said.

'When I was starting to get better, my mother would try to scare me by saying, "Would you prefer to be at home in a safe environment or in hospital where they control everything you do?" ' At the time Alice thought the hospital would be preferable, because at home her illness was constantly confronted; it couldn't hide. She believes her family's love played a huge role in her recovery. Because her family was around her 24/7, Alice began to feel guilty about their concern and wanted to try to get better:

At home you see how much this illness is destroying your family, if not yourself. So this small amount of me that was left wanted to make my mother and father a little happier, and the way to do this was to eat.

When I got to a certain weight and began thinking more like myself, I wanted to get better, though I couldn't really let myself. I continued to need the strong challenge from my parents to make me eat.

A new obstacle had to be overcome when Alice reached a safe weight, for she still had tormenting thoughts. 'People think that when you gain weight and look like your former self, you miraculously become you again', Alice said. 'But you don't. I thought "Why do I still have the thoughts of anorexia if I can't have the thin body?" This was very frustrating.'

Two years after completing her therapy program, Alice, at eighteen, had largely regained her sense of self. On completing secondary school she delayed university studies for a year to have fun with her friends and work as a lifeguard at a local swimming pool to save for an overseas trip. At times she continued to struggle in her mind, grappling with the concept of how anorexia manipulated her thoughts during her illness, for those thoughts belonged to her. Some days she overate and afterwards did not think kindly of herself. Surrounded by the love of her family, Alice worked on becoming more self-aware so that she could manage these problems. Her friends remained supportive through her illness and recovery, and if Alice was having a 'bad day' she felt free to share her feelings with family, especially Pip or Doug.

Choosing to eat, Alice said, was basically making a choice between having a life or not having a life, and being happy but in different ways.

When I was sick and isolated with anorexia nervosa, I was not really living my life. Getting better was the hardest thing I have ever done. At the time it was like a lose–lose situation – I did not want to eat, but I had to eat to get well. Once I did so I felt self-satisfied. Today I appreciate everything, like being able to go out with friends and not be consumed by thoughts, and being content with myself. Having the freedom to do what I want, eat when I want – the freedom others always have had but, having had it taken from me, I realise how precious this is.

Five years after developing anorexia nervosa, Alice continues to embrace her freedom and the joy of independence.

Shortly after celebrating her nineteenth birthday, she said 'goodbye' to family and friends and, realising a dream, set off to travel overseas and explore the world. 'She has turned into the beautiful butterfly I always thought was there', Cathy said.

PART 2

What are parents to do?

12

How to tell if your child has anorexia nervosa

Professor Daniel Le Grange

Having read this far, you have probably been able to identify with some of the trials and tribulations experienced by the ten families telling their stories for this book. If you have been through a dilemma like any one of those represented here, and the eating disorder in your family is something of the past, then congratulations! However, if your family is still struggling or you are concerned that your loved one might be developing an eating disorder, or in fact has been diagnosed with an eating disorder, this chapter will be a useful resource. This chapter is by no means a complete parent guide, but it does outline what symptoms and signs to look for, and what to do with this information.

A reminder of the diagnostic criteria for anorexia nervosa

Before we review many of the earlier symptoms and signs of anorexia nervosa, a brief review of the diagnostic criteria for this illness is in order. The *Diagnostic and Statistical Manual of Mental Disorders (DSM)* puts forward four criteria that should be met before a diagnosis of anorexia nervosa can be confirmed. These are: extreme weight loss (usually about 15 per cent or more of your ideal body weight) or a refusal to maintain a healthy weight for your age; overvaluing thinness insofar as nothing in life seems more important than the number on the scale; perceiving your body in such a way that only you think you are overweight or fat while everyone else can clearly see you are quite

emaciated; and finally, and for females, missing three consecutive menstrual periods when you are at an age where
regular menses are expected.

As you can see, these criteria are fairly strict and if one
examines the prevalence numbers for anorexia nervosa
among young women (about one in a hundred adolescent
girls), you might comment that relatively few teens meet
these strict criteria. This is correct! However, as many of the
parents in the preceding chapters have highlighted, early
recognition of signs of this disorder is paramount. Being
able to intervene even before someone presents with all four
of these criteria provides the sufferer a great advantage in
terms of quick and full recovery. In other words, many more
children and teens meet some criteria for anorexia nervosa,
or Eating Disorder Not Otherwise Specified (as per the
DSM), or sub-clinical anorexia nervosa. With this book, and
this chapter, we hope to emphasise the point that when you
notice the first signs of anorexia nervosa, you should act as
expeditiously as you would when you are presented with the
terrible news that your child indeed meets all criteria for
anorexia nervosa.

You are confused and unsure what to do

Your son or daughter has always been such an easy kid. The
possibility of an eating disorder is a frightening thought,
and you are confused and unsure about what you'd do if the
illness is confirmed. Your hope is that the eating difficulties
you are observing are only transient as you have seen these
fads come and go in your other kids, or other families have
shared similar stories about their kids with you. You want to
remind yourself that it's not the first time your child has had
a struggle with eating – being picky is not unusual, and
you've seen other times when he or she was eating too little
or perhaps too much, or complaining about an upset stomach
or difficulty going to the toilet.

Because you are concerned you have asked your relatives
or your friends, and they have reassured you that things
are okay and the problems you are observing are experienced by most adolescents, especially girls, and it will

probably blow over. You want to think that your child's concerns about weight and/or appearance are normal. After all, you have seen their friends express similar concerns and you are worried that, should you say something, you'll probably make things worse. So, you opt to do nothing even though your better judgment or gut feeling is telling you otherwise.

How are you to know that your concerns are well founded?

Any one of the family journeys you have read in this book – especially when the parents first suspect their child has an eating disorder – might sound familiar. If this is so, it is time to seek help. Anorexia nervosa is a serious disorder and left untreated or treated inadequately can lead to chronic medical and mental health problems and, in some instances, premature death. Severe weight loss associated with anorexia nervosa has numerous dire consequences. Among these are hypothermia (lowered body temperature), orthostatic hypotension (temporary light-headedness upon standing up), bradycardia (lowered resting heart rate), amenorrhea (loss of menstruation in young women), and osteopenia or osteoporosis (loss of bone density) to name but a few. In advanced stages of starvation, and due to lack of fuel, the body turns muscle into critically required energy. When this happens, extreme weakness and/or fatigue set in. Because the heart is a large muscle, a loss in cardiac mass can lead to critical changes in heart rhythms that can cause cardiac failure or death. Anorexia nervosa presents with the highest mortality rate of any psychiatric illness, and complications of anorexia are estimated to cause premature death in 5 to 15 per cent of all cases.

There are two subtypes of anorexia nervosa: restricting and binge/purge. It is unnecessary to speculate about whether the one form of the disorder is more lethal than the other; suffice to say that sufferers often 'migrate' from being a 'restrictor' to developing binge eating and purging episodes. When someone develops the binge/purge subtype, a whole series of additional complications can develop. The most common and serious concern is when the body becomes depleted of its stores of potassium (hypokalemia), an essential electrolyte that is lost when the content of the stomach is purged. Potassium is needed for several basic physical processes such as muscle contraction. The lack of such contractions can lead to cardiac arrhythmias, which in turn can lead to cardiac arrest and death. Frequent vomiting can also lead to the erosion of the lining of the esophagus and stomach, which can cause bleeding or ulcers to develop. In some instances this has been lethal if doctors are unable to stop the bleeding.

In addition to vomiting, some patients with anorexia nervosa will try to manage their weight by using laxatives and purgatives. These methods are highly ineffective in terms of weight loss; instead, the consequences are gastric complications such as pain and severe and unremitting constipation. Body fluid is lost through self-induced vomiting as well as the use of laxatives, resulting in dehydration. Such a critical depletion in water from the body can lead to a change in blood pressure (hypotension) and increase the likelihood of fainting and falling. The biggest risk from anorexia nervosa, however, would be for a parent to be complacent and not to take these symptoms and signs very seriously.

What are the characteristics of eating disorders when they develop?

From Chloe to Alice, you have been able to read about the development of anorexia nervosa in several teens. In your reading, you would have noticed that these teens did not develop an eating disorder overnight. Instead, the parents who have shared their experiences in this book almost all show how their child's anorexia nervosa developed gradually – sometimes in secret. With this final chapter, we hope to provide you with a road map of sorts – information that will allow you to evaluate where your child might be on the path of developing a serious eating disorder.

Not eating – on the path to anorexia nervosa?

Anorexia nervosa almost always starts in adolescence (around ages thirteen to fourteen years); however, it has become increasingly worrisome that more children under the age of twelve are developing anorexia nervosa. While the onset of this disorder is unique to each individual, it often starts with an episode of dieting, which can take on many forms, but almost always progresses to life-threatening starvation. It is often difficult to uncover what exactly is at the heart of the dieting or what caused the dieting, although in some instances an identifiable life event precedes the weight loss, such as a move to another state or school, the death of a favourite grandparent, the onset of puberty, the start of menstruation or what appears to be 'innocent' teasing about dieting, weight or shape. It is important to remember that these events are not the causes of anorexia nervosa as the illness is far too complex to be attributed to a single event, regardless of how meaningful or distressing the event might be. Nevertheless, it usually is the dieting that signals the start of the eating disorder.

You will recall that the parents who shared their experiences with their teen's eating disorder cited many different reasons why their daughter or son started dieting. These reasons varied from wanting to lose weight to be healthier or to be in better shape for a school sport. Others reported more ascetic purposes for embarking on a course of dieting; for instance, 'I will be a better person if I eat less'. What all these teens have in common, though, is that they wanted to diet as a way of improving themselves. This 'improvement' almost always takes on an outward expression – for example, being thinner, smaller or lighter – in that the teen wants to look different from the way they or others may view them. Many observers will emphasise the Western cultural environment in which this illness develops and blame social norms of beauty, especially female beauty, as at the heart of most dieting efforts. However, dieting to improve health or morality or sports performance might share a close connection with perfectionism, drive, dedication and ambition – all character traits that are often present in individuals who develop eating disorders.

Anorexia nervosa usually begins with a reduction in food intake or a schedule of increased exercise, or both. Because the onset of this illness is almost always insidious, the teen will almost always eliminate a certain food item – for example, no dessert or no fast foods – without their family noticing. Eventually entire food groups join the list of forbidden foods, such as no carbohydrates, no fats or no meat, and so on. In other teens, it could be a matter of just limiting quantities, a little at a time, or adjusting the range of foods 'allowed' to be consumed. The result of any one of these scenarios is a narrower range of foods and a much lowered consumption of calories than was the case prior to the onset of the dieting. This lowered energy intake often goes hand in hand with a detailed and precise set of rules that govern eating. Over the course of limiting calories more and more, the sufferer develops an elaborate system of counting calories or measuring or weighing the foods that are being consumed. This is all done in the service of making sure that less and less food is being consumed. At this stage, eating has become such an ordeal for some that the adolescent has removed themselves from social engagement around eating, instead preparing their own precise meal, in their own time, and in their own way. Occasionally, the adolescent may take on the role of 'chef' in their family, cooking elaborate and calorie-rich meals for everyone else, but refraining from participating in this feast!

Extreme dieting is seldom seen as 'sufficient' to achieve the strict weight-loss goals that sufferers with anorexia nervosa have set for themselves. The weight goals continue to shift downward and, as the teen's anxiety mounts, a punishing exercise schedule might be implemented to aid in this weight loss process. This can vary from doing thousands of push-ups and sit-ups daily, to going for one- or two-hour-long runs, to joining a gym and spending hours in aerobic exercises day after day. These attempts at additional weight loss are seldom 'sufficient' and many patients may attempt to rid themselves of even the small amounts of food they consume by inducing vomiting or abusing laxatives, diuretics or diet pills. At this stage, it is almost impossible for them to eat anything without feeling guilty, anxious or angry for having consumed even the most meagre amount of calories. The opposite is true in that when the teen manages not to eat anything, it is associated with a sense of accomplishment and pride. Hunger cues tend to dissipate with increased weight loss, making continued food restriction even easier. Not eating, though, keeps the sufferer captive because their mind becomes even more preoccupied with food-related thoughts.

In addition to repetitive thoughts about food, adolescents with anorexia nervosa can become so entangled in this disorder that most 'free' times are occupied by studying cookbooks, paging through recipes, visiting the supermarket, hoarding food, smelling food, and so on. At the same time, a variety of rituals around eating can develop; for example, only eating when using certain utensils, repeating specific encouraging or reassuring phrases, using unusual combinations of condiments, measuring food, and so on. At this point in the development of the illness, it is quite likely that the adolescent has come to cease her regular menses (if post-pubertal).

This turn of events can come about in as short a time as a few weeks for some, whereas for others the illness can slowly develop over a period spanning twelve months or more. Following is a list of some of the early warning signs that parents ought to be on the lookout for. Early-warning behaviours do not necessarily indicate that your child has an eating disorder but should not be overlooked either. In fact, it should indicate heightened vigilance on the part of the parents. The 'act-now' behaviours or symptoms are more alarming. The presence of these would indicate that parents should take immediate action and the first step would be to have your teen be evaluated by an eating disorder specialist.

Early signs and symptoms of anorexia nervosa [1]

Early-warning signs

- Dieting behaviour such as skipping meals

- Evidence of visiting pro-anorexia or eating disorder websites
- Reading cookbooks
- Becoming a vegetarian 'overnight' (without good philosophical or moral reasons)
- Picky eating (only eating 'healthy foods')
- Bathroom visits immediately after eating (for purging)
- Taking showers after a meal (for purging)
- A concerning or surprising number of stomach bug or flu episodes
- Signs of having missed a period

Act-now symptoms

- Fasting
- Dry skin, loss of hair
- Not eating with family or friends
- Having missed two periods in conjunction with weight loss
- Signs of binge eating or purging episodes
- Discovery of diet pills or laxatives
- Exercising to excess or in a driven way (>1 hour a day)
- Persistently refusing to eat non-diet foods
- Preparing own foods, weighing and measuring portions
- Calorie counting (persistently and to the last calorie)

Where do I go from here?

Parents are usually concerned for good reason and should be encouraged to trust their gut feelings. Therefore, if it appears that there is reason for worry, it is probably time to share your anxiety about your teen's eating habits with a professional who specialises in the treatment of adolescents with eating disorders. Your paediatrician might be a good start, but keep in mind that most family doctors or paediatricians are not experts in the treatment of eating disorders. However, they could assist you in finding a more appropriate referral.

Getting started will not be easy, but what should be clear is that a delay in addressing the teen's budding eating disorder will complicate recovery considerably. Like most other illnesses, medical or psychiatric, if an eating disorder is given half a chance to become established in a child's mind and body, it is incredibly complex to address effectively in treatment. The Maudsley Approach is the only treatment for which there is solid evidence of recovery for adolescents who have been ill with anorexia nervosa for a relatively short period of time. For now, this should be the treatment of choice for adolescents with anorexia nervosa.

The next chapter presents guidelines on where and how to find a family-based therapist. This is followed by an Appendix with details of treatment providers and resources.

13

Navigating the search for family-based treatment

As illustrated by the families in this book, the process of seeking treatment for a child's eating disorder can be overwhelming and emotionally draining. Confusion over terms and names for treatment approaches can make this process more difficult. In searching for a provider of family-based treatment, it helps to understand how to ask for it and how to determine which providers offer this treatment in its true form.

Family-based treatment for anorexia nervosa or family therapy?

The Maudsley Approach is more commonly known within the scientific community as family-based treatment for anorexia nervosa. This is to be distinguished from some other approaches to family therapy, which may lack some of the specific features of family-based treatment for anorexia nervosa. Family therapy is a broad term that encompasses a number of theoretical ideas and a range of therapeutic approaches. What they have in common is, first, the notion that individual problems and dilemmas are best understood in the social context in which they occur and, second, that the family is an important resource in finding constructive ways of dealing with individual problems.

A good definition of family therapy is:

A form of psychotherapy that is based on the idea that the behaviours of individuals and families is influenced and maintained by the way other individuals and systems interact with them both within and outside of the family. When a member of the family has a problem that is persistent it can often dominate family life and impact significantly on family function, interaction and communication. The aim of family therapy is to help family members recognise and understand how they function as a family and in particular how their patterns of interaction may have become organised around the symptoms or problems of one of their members. Where these patterns of interaction have become unhelpful and perhaps contribute to the maintenances of the problem, the family is helped to develop more functional patterns of organising and interacting within the family.[1]

Family-based treatment for anorexia nervosa – or as it has become popularly known, the Maudsley Approach – integrates ideas and interventions from a number of family therapy approaches, but also has some distinct features. The Maudsley Approach is very explicit in that the eating disorder is not an expression of family dysfunction but is seen as an illness, with the family being the solution to the problem rather than a target of treatment. Problematic patterns of family interaction – which may in some instances pre-date the development of the eating disorder but often will have arisen in response to the worries and pressures of living with a life-threatening illness – are addressed primarily in order to prevent them from interfering with the family's ability to eliminate the eating disordered symptoms and to return their child to a path of normal adolescent development.

One difference between the Maudsley Approach and some other family therapy approaches is that it integrates the medical, nutritional and psychological aspects of treatment. This requires a team approach with a paediatrician working as a consultant to the therapist (whether the therapist is a psychologist, psychiatrist, licensed clinical social worker or other therapist). This is particularly true in the case of children with anorexia nervosa. Eating disorders are life-threatening, so a paediatrician can help to monitor your child's health, provide nutritional information if needed, decide when it is appropriate to return to normal activities (such as gym class and sports teams) and help to determine a healthy body weight.

It is important to understand here that the term 'family' is not merely dictated by biology or law. The family engaging in Maudsley treatment can comprise parents, step-parents, long-term significant others, siblings, grandparents, aunts and uncles. Each week the therapist will want to meet with everyone who lives with the child with the eating disorder.

Also, the therapist might want to meet with people who are involved in caring for and feeding the child, but who do not live with the child with the eating disorder. For instance, if grandparents care for the child after school, or if there are no siblings and support is needed from close friends, it could be important for these people to join a few sessions to learn more about the Maudsley Approach. All caregivers are enlisted to be on 'the same page' with each other in the way the disorder is viewed and treated, and siblings play an important role, as do supportive peers.

Given the several names by which this method is called – Maudsley Approach, family-based treatment, and others – unsurprisingly many families have difficulty knowing whether a particular practitioner is trained in and provides the true Maudsley Approach. A formal credentialling system, established by Professor Daniel Le Grange and Professor James Lock, is facilitating this search (see page 217). Furthermore, here are a few ways to ensure you are receiving true Maudsley treatment:

- First, make sure the practitioner is a licensed mental health professional. This would include clinical psychologists, psychiatrists, licensed social workers, and marriage and family therapists. Be confident in asking about a professional person's credentials and training experiences in the Maudsley Approach. For example, this may comprise training from either Professor Daniel Le Grange or Professor James Lock at a workshop or through training with them at their respective universities. Other practitioners will have taught themselves the treatment through reading the treatment manuals (for example, the very helpful *Treatment Manual for Anorexia Nervosa* by James Lock, Daniel Le Grange, W Stewart Agras and Christopher Dare), which can also be a good source of training for talented therapists.

- Inquire about the practitioner's view of treatment. Professionals who have been trained in the Maudsley Approach will ask that all family members who live with the child or adolescent are present for sessions and will focus on the importance of parents taking charge of their child's eating. Treatment follows three phases with the first phase dedicated to weight restoration (in anorexia nervosa) and the elimination of any binge eating and purging. The therapist will initially focus almost exclusively on eating disorder symptom reduction, rather than discussing why the eating disorder started. Additionally, parents are not assigned any blame for the development or maintenance of the eating disorder.

- The therapist will put parents fully in charge of food choices and weight restoration at first, rather than leaving these decisions to the child. Therapists well trained in the Maudsley Approach will weigh the child at each appointment to determine progress and will share this information openly. The therapist will work with a physician to monitor the physical health of the child or adolescent. Finally, therapists offering true Maudsley treatment will ask that other therapies for the child or adolescent (for instance, an individual therapist or a nutritional counsellor) be discontinued until the family-based treatment has concluded.

- Think carefully if an in-patient or residential program advertises that they provide the Maudsley Approach or family-based treatment. A fundamental principle of the Maudsley Approach is that families can restore their child to health in their own home, providing their child is medically stable. To learn and use this approach in a setting that is not the home is extremely challenging, if not incompatible, with the basic philosophy of the Maudsley Approach. However, you will find that some in-patient or residential programs share a similar philosophy to the Maudsley Approach, where parents are taught to help re-feed their child in a blame-free environment.

- Following discharge from an in-patient or residential program, it is highly recommended that families find a skilled, outpatient therapist to guide them in the Maudsley Approach.

In late 2008, an institute offering accredited training in the treatment of child and adolescent eating disorders was founded in the United States. The Training Institute for the Treatment of Child and Adolescent Eating Disorders is based at Stanford University and the University of Chicago, with James Lock, MD, PhD, and Daniel Le Grange, PhD, as co-directors. The institute's first formal training for accreditation, including that for family-based treatment for adolescent eating disorders, began in early 2009.

For further information, visit www.train2treat4ed.com. The www.maudsleyparents.org website provides supportive information and a listing of family-based treatment providers.[2]

The Australian experience

My Kid is Back is testimony to the willingness of Australia's pioneering health practitioners to adopt the Maudsley Approach, an effective family-based treatment for early intervention of anorexia nervosa in adolescents.

It was through the Children's Hospital at Westmead, Sydney, and a private outpatient eating disorder clinic, The Oak House, in Melbourne, that I sourced the families whose stories appear in this book. Westmead began adopting the Maudsley Approach in 2002 and The Oak House in 2004. In both cases, introducing family-based treatment into a situation where an eating disorder service is already established has been shown to produce encouraging results.

The treatment has provided an ongoing injection of hope to families with a child suffering anorexia nervosa. The strength of the evidence base and the integration of family therapy theory have made the treatment particularly appealing to both medical and allied health professionals who work together with the patients or clients.

Paul Rhodes was a clinical psychologist with the Eating Disorder Service at the Children's Hospital, Westmead, when he heard a talk about the Maudsley Approach in 2001 and became interested in learning more about it.

My Kid is Back collaborator Professor Daniel Le Grange, together with Professor James Lock and W Stewart Agras from the United States and Christopher Dare from the United Kingdom, had written a manual for a family-based treatment of anorexia nervosa in adolescents, *Treatment Manual for Anorexia Nervosa*, which made learning about the treatment widely available to interested clinicians.

The evidence base for family-based treatment effectiveness was a key factor in deciding that the approach was worth trying. Another important factor was that the approach was family-based and would be a good fit for both the family therapists and doctors. Paul gathered three like-minded clinicians together (Andrew Wallis, Andrea Worth and Tahn Le) and, with child and adolescent psychiatrist Dr Sloane Madden and paediatrician Dr Michael Kohn, discussed how the treatment could be introduced at the Children's Hospital.

Prior to the implementation of family-based treatment in January 2003, a range of different individual and family therapy models, including medical and psychiatric management, were used for both in-patients and outpatients in the Eating Disorder Program. These traditional models were successful in terms of medical stability and weight gain in the hospital setting, but many of these gains were not maintained for a significant number of patients on discharge. Likewise, while a number of outpatients did well, a significant number of patients were returning to hospital for multiple admissions.

The Eating Disorders Family-based Treatment team was formed in September 2002 in an attempt to break the cycle of readmissions by implementing the Maudsley Approach of family-based treatment for anorexia nervosa. Training took place in two stages. First, the team members who were experienced family therapists learnt together from the treatment manual, experimenting with the approach on a small number of families. Next, Professor James Lock and Professor Daniel Le Grange travelled to Sydney to present a training workshop on the Maudsley Approach of family-based treatment.

The change in treatment was challenging in that it required the health practitioners to adopt a shift in their own beliefs and views of families. This meant seeing the family as the essential resource in the child's recovery despite the family interaction difficulties the team experienced or perceived. The team soon came to learn that many of the difficulties families seemed to have were a consequence of trying to manage the anorexia nervosa and the stress this entailed, rather than the cause of the child's illness.

It also meant that if they were asking the family to be a united front against the anorexia, and to be in agreement to get their child well, the team needed to do the same. Current team leader of the family-based treatment team at the Children's Hospital, Andrew Wallis, said:

> We worked very hard on enhancing communication between team members and ensuring that everyone could participate in decision making.
>
> The essential starting point for the successful implementation of family-based treatment is the team's own communication and values. Without these systemic prerequisites it will not be easy to implement the model. The medical and psychiatric care provided by the medical part of the team is as crucial as the family therapists' input if the model is to be implemented successfully, given the life-threatening nature of the illness.
>
> Since the implementation of family-based treatment we have seen the majority of young people in our care get well through the therapy. Readmission rates have almost halved since 2001–02[3] and the group of patients having multiple admissions has become significantly smaller. It has been an incredibly exciting time that has been professionally and personally satisfying for the team, and we have learnt a lot from the families we have worked with during the past five years.

Since the early days of implementing the model, the Children's Hospital team has provided workshops, consultation, training and clinical supervision to teams from across Australia, from Cairns in North Queensland to Launceston in Tasmania, training hundreds of health practitioners to implement the Maudsley Approach of family-based treatment consistent with the manual published in 2001. This has allowed the treatment to become more prominent in Australia, and a number of teams and services are now using the approach.

Among these is The Oak House, based in Surrey Hills, Melbourne. This specialist outpatient facility provides recovery programs in a supportive home-like setting for sufferers of eating disorders. When founder and director Belinda Dalton learnt about the Maudsley Approach in 2004, she was so impressed she arranged for the family-based treatment team from Westmead to travel to Melbourne to hold a three-day intensive training workshop for her entire multi-disciplinary team. Following the initial training a commitment was made to regular supervision, initially provided by members of the Children's Hospital, Westmead, family-based treatment team, and then within The Oak House, headed by family therapist Vicki O'Dwyer. Many clients attend The Oak House from regional Victoria, other states of Australia and overseas.

Like Andrew, Belinda emphasised that just as a family needs to be united in the fight against anorexia nervosa, so, too, does the therapy team:

At The Oak House we apply ongoing peer support and supervision that allows us to protect and maintain the integrity of the treatment and to work most effectively with each family. It is truly a united team approach – just like Maudsley is with the parents, so it is with the treatment team. To aid success, we regularly participate in role-play situations and case presentations behind the scenes in team meetings. The team members' enthusiasm for supporting, guiding and encouraging each other and embracing this model has been crucial in the successful adoption of the Maudsley Approach.

Practitioners learning the intricacies of the model work as co-therapists as part of their training at The Oak House. This enables staff to support each other in their work with the approach, to learn from each other and to form a reflecting team for the family. Practitioners find the skills they develop in implementing the treatment transfer well to their work in engaging families of adult clients.

The Oak House staff work collaboratively with paediatric and psychiatric colleagues, some who are unaware of (or have not trained in implementing) family-based treatment. This means that educating practitioners unfamiliar with the Maudsley Approach principles is a challenge, and The Oak House staff appreciates the support of like-minded practitioners at, for example, the Centre for Adolescent Health at the Royal Children's Hospital in Melbourne.

The British experience

Dr Ivan Eisler provides the following explanation of family-based treatment in the United Kingdom, and suggestions for accessing this treatment.

While this book was being written, June emailed me for help, as she was puzzled by the mystery of a lack of 'Maudsley treatment centres' in the United Kingdom. There are several reasons for this. First, few clinicians here use the term Maudsley Approach. This is mainly because, unlike for instance in North America, the tradition among clinicians in the United Kingdom tends to be to define treatments quite broadly and the 'Maudsley Approach' would be seen as a specialist form of family therapy rather than a different kind of treatment. In North America, treatments are often defined in a more narrow way and given a label or brand name. This has the advantage of making treatments more amenable to systematic research evaluation, but has the disadvantage that often quite similar approaches are being promoted as quite distinct when in reality there is often a considerable overlap between supposedly different treatments. In the absence of a more narrowly defined (and labelled) treatment, the client or family seeking help may have to work harder to find out what is being offered as they will need to ask more detailed questions about the main principles underpinning what different treatment centres do, rather than rely on what they call their treatment.

Second, the way services are organised in the United Kingdom means that most people who seek treatment (including for eating disorders) use the National Health Service. There are still relatively few specialist services for children and adolescents with an eating disorder here: they are often in the private sector and are nearly exclusively residential. While many of them will work with families, the points made earlier in this chapter about the difficulty of combining a residential treatment philosophy with empowering families to help their child applies in the United Kingdom as much as in any other country. There are also, of course, many private therapists who, like everywhere else, can be good, indifferent or bad, but on the whole I tend to advise people not to use them for anorexia nervosa because I believe that you get better treatment from a service with a multi-disciplinary team.

The usual route to treatment for adolescent anorexia nervosa in the UK is via the family doctor to the local Child and Adolescent Mental Health Service (CAMHS). Many of these will be good and they will nearly always have family therapy expertise. The downside is that they may often have fairly limited or at best moderate expertise in eating disorders as a typical CAMHS service (covering a population of around 250 000) will probably have no more than four to six eating disorder referrals a year. Many adolescents will do well with the help they get in CAMHS, but 35 per cent or more will not and will end up being referred for in-patient treatment. A growing number of CAMHS services are trying to develop mini-specialist eating disorder clinics, and a growing number of areas are recognising it is better to have larger specialist outpatient eating disorder services (covering a population of one million or more). The specialist out-patient services, mini or large, are what I would encourage people to look for as these days they will nearly always use a family-based approach and will generally refer to in-patient treatment in less than 10 per cent of cases. Many of them are also including other ways of working with families such as parent support groups or multi-family workshops which can be very helpful. Many services are setting up multi-family group programmes, an approach that we have been developing and researching at the Maudsley Hospital over the past ten years. These programmes provide an opportunity for a group of families to come together for an intensive workshop usually over four days where they can provide support and learn from each other as well as getting expert input from the clinicians running the workshop. While the evaluation of the effectiveness of this treatment is not complete, the several hundred families that have taken part in these programmes have been extremely positive about their experiences. I am unaware of any comprehensive listing of specialist outpatient services for child and adolescent eating disorders across the United Kingdom; however, the good news is that these are growing in number. It is important that parents get as much information as possible about what help is available to them, and that they ask informed questions. As a guide, answers to the following questions will be useful when seeking help for your child:

- What eating disorder expertise is available in my local CAMHS?
- Does the treatment in CAMHS encourage an active involvement of the family as partners in the treatment process?
- What medical expertise does the team have to ensure that outpatient treatment can be carried out safely and unnecessary admissions to hospital can be avoided? (This is a tricky question to ask because sometimes a hospital admission is necessary and parents have to be able to feel confident that the medical risk is being assessed in the best possible interest of their child. However, the ability to have an open and frank conversation about difficult issues is part of what you should expect from a good clinical team.)
- Is there a specialist eating disorder service my child can be referred to for outpatient treatment?
- If there is such a service (locally or regionally), is it

worth trying to get referred directly? Sometimes, this may require an assessment by the local CAMHS, but parents should not accept too readily any protracted wait before treatment is available.

The same kind of questions suggested above concerning CAMHS can be asked about any specialist service.

If specialist treatment is not available as a first step it is probably sensible to make use of what is offered by local CAMHS, but parents should be prepared to make a strong case that they want to be actively involved in the treatment of their child.

Parents should read guidelines published by the National Institute for Health and Clinical Excellence (NICE) as they recommend family-oriented treatment for adolescent anorexia nervosa. Getting advice from beat (see below) is also often a useful step.

- For information on the National Institute for Health and Clinical Excellence (NICE) website go to www.nice.org.uk.
- The working name of the Eating Disorders Association is beat. Eating disorders are a serious mental illness affecting 1.1 million people in the United Kingdom. Both young people and adults affected by eating disorders and, in particular, anorexia and bulimia nervosa, turn to beat's website. This site lists a country-wide network of self-help groups, where participants support each other by sharing experiences, thoughts, successes and problems. For details visit www.b-eat.co.uk.

Appendix

Listing of providers and support services

Families and sufferers may find Dr Eisler's suggestions, in the United Kingdom section of the previous chapter, very helpful when taking the first step in seeking assistance. Dr Eisler's guidance for parents and carers on what questions to ask when seeking information and treatment for a child is relevant for families everywhere.

Jane Cawley, a co-founder of Maudsley Parents, reiterates the importance of thorough preparation when making the initial approach. Jane suggests that parents and carers consider the provider listing as a guide only, and says, 'Parents will get the best result by being well informed and being prepared to ask a lot of questions. It is important to be clear about what you want when arranging treatment'.

The number of family-based treatment/Maudsley Approach providers is growing all the time; the listing in this Appendix is current as of December 2009 and details are provided on where to seek updates.

Note: (Cert.) denotes graduates in Family-Based Treatment (FBT) from the Training Institute for Child and Adolescent Eating Disorders founded by Prof. Daniel Le Grange and Dr James Lock. Certification = completion of three steps set by the Institute: (1) two-day workshop (2) 25 hours of post-workshop supervision by Institute faculty, and (3) advanced workshop. Website: train2treat4ed.com

United Kingdom

For information on the National Institute for Health and Clinical Excellence (NICE) website visit www.nice.org.uk. beat provides helplines for adults and young people, online support and a UK-wide network of self-help groups. For details visit www.b-eat.co.uk/

Europe

Germany

Roslyn Binford Hopf, PhD, LP (Cert.)
Im Haderheck 40a
61462 Koenigstein im Taunus (near Frankfurt)
Phone: +49 (0) 61 742556140
Email: roslyn.hopf@t-online.de

North America

Canada

Ontario

D Blake Woodside MD FRCPC (Cert.)
Medical Director, Program for Eating Disorders,
8EN-219, Toronto General Hospital,
200 Elizabeth St., Toronto, Ontario M5G 2C4

Gina Dimitropoulos, PhD, RSW (Cert.)
Clinical Social Worker and Researcher
Eating Disorder Program
Toronto General Hospital
Phone: (416) 340-3749
Email: gina.dimitropoulos@uhn.on.ca

Ester Wagner
Registered Psychologist
Ste 419, 45 Sheppard Ave East, Toronto, Ontario M2N 5W9
Phone: (416) 229-1477, Ext. 234

McMaster Children's Hospital
Pediatric Eating Disorders Program
1200 Main St. West, Hamilton, Ontario L8N325
Phone: (905) 521-2100, Ext. 73497
Website: http://www.mcmasterchildrenshospital.ca

North York General Hospital
4001 Leslie St., Toronto, Ontario M2K 1E1
Phone: (416) 756-6000
Website: www.nygh.on.ca

Sherry Van Blyderveen, C. Psych.
Halton Psychological Services
14A Martin Street, Milton, Ontario L9T 2P9
Phone: (905) 878-6650
Fax: (905) 905-878-2205
Website: www.haltonpsychologists.ca

The Hospital for Sick Children
555 University Ave, Toronto, Ontario M5G 1X8
Phone: (416) 813-1500
Website: www.sickkids.ca

Lindsay Ross MSW RSW (Cert.)
Social Worker (The HSC)
Phone: (416) 813-5598
Email: lindsay.ross@sickkids.ca

United States

California

Alexia Anderson, DO
Child, Adolescent and Adult Psychiatry
Ste 185, 21 Tamal Vista Blvd, Corte Madera, CA 94925
Phone: (415) 734-8727

James Lock, MD, PhD
Director
Stanford Child and Adolescent Eating Disorder Program

Division of Child Psychiatry
Dept Psychiatry and Behavioral Sciences Stanford
    University

Athena Robinson, PhD (Cert.)
Instructor, School of Medicine
401 Quarry Rd, Stanford, CA 94305-5722
Phone: (650) 736.0943
Email: athenar@stanford.edu

Kara Fitzpatrick (Cert.)
Comprehensive Eating Disorders Program
Lucile Packard Children's Hospital
Stanford University Medical Center
725 Welch Rd, Palo Alto, CA 94304
Phone: (650) 498-4468
Website: http://www.lpch.org/clinicalSpecialtiesServices/
    ClinicalSpecialties/EatingDisorders/eatingDisorders
    Index.html

Haleh Kashani, PhD
Ste 120, 350 Bon Air Rd, Greenbrae, CA 94904
Phone: (415) 898-9839
Email: haleh@kashaniphd.com

Jill Rodgers-Quaye, PhD
Bay Area Eating Disorder Associates
4281 Piedmont Ave, Oakland, CA 94611
Phone: (510) 282-2197
Email: jill.rodgers.quaye@ sbcglobal.net
Website: www.drjillrodgersquaye. com

Joy Jacobs, J.D., PhD
Ste 157, 11772 Sorrento Valley Rd, San Diego, CA 92121
Phone: (858) 922-4383
Email: joy@drjoyjacobs.com
Website: http://drjoyjacobs.com

Sari Shepphird, PhD
Ste 100, 2550 Overland Ave, West Los Angeles, Ca. 90064

Phone: (310) 826-4300
Website: www.drshepp.com

Starr Kelton-Locke, PhD
Ste 120, 1030 Sir Francis Drake, Kentfield, CA 94904
Phone: (415) 453-2782
Email: starr@keltonlocke.com

Taya Cromley, Ph.D. (Cert.)
Post Doctoral Scholar
University of California, Los Angeles
Email: tcromley@ucla.edu

University of California San Diego
Medical Center Eating Disorder Treatment Center
Ste C-207, 8950 Villa La Jolla Dr., La Jolla, CA 92037
Phone: (858) 228-7023
Website: http://eatingdisorders.ucsd.edu

Kerri Boutelle, Ph.D., L.P. (Cert.)
Associate Professor of Pediatrics and Psychiatry, UCSD
Ste B-122, 8950 Villa La Jolla Dr.
Phone: (858) 966-8904: direct: (858) 534-8037
Email: kboutelle@ucsd.edu
Website: www.obesitytreatment.ucsd.edu

Vandana Aspen, M.A. (Cert.)
Dept of Psychiatry, UCSD
Ste C-207, 8950 Villa La Jolla Dr.
Phone: (858) 534-8053

Florida

Sarah Ravin, PhD
1550 Madruga Ave Suite #414, Coral Gables, FL 33146
Phone: (305) 668-5755
Website: drsarahravin.com

The Boswell Center for Life Enrichment
Ste 904, 6817 Southpoint Parkway, Jacksonville, FL 32216
Phone: (904) 332-9100
Website: www.boswellcenter.com

Illinois

Daniel Le Grange, PhD
Director, Eating Disorders Program
Department of Psychiatry
The University of Chicago
5841 S. Maryland Ave, Chicago, IL 60637
Phone: (773) 702-0789
Email: edclinic@yoda.bsd.uchicago.edu
Website: www.eatingdisorders.uchicago.edu

Angela Celio Doyle, PhD (Cert.)
Department of Psychiatry
The University of Chicago
5841 S. Maryland Ave, Chicago, IL 60637
Phone: (773) 834-4114
Email: acelio@yoda.bsd.uchicago.edu

Renee Rienecke Hoste, Ph.D. (Cert.)
Department of Psychiatry
The University of Chicago
5841 S. Maryland Ave, Chicago, IL 60637
Phone: (773) 702-9683
Email: rhoste@yoda.bsd.uchicago.edu

Linda K. Castor, RN, LCPC
Clocktower Therapy Center
2663 Farragut Drive, Springfield, IL 62704
Phone: (217) 793-0680

Kansas

Susan Cowden, MS, LMFT
Renew Eating Disorder Recovery
Ste B, 11695 S. Black Bob Rd, Olathe, KS 66062
Phone: (913) 768-6606, Ext. 319
Email: scowden@renewkc.com

Maryland

Ann Jacob Smith, Ph.D., LCPC, NCC
5480 Wisconsin Ave, Suite 204, Chevy Chase, MD 20815
Phone: (240) 753-3775

Center for Eating Disorders
Sheppard Pratt Health System
Ste 300, Physicians Pavilion North, 6535 North Charles St.,
    Baltimore, MD 21204
Phone: (410) 938-5252
Website: www.eatingdisorder.org

Dina Wientge, LCSW-C (Cert.)
Senior Social Worker
C for ED (SPHS)
6501 North Charles St., Towson, Maryland 21204
Phone: (410) 938-5455
Email: dwientge@sheppardpratt.org

Jennifer Moran, Psy.D. (Cert.)
Licensed Psychologist
C for ED (SPHS)
6501 North Charles Street, PPN I Ste 300, Towson, MD 21204
Phone: (410) 938-5252
Email: Jmoran14@jhu.edu

Laura K. Ratner, LCSW-C, BCD
Ste 230, 4701 Willard Ave, Chevy Chase, MD 20815
Phone: (301) 652-0695
Email: LKRatner@aol.com

Washington Center for Eating
Disorders and Adolescent Obesity
Ste 410, 6410 Rockledge Drv, Bethesda, MD 20817
Phone: (301) 530-0676
Website: www.washingtoncenteronline.com

Massachusetts

Catherine Steiner-Adair, EdD
Clinical Psychologist
25 Wachusett Rd, Chestnut Hill, MA 02467,
Phone: (617) 332-2001
Email: csadair@comcast.net

Michigan

Stephanie B Milstein, PhD
Dennis & Moye & Associates, PC
Ste 101, 1750 S. Telegraph Rd, Bloomfield Hills, MI 48302
Phone: (248) 451-9085
Email: Samsi77@aol.com

Rhonda Overberger, LPC, LMFT
Center for Counseling and Wellness
605 Howard St., Kalamazoo, MI 49008
Phone: (269) 341-9629; mobile: (269) 207-7549
Email: overbergerr@yahoo.com

Minnesota

Diann M Ackard, PhD, LP, FAED
Licensed Psychologist, Private Practice
Fellow, Academy for Eating Disorders Adjunct Assistant
    Professor,
University of Minnesota Division of Epidemiology and
    Community Health
Research Scientist, Eating Disorders Institute
Ste 4001, 5101 Olson Memorial Hwy, Golden Valley, MN
    55422
Phone: (763) 595-7294, Ext. 111
Website: www.diannackard.com

The Emily Program
Ste 314 N, 2550 University Ave W., St Paul, MN 55114
Ste 250, 1660 S. Hwy 100, St Louis Park, MN 55416
Ste 202, 200 E. Chestnut St., Stillwater, MN 55082
Phone: (651) 645-5323

Kathleen Jacobson, PhD, LP
Ste 4003, 5101 Olson Memorial Hwy, Golden Valley,
    MN 55422
Phone: (763) 595-7294, Ext. 112
Email: kajphd@mail.com

Kathryn Miller, PhD
Licensed Psychologist
Ste 4004, 5101 Olson Memorial Hwy, Golden Valley,
    MN 55422
Phone: (763) 595-7294, Ext. 114

STAR Center
University of Minnesota
Department of Pediatrics
Ste 160, 200 Oak St SE, Minneapolis, MN 55455
Phone: (612) 626-4260

Missouri

Dorothy J. Van Buren, Ph.D.
Assistant Research Professor, Department of Psychiatry
Washington University School of Medicine, Campus Box
    8134, 660 S. Euclid, St Louis, MO 63110
Phone: (314) 286-2097 (office phone)
Email: vanbured@psychiatry.wustl.edu

Eating Disorder Recovery Center
Director: Deborah J Kuehnel, LCSW
Ste 694, 1034 S. Brentwood Blvd, St Louis, MO 63117
Phone: (866) 706-7111
Email: dk@addictions.net
Website: www.addictions.net

New Mexico

Deborah Okon, PhD
315-C West Reinken Ave, Belen, NM 87002
Phone: (505) 861-3894
Email: dmokon@highstream.net

New York

Dara Bellace, PhD
Eating Disorders Program
Weill Cornell Medical College
New York-Presbyterian Hospital
21 Bloomingdale Rd, White Plains, NY 10605
Phone: (914) 997-5974

Katherine Halmi, MD
Weill Medical College of Cornell University
21 Bloomingdale Rd, White Plains, NY 10605
Contact: Samantha Berthod, MA
Phone: (914) 997-4395
Email: sab2024@med.cornell.edu

Cris Haltom, PhD
Licensed Psychologist
215 N. Geneva St., Ithaca, NY 14850
Phone: (607) 272-6750
Website: www.EDsurvivalguide.com

Jennifer Jones, PhD (Cert.)
31 West 9th St, 1st Floor, New York, NY 10011
Phone: (212) 604-4643

Mount Sinai Eating and Weight Disorders Program
One Gustave L. Levy Place, Box 1230, New York,
    NY 10029
Phone: (212) 659-8724
Website: www.mountsinai.org/eatingdisorders

Katharine L. Loeb, Ph.D. (Cert.)
Fairleigh Dickinson University and Mount Sinai EWDP
Phone: (212) 659-8727
Email: katharine.loeb@mssm.edu

Unity Health System
Eating Disorders Partial
Hospitalization Program
Intake Coordinator: Erica Thomas
89 Genesee St., Rochester, NY 14611

Phone: (585) 368-3709
Email: ethomas@unityhealth.org

North Carolina

Heidi M Limbrunner, PsyD
Southeast Psychological Services
6115 Park South Drv, Charlotte, NC 28210
Phone: (704) 552-0116
Website: www.southeastpsych.com

Nancy Zucker, PhD, Director
Duke Eating Disorders Program
Duke University Medical Center
PO Box 3842, Durham, NC 27710
Phone: (919) 668-2281
Website: http://eatingdisorders.mc.duke.edu

Ohio

Center for Balanced Living
Laura Hill, PhD, CEO/CCO, FAED
445 E. Granville Rd, Bldg N, Worthington, OH 43085
Phone: (614) 293-9550
Website: www.centerforeatingdisorders.org

Ellen S Rome, MD, MPH
Laura Gillespie, MD
Children's Hospital
Cleveland Clinic
Desk A120, 9500 Euclid Ave, Cleveland, OH 44195
Phone: (216) 444-3566
Website: cms.clevelandclinic.org/childrenshospital

Lucene Wisniewski, PhD, FAED,
Clinical Director
Cleveland Center for Eating Disorders
25550 Chagrin Blvd, Ste 200, Chagrin Richmond Plaza,
    Cleveland, OH 44122
Phone: (216) 765-0500
Website: http://www.eatingdisorders cleveland.org/

Oklahoma

Nichole Wood-Barcalow, PhD (Cert.)
Licensed Psychologist
Clinical Supervisor for the Adolescent Eating Disorders
   Program
Laureate Psychiatric Clinic & Hospital
6655 S. Yale Ave, Tulsa, OK 74136
Phone: (918) 491-5940
Email: nlbarcalow@saintfrancis. com
Website: www.laureate.com

Pennsylvania

Jill Cohen MSW, LCSW, BCD
Hamilton & Miraglia Associates
105 Sibley Ave, Ardmore, PA 19003
Phone: (215) 681-6363

Rachel Millner, PsyD
Ste 402B, 301 Oxford Valley Rd, Yardley, PA 19067
Phone: (215) 321-1920
Email: rachel@rachelmillner.com

South Carolina

Timothy D Brewerton, MD, DFAPA, FAED
Clinical Professor of Psychiatry & Behavioral Sciences
Medical University of South Carolina
216 Scott St., Mt Pleasant, SC 29464
Phone: (843) 509-0694
Email: tbrewerton1@comcast.net
Website: www.drtimothybrewerton.yourmd.com

Texas

Allison K. Chase, PhD
Clinical Psychologist Department of Psychology
University of Texas, Austin
Ste 295, Capital of Texas Hwy, Bldg, Austin, TX 78746
Phone: (512) 347-9992

Karyn D Hall, PhD
Dialectical Behavior Therapy Center
Ste 750, 820 Gessner Rd, Houston, TX 77024
Phone: (713) 973-2800
Website: www.karynhallphd.com

Stacie McKenna-Crochet
Ste U-4, 13740 Research Blvd, Austin, TX 78750
Phone: (512) 921-5925
Website: www.staciecrochet.com

Theresa Fassihi, PhD, PLLC
3730 Kirby Drive, Suite 925, Houston, TX 77098
Phone: (832) 794-1280
Email: terryfassihi@earthlink.net

Utah

Mary K Hales, PhD
Clinical Neuropsychologist
Neurodynamics, LLC
Ste L1, 1060 E. 100 S., Salt Lake City, UT 84102
Phone: (801) 359-6069

Virginia

Carolyn Reed Hersh, MA, LPC
Ste 206, 117 W. 21 St., Norfolk, VA 23517
Phone: (757) 404-3010
Email: crhmail@verizon.net

Washington DC

Donald Delaney Eating Disorders Program
Children's Outpatient Center in Spring Valley
Director: Darlene Atkins, PhD
4900 Massachusetts Ave, NW, Washington, DC 20016
Phone: (202) 884-3066

Washington State

Karen Pavlidis
2910E Madison St., Seattle, WA 98112
Phone: (206) 729-2829

Wisconsin

Nancy A Cannon, PsyD, LLC
Private Practice
Ste 180, 11520 N. Port Washington Rd, Mequon, WI 53092
Phone: (414) 803-9967
Email: ncannon2@wi.rr.com

Susan Neff, RN
Mental Health Resources
Ste 290, 402 Gammon Pl, Madison, WI 53719
Email: sneff@tds.net

Stacey Nye, PhD, FAED
Ste 203, 10303 N. Port Washington Rd, Mequon, WI 53092
Phone: (262) 241-5955, Ext. 210
Website: www.nodietdoc.com

For provider updates go to: train2treat4ed.com
Guidance is also available through support organizations including: National Eating Disorders Association (NEDA: www.nationaleatingdisorders.org); National Association of Anorexia Nervosa and Associated Disorders (ANAD: www.anad.org); Families Empowered and Support Treatment of Eating Disorders (FEAST: www.feast-ed.org) and Maudsley Parents (www.maudsleyparents.org).

(Maudsley Parents has provided the listing for Canada and the US in this Appendix).

Asia/Pacific

Australia

New South Wales

Central Coast Eating Disorders Service
Wyong Central Community Health Centre
Co-ordinator: Judith Leahy
38a Pacific Hwy, Wyong, NSW 2259
Phone: (02) 4356 9418
Email: jleahy@nsccahs.health.nsw.gov.au

Eating Disorders Family-based Treatment Team
Children's Hospital at Westmead
Locked Bag 4001, Westmead, NSW 2145
Phone: (02) 9845 2005
Email: andreww7@chw.edu.au

Newcastle Child and Adolescent
Mental Health Service
621 Hunter St., Newcastle, NSW 2300
Phone: (02) 4925 7800

Sydney Children's Hospital, Randwick
High St., Randwick, NSW 2031
Phone: (02) 9382 1111
Website: www.sch.edu.au/health

Queensland

Child and Youth Mental Health Service
130 McLeod St., Cairns
Postal: PO Box 268N
North Cairns, QLD 4870
Phone: (07) 4015 0600
Email: CairnsCYMHSIntake@ health.qld.gov.au

Eating Disorders Program
Child and Youth Mental Health Service
Gold Coast Health Service District

Ste 11, Riverwalk Place, 238 Robina Town Centre Drive,
    Robina, QLD 4226
Phone: (07) 5667 1700

Eating Disorders Team (Maudsley)
Child and Youth Mental Health Services
Royal Children's Hospital Children's Health Service
    District
Contact: Co-ordinator Specialist Intervention Teams, or
    Director
Eating Disorders Team
PO Box 1507, Fortitude Valley, QLD 4006
Phone: (07) 3310 9444

Victoria

Oak House
PO Box 210, Surrey Hills, VIC 3127
Phone: (03) 9888 4737
Website: www.theoakhouse.com.au

Royal Children's Hospital Eating Disorders Program
Centre for Adolescent Health
William Buckland House
2 Gatehouse St., Parkville, VIC 3052
Phone: (03) 9345 5890
Website: www.rch.org.au/cah

Southern Health Psychiatric Triage Service
Melbourne
Phone: 1300 369 012

Child and Adolescent Mental Health Services (CAMHS)
For local CAMHS triage details go to:
http://www.health.vic.gov.au/mentalhealth/services/child/

For updates, contact your state-based eating disorder association:

New South Wales

The Butterfly Foundation
Phone: (02) 9412 4499
Email:info@thebutterflyfoundation.org.au
Website: www.thebutterflyfoundation.org.au

Queensland

Eating Disorders Association
Phone: (07) 3891 3660
Email: eda.inc@uq.net.au
Website: www.eda.org.au

Victoria

Eating Disorders Foundation of Victoria
Phone: (03) 9885 0318
Email: edfv@eatingdisorders.org.au
Website: www.eatingdisorders.org.au

South Australia

Eating Disorder Association of South Australia
Phone: (08) 8332 3466
Email: information@edasa.org.au
Website: www.edasa.org.au

Western Australia

Eating Disorders Association of Western Australia
Phone: (08) 9221 0488

Eating Disorders Alliance
Phone: (08) 9444 5922
Website: www.wchm.org.au

ACT

Women's Centre For Health Matters
Phone: (02) 6290 2166
Website: www.wchm.org.au

Tasmania

Community Nutrition Unit
Phone: (03) 6222 7222
Email: tas.eatingdisorders@dhhs.tas.gov.au
Website: www.tas.eatingdisorders.org.au

National links to support services for families and sufferers of eating disorders and for people working in and studying the field of eating disorders are provided on the NSW Centre for Eating and Dieting Disorders (CEDD) website: www.cedd.org.au

CEDD also provides a listing of eating disorder clinical support services across Australia. An example is the Victorian Centre of Excellence in Eating Disorders (CEED), which offers professional resources, training and education: www.rch.org.au/ceed

Assistance for families and sufferers is available through The Butterfly Foundation website: www.thebutterflyfoundation.org.au

New Zealand

The Eating Disorder Association of New Zealand (EDANZ) offers support and information for parents and caregivers:

Eating Disorder Association of New Zealand
PO Box 37-943, Parnell, Auckland
Phone: (03) 522 2679
Email: info@ed.org.nz
Website: www.ed.org.nz

To contact June Alexander, author of this book, go to www.junealexander.com or email june@junealexander.com.

Notes

Acknowledgements

1 Claire Vickery established The Butterfly Foundation in 2002 after she found many 'gaps' in the Australian public health system for those suffering from eating disorders and negative body image. Butterfly is a non-government, community-based charitable organisation that has been a significant agent for change in the field of eating disorders. Accomplishments include the establishment of the first publicly funded day treatment centre for adolescents with eating disorders in Australia, and the establishment of the first National Research Institute for Eating Disorders. Core services for Butterfly include direct financial relief to individuals, enhancement of treatment services, delivery of body image and media literacy education in schools, and health promotion. In 2009 Butterfly is expanding its services to include phone and internet counselling nationally. Visit www.thebutterflyfoundation.org.au.

2 Maudsley Parents was created in 2006 by parents in the United States who helped their children recover with family-based treatment, to offer hope and help to other families confronting eating disorders. The website includes information on eating disorders and family-based treatment, family stories of recovery, parent-to-parent advice, videos on both anorexia nervosa and bulimia nervosa, and a treatment provider listing. For details visit www.maudsleyparents.org.

Introduction

1 This externalisation technique is also used in the Maudsley family-based treatment to empower acceptance of self and focus efforts on disempowering the eating disorder.

1 Family-based treatment of adolescent anorexia nervosa: The Maudsley Approach

1 Hoek and van Hoeken, 2003, pp. 383–96; Woodside et al., 2001, pp. 570–4.
2 American Psychiatric Association, 1994.
3 Katzman, 2003, pp. 11–15; Kreipe et al., 1994, pp. 159–65; Winston and Stafford, 2000, pp. 117–25.
4 Zipfel, Lowe and Herzog, in Treasure and Schmidt, 2003, pp. 191–206.
5 Katzman et al., 2001, pp. 146–52.
6 Flament et al., 2001, pp. 99–106; Rorty et al., 1999, pp. 1–12.
7 Beumont, 2002, p. 141.
8 Grilo et al., 1996, pp. 754–7; Wonderlich and Mitchell, 1997, pp. 381–90.
9 Steinhausen et al., 2003, pp. 91–8.
10 Ratnasuriya et al., 1991, pp. 495–502; Sullivan, 1995, pp. 1073–4.
11 Minuchin et al., 1975, pp. 1031–8; Minuchin, Rosman and Baker, 1978.
12 ibid.
13 See Loeb et al., 2005; Loeb et al., 2006; Geist et al., 2000, pp. 173–8; Dare, 1983, pp. 28–37; Herscovici and Bay, 1996, pp. 59–66; Le Grange and Gelman, 1988, pp. 182–6; Martin, 1984, pp. 509–14; Mayer, 1994; Rhodes and Madden, 2005, ch. 27(2), pp. 171–82; Stierlin and Weber, 1988, pp. 120–57; Stierlin and Weber, 1989; Wallin and Kronwall, 2002, pp. 363–9.
14 Hoek and van Hoeken, 2003, pp. 383–96; Woodside et al., 2001, pp. 570–4.
15 Russell et al., 1987, pp. 1047–56; Dare et al., 1990, pp. 39–57.
16 Eisler et al., 1997, pp. 1025–30.
17 Eisler et al., 2000, pp. 727–36; Le Grange et al., 1992a, pp. 347–57.
18 Le Grange et al., 1992a, pp. 347–57.
19 Eisler et al., 2000, pp. 727–36.
20 ibid.
21 Lock, Le Grange, Agras and Dare, 2001.
22 Lock, Agras, Bryson and Helena, 2005, pp. 632–9.
23 Lock and Le Grange, 2001, pp. 253–61.
24 Lock, Agras, Bryson and Helena, 2005, pp. 632–9.
25 Le Grange, Binford and Loeb, 2005, pp. 41–6.
26 Loeb et al., 2007, pp. 792–800.
27 Lock, Le Grange, Fordsburg and Hewell, 2006, pp. 1323–8.
28 Eisler et al., 1997, pp. 1025–30; Eisler, Simic, Russell and Dare, 2007, pp. 552–60; Lock, Couturier, Agras and Bryson, 2006, pp. 666–72.
29 Robin et al., 1994, pp. 111–16; Robin et al., 1999, pp. 1482–9.

30 Dare and Eisler, 2000, pp. 4–18; Scholz and Asen, 2001, pp. 33–42.
31 Dare and Eisler, 2000, pp. 4–18.
32 Scholz and Asen, 2001, pp. 33–42.
33 Dare and Eisler, 2000, pp. 4–18; Scholz and Asen, 2001, pp. 33–42.
34 Scholz and Asen, 2001, pp. 33–42; Lim, 2000.
35 Le Grange and Lock, 2007.
36 Le Grange, Crosby, Rathouz and Leventhal, 2007, pp. 1049–56.
37 Le Grange and Lock, 2007.
38 Loeb et al., 2005.
39 Loeb et al., 2006.
40 Eisler et al., 1997, pp. 1025–30; Eisler, Simic, Russell and Dare, 2007, pp. 552–60; Lock, Couturier, Agras and Bryson, 2006, pp. 666–72.
41 Eisler et al., 2000, pp. 727–36; Le Grange et al., 1992a, pp. 347–57.
42 Le Grange et al., 1992b, pp. 177–92; Szmukler et al., 1985, pp. 265–71.
43 Squire-Dehouck, 1993.
44 Lock, Le Grange, Agras and Dare, 2001; Lock and Le Grange, 2001, pp. 253–61.
45 Lock, Le Grange, Agras and Dare, 2001.
46 Le Grange and Lock, 2007.
47 Lock, Agras, Bryson and Helena, 2005, pp. 632–9.
48 James Lock and Daniel Le Grange, *Help Your Teenager Beat an Eating Disorder*, Guilford, New York, 2004. This book introduces parents to and guides them through the Maudsley Approach. It helps parents understand why they need to act now, and explains what research says about which treatments work. The authors offer guidance in taking charge of changes in eating habits and exercise and in presenting a united family front to prevent relapse.

2 Chloe

1 What the therapist says: It is common for young people with anorexia to feel afraid of making their own decisions and to rely on anorexia's rigid, demanding rules for comfort. No matter what decision the young person tries to make around eating or food, anorexia judges this as being 'wrong' or 'bad', leaving the young person's confidence in tatters, and heavily relying on anorexia's harsh 'all-or-nothing' style of rules to feel comfortable. These young people may be quite adept at making independent decisions in other areas of their lives such as friends, schooling or clothing, but anorexia demands they behave in life-threatening ways (such as restrictive eating,

bingeing or purging) that result in the absolute necessity for parents to intervene with appropriate food, initially to save their life, then to teach them how to eat again.

Although this initial 'parents in charge of all food' approach is entirely necessary, parents learn how to create a firm foundation for their child to try new behaviours, first with support then on their own; and for their son or daughter to launch into a more independent life free from anorexia.

2 What the therapist says: The appropriate inclusion of siblings is a central aspect of family-based treatment. Younger siblings may become frightened by their brother's or sister's behaviour, and will need to be guided by their parents to understand the behaviour of anorexia versus that of their brother or sister. It is also important that older siblings do not step in and act as 'an extra parent' but maintain a supportive role as a brother or sister. It is common that siblings also feel helpless and powerless in this difficult family situation and, if given a role, the anxieties of siblings can be reduced. This can also help the parents take a firm loving stance when they know that siblings are supporting their sister or brother. An example of this is that the family-based treatment therapist encourages Chloe's brother to do regular things with his sister such as playing on the computer, watching a DVD or even getting up to fun family mischief!

4 Kelly

1 What the therapist says: Keeping a clear separation between the illness and the child is essential in order to target the behaviours of the illness while loving the person underneath. It is also essential to help the child to see the separation, as this will eventually help them to face the situation. One of the most useful aspects of separating the illness from the person is that it can help reduce negative emotions towards the child. When the child feels blamed, the symptoms of anorexia often get worse.

2 What the therapist says: A strength of family-based treatment is the sequencing of the treatment so that the health emergency is the first issue focused on. This means that a complex and distressing situation can be broken down at the start and all the red herrings, such as 'why', can be eliminated so that the child gains weight. Then, when this has occurred, everyone feels more confident to progress to the reintroduction of adolescence and the important tasks required such as friends, school and independence.

3 What the therapist says: This is a great example of how each family has to find the strategies that will work for them. An essential part of family-based treatment is that the therapist is

not prescribing what should happen but the family decides on the strategies they think will succeed.

4 Bridget is now a member of the parent council of FEAST (Families Empowered And Supporting Treatment of eating disorders). FEAST is an international organisation of, and for, parents and caregivers to help loved ones recover from eating disorders by providing information and mutual support, promoting evidence-based treatment, and advocating for research and education to reduce the suffering associated with eating disorders.

FEAST, which has a strong professional advisory panel that includes Professor Daniel Le Grange and Andrew Wallis, runs an active internet forum offering support for parents and carers of young people suffering from eating disorders. Bridget is a moderator on this forum and explains how the forum was extremely helpful to her family when Kelly was ill:

> The parents on the forum are supportive, with many offering
> well-informed and constructive ideas. It was the first place
> where I heard of other children with anorexia showing the
> kind of fear, anger and resistance to treatment shown by Kelly.
> It was reassuring to know that others had been in the place we
> were and had emerged from the other end. I would recommend
> the FEAST website and forum to any parent or carer looking
> after someone with an eating disorder whether or not they are
> re-feeding at home.

For more details visit the FEAST website at www.feast-ed.org

5 Kristen

1 What the therapist says: It is a central part of family-based treatment that parents connect with their intuition in the feeding and nourishing of their child. It is likely that the young person has siblings who are well nourished and have grown normally, therefore illustrating the parents' ability to sufficiently provide the appropriate nutrition for their children. We often use the example that if your child had cancer or diabetes and refused to take the medication needed to save their life, what would you do? In this example, food is the medication necessary to support the young person back to health and a full and normal life. And it is the role of the parents to firmly insist, in a loving, persistent and consistent way, that their child does need to eat everything that is presented to them.

2 What the therapist says: It is very common for anorexia to attempt to encourage protracted and physical 'battles' in an effort to dissuade parents from insisting that a meal needs to be

eaten to completion. A strong philosophy of family-based treatment is that this is 'hands-off' and therefore any attempts by the young person to engage parents in anorexia-initiated physical contact is seen as counter-productive to the parents' efforts in providing a safe, secure environment for their child to eat, live and become stronger.

3 What the therapist says: The immense commitment Karen and Greg demonstrated in seeking the best treatment approach for their family was echoed in their efforts to restore Kristen to health. The Maudsley Approach tests the family in many ways. Yet despite the distress, trauma and disruption, Karen and Greg's strength, commitment and parental unity never strayed. Each therapy session is confronting and challenging, and therapists certainly 'upset the apple cart' week after week to prevent anorexia lulling the family into a false sense of security. Yet with every suggested new challenge, whether it be to introduce a new food or to confront an eating disorder behaviour, Karen and Greg stepped up to the task, returning the following week to report on their successes.

6 Hayley

1 What the therapist says: It is common at the start of family-based treatment for the young person to be uncooperative and say some difficult things for the family to face. Anorexia fights back when made uncomfortable and one of its main tricks is to hurt people's feelings and to try to reduce their efforts to get their child well.

2 What the therapist says: Beating anorexia for most families involves finding all the ways that it is being maintained and then putting practical strategies in place, like eating with the child at school as required. It is all about taking practical steps and problem solving at every turn, just as Kathryn and Evan highlight.

3 What the therapist says: An important aspect of getting started with fighting anorexia is for the parents to work together. All parents have strengths to bring to the fore. It is unfortunate that some therapists have blamed families for the development of anorexia. On meeting people in crisis, family difficulties look obvious and part of the problem, but family-based treatment therapists know that cracks will appear in all families who have been fighting difficulties for a long time. Getting parents working together and involved with a clear role (just as Evan and Kathryn did) is always step one.

4 What the therapist says: One of the considerable paradoxes we have experienced in the family-based treatment is that emotional recovery occurs in the context of parental firmness. Children are more likely to find their feet again or for the first time when

parents maintain an authoritative position that allows them to recover from anorexia without feeling they have to initiate the process. Family-based treatment argues that it is too risky to wait for the child to want to get well. However, during the process, as the child becomes less involved with the illness (because the parents are not allowing it), they will start to separate themselves and feel more like they want to get well. Just as Hayley said, 'I'm feeling more me'.

7 Claire

1 What the therapist says: This is a common framing of the problem: that it represents a struggle of the adolescent to achieve independence and autonomy. However, those framing the problem this way assume two things. One is that the adolescent is securely attached to her parents, and that this secure base then allows them the freedom to explore their emerging adult identity. The other assumption is that separation from parents occurs by 'cutting them off'. For well-adjusted adolescents, attachment needs to be secure, and separation needs to occur within relationships through a process of differentiation. The family-based treatment aims to achieve both of these things.
2 What the therapist says: Silence proved to be a powerful tool of Claire's anorexia, especially as Jennifer relied so much on verbal communication to try to understand her daughter and what was happening.
3 What the therapist says: Persistence is a key feature of the successful parental stance – the parents have to be more determined than the eating disorder, which means lasting longer while at the same time maintaining a firm and loving attitude. This can be difficult in the face of the young person's fear-driven responses and the eating disorder's determination to outmanoeuvre the parents using whatever means it can.
4 What the therapist says: The therapist uses opportunities provided during the restoration of the child to health to ensure a secure attachment. This is achieved when parents provide 'good enough' emotional regulation and consistency, and emotional and physical availability. At the same time, the parents are working on a supportive spousal relationship that transfers to positive parenting, a child's development of emotional expression, successful adaptation and closeness to both parents. Parental collaboration is a crucial attribute, joining attachment relationships into a functioning network, and providing a secure base for all members of the family to explore their potential.
5 What the therapist says: Separating the eating disorder involves thinking of the problem as separate to the person; that is,

considering them as a person first, who happens to have a problem. Separating is also known as externalising the problem. It helps because it keeps you focused on the problem as the problem and not the person (you attack the problem and not the person). It also reduces defensiveness and guilt from feeling 'blame', so it opens space for action to be taken against the problem and to work cooperatively. Also of benefit is the potential for separation to make the problem appear less fixed and less restricting, so that skills, abilities, interests, competencies and commitments become more visible and therefore more accessible. Importantly, separation disempowers the effects of labelling, allowing Claire's identity to preclude that of being called 'anorexic'.

6 What the therapist says: Phase Two of family-based treatment promotes the gradual independence for the adolescent from their illness and their family (in age-appropriate ways). During this phase there is a shift from alliance with anorexia dictating a total focus on restrictive eating and weight loss, as seen in Phase One, to self-doubt and some confusion as the young person develops their own sense of self without anorexia's rules to guide them. Some of the thoughts from anorexia are still present, however, yet less intrusive and strong, and often the young person can stand up to them without the parental authority required in Phase One. The focus of Phase Two is to support the young person in gradually developing their own independence from the eating disorder and their parents' stance against the anorexia. In addition, the therapist supports the parents and siblings to gradually step back and re-engage in life, more as it was prior to anorexia. Time is required for all members of the family to adjust to their new roles, as anorexia is less dominant and the young person needs the life experience to grow into their self. As with all transitions in life, there are many thoughts and feelings of self-doubt, worry and uncertainty mixed with hopes and excitement about the future. These are addressed as more evidence is mounted against anorexia and trust is gradually restored within the family.

8 Kylie

1 What the therapist says: It is unfortunate that in our society there is a strong focus on children being over their most healthy weight and only slight recognition of children failing to thrive. As such, we often hear similar reports from families following consultation with a medical professional. Just as Naomi and Sean did, it is essential that parents trust their own instincts about their child's well-being and pursue the course of action they feel necessary.

2 What the therapist says: Reflecting on such incidences is a feature of weekly family-based treatment therapy sessions. Together, the therapist and the family look at the ways in which anorexia has attempted to trick the family into taking the easier option. Sean and Naomi quickly became aware of the tricks of anorexia and are vigilant of the games it attempts to play.

3 What the therapist says: In sessions therapists sometimes use the analogy of taking a Band-Aid off the wound of a young child. There are two options: it can be rapidly ripped off, which is traumatic at first but ultimately shortens the duration of the pain, or, alternatively, it can be slowly and gently peeled off, which seemingly decreases the distress, but ultimately drags out the task. Anorexia generally prefers the latter option as it causes a greater degree of torment; family-based treatment therapists work with the parents to see the former option as desirable and, as such, will continually encourage parents to push against the restraints of anorexia.

4 What the therapist says: Parental unity is the key to success in the Maudsley Approach. There must be no room for the illness to 'divide and conquer' the parenting team. Sean and Naomi have worked hard to stand firm and support the stance made by the other. This consistency in expectation and consequence provides stability and trust. It encourages the young person to turn away from the eating disorder, which tries to constantly shift the goalposts, and place their trust in the hands of their parents.

5 What the therapist says: Anorexia certainly attempts to match the strength and determination demonstrated by Sean and Naomi. However, their family-based treatment therapist fully expects that Kylie and her family will triumph.

6 What the therapist says: The concept of externalisation and separation of the illness from Kylie has been an essential tool for the family. The ability to muster the strength to persist through another meal is excruciatingly difficult at times, particularly when they're met with outcries of hatred and detestation. However, Naomi and Sean know that their daughter is not the 'monster' they meet at the dinner table, and having the skills to separate this horrid illness from their beautiful daughter gives them the strength to battle through another meal.

9 Billie

1 What the therapist says: At the time of Billie's admission the therapy team had only one patient more chronic in family-based treatment and had never before treated a child who had been on nasogastric feeding for a year at home prior to treatment. All team members asked the question, 'Will family-based treatment

work for someone so unwell?' Billie demonstrated to her therapy team a very important lesson: if the family has the desire and the perseverance, this can balance out the severity and length of illness.

2 What the therapist says: The initial plan with Billie was to increase her weight and remove the nasogastric tube during a routine in-patient admission and then begin outpatient family-based treatment. However, the anorexia proved too strong for the normal in-patient program. This is what led to a new way to do things – a true collaboration between the family and the team.

3 What the therapist says: The family-based treatment with Billie and her family had a number of aspects unique to that situation. Her length of illness, severity of illness and the distance the family lived from the therapy team meant changing some aspects of the treatment while always relying on the core concepts. It demonstrates what can be achieved when the medical and therapy team create a deep and enduring collaboration with the family to fight anorexia, no matter where it takes them or what needs to be confronted. The heart of family-based treatment is working together, no matter how things appear on the surface, and believing that the family will find a way.

10 Annabelle

1 What the therapist says: The rejection of parents is a typical strategy of anorexia, hoping that in response the parents will soften their approach for fear of 'losing their relationship' with their daughter. The parents are really tested with this perceived attack on their treasured parent–child bond, and it takes great resolve on the parents' part to remain in the role of 'parent' and not of 'friend'. Of course, the bond isn't being lost with their child, but with the eating disorder.

2 What the therapist says: Anorexia nervosa, like other eating disorders, loves to enter the home of families not accustomed to conflict. It can just threaten conflict, and make family members very uncomfortable, so it can have its way with their child. It relies on the parents' discomfort with conflict, and normal desire to avoid it. Supporting the parents to accept and manage conflict in a healthy way is a key aspect of family-based treatment. When the parents can accept conflict as normal and a part of the treatment, model and set expectations and limits on how conflict is expressed, and manage their levels of emotional expression, it fails as a trick of anorexia to disrupt parent–child bonds.

3 What the therapist says: This is often a difficult yet incredibly important shift for parents to make, as they must acknowledge that their previously well-functioning, independent daughter is

now dependent on them fully to save her life. Simple decisions now create inordinate amounts of distress, and insecurity reigns supreme. It hurts and is a great loss for all family members. Once the shift is made, the parents can cease to be 'disappointed' in their child's lone attempts to fight the eating disorder, and the child can cease to feel guilt and shame from continually disappointing their parents. The opportunity for teamwork between parents and child is thus created.

4 What the therapist says: The family-based treatment is very successful, and recovery can occur within one year providing that the young person has been unwell less than three years. Once weight restoration has been achieved, providing all feared foods have been confronted during restoration, it can take up to a year for a very comfortable relationship with food and body to develop without much fear or relapse. It can also be successful in those who have been unwell for longer, like Annabelle who had been developing anorexia for more than three years before starting treatment. In this case recovery takes longer, so it makes sense that Annabelle, brought to a much healthier place by her parents' efforts, can now benefit from ongoing individual therapy.

11 Alice

1 What the therapist says: Sibling or other support is essential to the young person in family-based treatment. It allows the parents to fight the illness knowing that the young person is emotionally supported. It also helps the young person realise that the family is not against them and each person has a role in the fight against anorexia nervosa.

2 What the therapist says: The relationship the therapist has with the family is crucial. The bond is important because it is the primary source of support and confidence for the parents at the beginning of treatment. The therapist has to be equally committed to the process, and willing to go the distance with the family.

3 What the therapist says: During family-based treatment the family needs to uncover all the ways in which anorexia is staying strong for their child. While all young people experience some similar behaviour, the key is the parents using their knowledge of their child to assess and work out how the anorexia is affecting their child so it can be stopped. The small crumbs and weights in the bra are two examples of how all the little things add up and need to be sorted out if the child is to eventually divorce anorexia. In one family's words, it must be 'zero tolerance'.

12 How to tell if your child has anorexia nervosa

1 The dot points listed under the heading 'Early signs and symptoms of anorexia nervosa' were adapted from James Lock and Daniel Le Grange, *Help Your Teenager Beat an Eating Disorder*, Guilford, New York, 2004.

13 Navigating the search for family-based treatment

1 National Institute for Health and Clinical Excellence, 2005.
2 Information also has been sourced from the article 'Navigating the Search for True Maudsley Treatment' by Dr Angela Celio Doyle and Dr Renee Rienecke Hoste of the University of Chicago Eating Disorders Program, with permission from www.maudsleyparents.org. The Maudsley Parents website includes a guide to treatment (www.maudsleyparents.org.maudsleyparents-advice.html) and a list of family-based treatment providers in the United States, Australia and Canada, and was a source for the listings in the Appendix. Check the website for regular updates and other support information.
3 Wallis, Rhodes, Kohn and Madden, 2007, p. 3.

Bibliography

American Psychiatric Association, *Diagnostic and Statistical Manual of Mental Disorders*, 4th edn, American Psychiatric Association, Washington, 1994.

Beumont, P, 'The Mental Health of Young People in Australia: Report by the National Mental Health Strategy', *Australian and New Zealand Journal of Psychiatry*, 2002, vol. 36, p. 141.

Bowers, WA, K Evans, D Le Grange et al., 'Treatment of Adolescent Eating Disorders', in MA Reinecke, FM Dattilio and A Freeman A (eds), *Cognitive Therapy with Children and Adolescents: A Casebook for Clinical Practice*, 2nd edn, Guilford Press, New York, 2003, pp. 247–80.

Dare, C, 'Family Therapy for Families Containing an Anorectic Youngster', in *Understanding Anorexia Nervosa and Bulimia*, Ross Laboratories, Columbus, OH, 1983, pp. 28–37.

Dare, C and I Eisler, 'A Multi-family Group Day Treatment Programme for Adolescent Eating Disorder', *European Eating Disorders Review*, vol. 8, 2000, pp. 4–18.

Dare, C, I Eisler, GFM Russell et al., 'Family Therapy for Anorexia Nervosa: Implications from the Results of a Controlled Trial of Family and Individual Therapy', *Journal of Marital and Family Therapy*, vol. 16, 1990, pp. 39–57.

Doyle, AC and R Rienecke Hoste, 'Navigating the Search for True Maudsley Treatment', the University of Chicago Eating Disorders Program, 2007, with permission from www.maudsleyparents.org (viewed December 2008).

Eisler, I, C Dare, M Hodes et al., 'Family Therapy for Adolescent Anorexia Nervosa: The Results of a Controlled Comparison of Two Family Interventions', *Journal of Child Psychology and Psychiatry*, vol. 41, 2000, pp. 727–36.

Eisler, I, C Dare, GFM Russell et al., 'Family and Individual Therapy in Anorexia Nervosa: A 5-year Follow-up', *Archives of General Psychiatry*, vol. 54, 1997, pp. 1025–30.

Eisler, I, D Le Grange and KE Asen, 'Family Interventions', in J Treasure, U Schmidt and E van Furth (eds), *Handbook of Eating Disorders*, 2nd edn, Wiley, Chichester, United Kingdom, 2003, pp. 291–310.

Eisler, I, M Simic, G Russell and C Dare, 'A Randomized Controlled Treatment Trial of Two Forms of Family Therapy in Adolescent Anorexia Nervosa: A Five-year Follow-up', *Journal of Child Psychology and Psychiatry*, vol. 48, 2007, pp. 552–60.

Flament, MF, NT Godart, J Fermanian et al., 'Predictive Factors of Social Disability in Patients with Eating Disorders', *Eating & Weight Disorders*, vol. 6, 2001, pp. 99–106.

Geist, R, M Heineman, D Stephens et al., 'Comparison of Family Therapy and Family Group Psychoeducation in Adolescents with Anorexia Nervosa', *Canadian Journal of Psychiatry*, vol. 45, 2000, pp. 173–8.

Gowers, SG and B Smyth, 'The Impact of a Motivational Assessment Interview on Initial Response to Treatment in Adolescent Anorexia Nervosa', *European Eating Disorders Review*, vol. 12, 2004, pp. 87–93.

Grilo, CM, DF Becker, ML Walker et al., 'Gender Differences in Personality Disorders in Psychiatrically Hospitalized Young Adults', *Journal of Nervous and Mental Disease*, vol. 184, 1996, pp. 754–7.

Herscovici, CR and L Bay, 'Favourable Outcome for Anorexia Nervosa Patients Treated in Argentina with a Family Approach', *Eating Disorders Journal of Treatment and Prevention*, vol. 4, 1996, pp. 59–66.

Hoek, HW and D van Hoeken, 'Review of the Prevalence and Incidence of Eating Disorders', *International Journal of Eating Disorders*, vol. 34, 2003, pp. 383–96.

Jeammet, P and C Chabert, 'A Psychoanalytic Approach to Eating Disorders: The Role of Dependency', in AH Esman (ed.), *Adolescent Psychiatry: Developmental and Clinical Studies*, vol. 22, Analytic Press, Hillsdale, New Jersey, 1998, pp. 59–84.

Katzman, DL, 'Osteoporosis in Anorexia Nervosa: A Brittle Future? Current Drug Targets', *CNS & Neurological Disorders*, vol. 2, 2003, pp. 11–15.

Katzman, DL, B Christensen, AR Young et al., 'Starving the Brain: Structural Abnormalities and Cognitive Impairment in Adolescents with Anorexia Nervosa', *Seminars in Clinical Neuropsychiatry*, vol. 6, 2001, pp. 146–52.

Kreipe, RE, B Goldstein, DE DeKing et al., 'Heart Rate Power Spectrum Analysis of Autonomic Dysfunction in Adolescents with Anorexia Nervosa', *International Journal of Eating Disorders*, vol. 16, 1994, pp. 159–65.

Le Grange, D, R Binford and K Loeb, 'Manualized Family-based

Treatment for Anorexia Nervosa: A Case Series', *Journal of American Academy of Child and Adolescent Psychiatry*, vol. 44, 2005, pp. 41–6.

Le Grange, D, RD Crosby, PJ Rathouz and BL Leventhal, 'A Randomized Controlled Comparison of Family-Based Treatment and Supportive Psychotherapy for Adolescent Bulimia Nervosa', *Archives of General Psychiatry*, vol. 64, 2007, pp. 1049–56.

Le Grange, D, I Eisler, C Dare et al., 'Evaluation of Family Therapy in Anorexia Nervosa: A Pilot Study', *International Journal of Eating Disorders*, vol. 12, 1992a, pp. 347–57.

—— 'Family Criticism and Self-Starvation: A Study of Expressed Emotion', *Journal of Family Therapy*, vol. 14, 1992b, pp. 177–92.

Le Grange, D, and T Gelman, 'Patients' Perspective of Treatment in Eating Disorders: A Preliminary Study', *South African Journal of Psychology*, vol. 28, 1988, pp. 182–6.

Le Grange, D, and J Lock, *Treating Bulimia in Adolescents: A Family-based Approach*, Guilford Press, New York, 2007.

Lim, C, 'A Pilot Study of Families' Experiences of a Multi-family Group Day Treatment Programme', MSc Dissertation, Institute of Psychiatry, King's College, University of London, 2000.

Lock, J, WS Agras, S Bryson and K Helena, 'A Comparison of Short- and Long-term Family Therapy for Adolescent Anorexia Nervosa', *Journal of the American Academy of Child and Adolescent Pyschiatry*, vol. 44, 2005, pp. 632–9.

Lock, J, J Couturier, WS Agras and S Bryson, 'Comparison of Long-term Outcomes in Adolescents with Anorexia Nervosa Treated with Family Therapy', *Journal of the American Academy of Child and Adolescent Pyschiatry*, vol. 45, no. 6, 2006, pp. 666–72.

Lock, J and D Le Grange, 'Can Family-based Treatment of Anorexia Nervosa Be Manualized?', *Journal of Psychotherapy Practice and Research*, vol. 10, 2001, pp. 253–61.

Lock, J, D Le Grange, WS Agras and C Dare, *Treatment Manual for Anorexia Nervosa: A Family-based Approach*, Guilford Press, New York, 2001.

Lock, J, D Le Grange, S Fordsburg and K Hewell, 'Is Family Therapy Effective for Children with Anorexia Nervosa?', *Journal of the American Academy of Child and Adolescent Psychiatry*, vol. 45, 2006, pp. 1323–8.

Loeb, KL, AC Doyle, D Le Grange et al., 'Family-based Treatment for Child and Adolescent Overweight: A Transdevelopmental Approach', Unpublished Manual, Mount Sinai School of Medicine, New York, 2006.

Loeb, K, D Le Grange, J Lock et al., 'Family-based Treatment for Adolescents with Subsyndromal Anorexia Nervosa', Unpublished Manual, Mount Sinai School of Medicine, New York, 2005.

Loeb, K, B Walsh, J Lock et al., 'Open Trial of Family-based Treatment for Adolescent Anorexia Nervosa: Evidence of Successful Dissemination', *Journal of the American Academy of Child and Adolescent Psychiatry*, vol. 46, 2007, pp. 792–800.

Martin, FE, 'The Treatment and Outcome of Anorexia Nervosa in Adolescents: A Prospective Study and Five-year Follow-up', *Journal of Psychiatric Research*, vol. 19, 1984, pp. 509–14.

Mayer, RD, 'Family Therapy in the Treatment of Eating Disorders in General Practice', MSc Dissertation, Birkbeck College, University of London, 1994.

Minuchin, S, L Baker, BL Rosman et al., 'A Conceptual Model of Psychosomatic Illness in Childhood', *Archives of General Psychiatry*, vol. 32, 1975, pp. 1031–8.

Minuchin, S, BL Rosman and L Baker, *Psychosomatic Families: Anorexia Nervosa in Context*, Harvard University Press, Cambridge, MA, 1978.

Morgan, HG and AE Hayward, 'Clinical Assessment of Anorexia Nervosa: The Morgan-Russell Outcome Assessment Schedule', *British Journal of Psychiatry*, vol. 152, 1988, pp. 367–71.

National Institute for Health and Clinical Excellence, *Obsessive-Compulsive Disorder: Core Interventions in the Treatment of Obsessive-Compulsive Disorder and Body Dysmorphic Disorder*, NICE, London, 2005.

Ratnasuriya, RH, I Eisler, GI Szmukler et al., 'Anorexia Nervosa: Outcome and Prognostic Factors After 20 Years', *British Journal of Psychiatry*, vol. 158, 1991, pp. 495–502.

Rhodes, P and S Madden, 'Scientific Family Therapists, Postmodern Medical Practitioners, and Expert Parents: Second Order Change in the Eating Disorders Program at the Children's Hospital at Westmead', *The Journal of Family Therapy*, 2005, Chapter 27(2), pp. 171–82.

Robin, AL, PT Siegel, T Koepke et al., 'Family Therapy versus Individual Therapy for Adolescent Females with Anorexia Nervosa', *Journal of Developmental Behavioral Pediatrics*, vol. 15, 1994, pp. 111–16.

Robin, AL, PT Siegel, A Moye et al., 'A Controlled Comparison of Family versus Individual Therapy for Adolescents with Anorexia Nervosa', *Journal of the American Academy of Child and Adolescent Psychiatry*, vol. 38, 1999, pp. 1482–9.

Rorty, M, J Yager, J Buckwalter et al., 'Social Support, Social Adjustment, and Recovery Status in Bulimia Nervosa', *International Journal of Eating Disorders*, vol. 26, 1999, pp. 1–12.

Russell, GFM, GI Szmukler, C Dare et al., 'An Evaluation of Family Therapy in Anorexia Nervosa and Bulimia Nervosa', *Archives of General Psychiatry*, vol. 44, 1987, pp. 1047–56.

Scholz, M and KE Asen, 'Multiple Family Therapy with Eating

Disordered Adolescents', *European Eating Disorders Review*, vol. 9, 2001, pp. 33–42.

Squire-Dehouck, B, 'Evaluation of Conjoint Family Therapy versus Family Counselling in Adolescent Anorexia Nervosa Patients: A 2-year Follow-up Study', MSc Thesis, University of London, 1993.

Steinhausen, HC, S Boyadjieva, M Griogotoiu-Serbanescu et al., 'The Outcome of Adolescent Eating Disorders: Findings from an International Collaborative Study', *European Child and Adolescent Psychiatry*, vol. 12 (supp. 1), 2003, pp. 91–8.

Stierlin, H and G Weber, 'Anorexia Nervosa: Lessons from a Follow-up Study', *Family Systems Medicine*, vol. 7, 1988, pp. 120–57.

—— *Unlocking the Family Door*, Brunner/Mazel, New York, 1989.

Sullivan, PF, 'Mortality in Anorexia Nervosa', *American Journal of Psychiatry*, vol. 152, 1995, pp. 1073–4.

Szmukler, GI, I Eisler, GFM Russell et al., 'Anorexia Nervosa, Parental Expressed Emotion and Dropping Out of Treatment', *British Journal of Psychiatry*, vol. 147, 1985, pp. 265–71.

Wallin, U and P Kronwall, 'Anorexia Nervosa in Teenagers: Change in Family Function After Family Therapy at 2-Year Follow-up', *Nordic Journal of Psychiatry*, vol. 56, 2002, pp. 363–9.

Wallis, A, P Rhodes, M Kohn and S Madden, 'Five-years of Family-based Treatment for Anorexia Nervosa: The Maudsley Model at the Children's Hospital at Westmead', *International Journal of Adolescent Medicine & Health*, vol. 19, 2007, p. 3.

Winston, AP and PJ Stafford, 'Cardiovascular Effects of Anorexia Nervosa', *European Eating Disorders Review*, vol. 8, 2000, pp. 117–25.

Wonderlich, SA and JE Mitchell, 'Eating Disorders and Comorbidity: Empirical, Conceptual, and Clinical Implications', *Psychopharmacology Bulletin*, vol. 33, 1997, pp. 381–90.

Woodside, DB, PE Garfinkel, E Lin et al., 'Comparisons of Men with Full or Partial Eating Disorders, Men without Eating Disorders, and Women with Eating Disorders in the Community', *American Journal of Psychiatry*, vol. 158, 2001, pp. 570–4.

Zipfel, S, B Lowe and W Herzog, 'Medical Complications', in J Treasure and U Schmidt (eds), *Handbook of Eating Disorders*, Wiley, Chichester, United Kingdom, 2003, pp. 191–206.